T H E A R T O F
ENTERPRISE ARCHITECTURE
FOR BUSINESS ARCHITECTS

C J C O O N E Y

{ REAL ENGINE }

Regina. MMX.

PUBLISHED BY FORWARD-THINKING PRESS
Regina, SK, Canada
www.forwardthinkingpress.com

Library and Archives Canada Cataloguing in Publication

Cooney, C. J., 1965-
    The art of enterprise architecture for business
architects / C J Cooney.

Includes index.
ISBN 978-0-9865087-5-2

    1. Management information systems. 2. Industrial management. 3. System analysis. I. Title.

HD30.213.C65 2010   658.4'038011   C2010-901362-X

VISIT: www.TheArtofEA.com

"Things which matter most must never be at the mercy of things which matter least." — Goethe

"Measure twice. Cut once." — A Carpentry Maxim

Table of Contents

INTERACTIONS

THE POWER OF ALIGNMENT

INTRODUCTION

Fortune Favours the Aligned

It is possible for an enterprise to deal with overwhelming complexity and unprecedented change and massive competition and still perform brilliantly with rising profits, rising stock prices, growing market share, and high levels of stakeholder and employee satisfaction. It's great when that happens. Unfortunately, it's just not all that common.

In the real world, enterprise performance is degraded by a shockingly long list of things, not least of which are: increasing complexity, rapid business and technological change, cut-throat competition, ever rising costs, strategy confusion, chronic project failures, the vexing phenomenon known as the business-IT gap, and unstable economic conditions.

Empty storefronts in the mall and on Main Street remind us that poor performance leads to failure. The ups and downs of the stock market tells us that some companies perform better than others. Everyday, some stocks spike and other tank. When a company collapses, its stock becomes worthless, investors lose their money, employees lose their livelihood, many lose their pensions, some lose their life's savings, others lose everything. If the recent meltdown on Wall Street teaches us anything, it's that worst case scenarios happen with alarming regularity. It took trillions to bail out the world's once rock-solid banks and billions to bail out Detroit's former blue chip automakers. There are lots of lessons to draw from this. Here's one: Just because a company did well in the past does not automatically mean it will do well tomorrow. The only success an enterprise can count on is the success it is working hard to make happen today.

Most of the CxOs running today's enterprises are not on the golf course, they're in the office *leading* their organizations and working hard to make success happen. These CxOs know something crucial about success in the modern world. They know that fortune favours organizations that align their IT capabilities with their business. For the modern organization, success and information technology are tightly coupled—aligning IT with the business is not a nice idea, it's a pre-requisite for success. These CxOs know that having a strategy is not enough; success and survival are a function of strategy *execution*.

Enterprise architecture is a strategy put into place by today's CxOs in order to accelerate the effectiveness of strategic initiatives and to achieve high organizational performance, and at the heart of enterprise architecture is enterprise business architecture.

The primary function of *enterprise business architecture* is to bring business capabilities and IT capabilities into alignment: by creating a value-adding enterprise reference architecture, by aligning business strategy with IT risks and opportunities, by aligning the strategic IT plan with the strategic business plan, by aligning business and IT tactical plans, by aligning IT project, program, and change management plans with IT strategic and tactical plans.

The mission of *The Art of Enterprise Architecture for Business Architects* is to put the tools of enterprise business architecture into the hands of business architects so that they can create strategic alignment between their organization's business and IT capabilities, take a leading role in creating value for their organizations, and help create organizations that generate value for clients, shareholders, stakeholders, and employees.

Framework Independence

The Art of Enterprise Architecture for Business Architects makes no assumptions about which frameworks are used by the reader, if any.

The *models*, *catalogs*, and *interactions* presented in this book can easily be adapted for use with:

- The Zachman Framework,
- The Open Group's Architecture Framework (TOGAF),
- Federal Enterprise Architecture Framework (FEAF),
- Department of Defence Enterprise Architecture (DoDEA) Framework,
- almost any 'big consultancy' framework, or
- any custom framework developed for an enterprise's specific purposes.

The enterprise business architecture tools presented in this book are highly specific to the work of enterprise business architecture, but not so specific that they're tied to any of the ever changing landscape of enterprise architecture frameworks . . . and not so specific that they cannot be adapted to a wide-variety of business, architecture, and IT uses.

The Target Audience

This book makes one very important assumption about its target audience, namely, that they are smart, curious, and capable people able to take this book of ideas and tools and adapt them to a wide variety of enterprises and an even wider variety of business circumstances.

This book will prove useful to:

- enterprise and business architects,
- CxOs (CIOs, COOs, CEOs),
- strategic planners,
- data, applications, technology, and security architects,
- change management and innovation management professionals,
- project directors and managers,
- program directors and managers, and
- anyone interesting in understanding the value of enterprise alignment and the important relationships between strategic outcomes and strategic plans, tactical plans, and project/program/change management plans.

The Structure of this Book

The Art of Enterprise Architecture for Business Architects is divided into four parts: the Power of Alignment, Models, Catalogs, and Interactions.

Part 1: The Power of Alignment

The first part "The Power of Alignment" (*Chapter 001* to *Chapter 003*) sets the context for enterprise business architecture. This section answers fundamental questions about enterprise business architecture, such as: why EBA is important, how EBA works, how to avoid the pitfalls of the enterprise architecture framework wars, what the key principles of enterprise business architecture are, and, finally, introduces the EBA tools and techniques—the models, catalogs, and interactions—that are indispensable to achieving enterprise-wide alignment and, as a by-product of that alignment, a high-performing, successful enterprise.

Part 2: Models

The second part "Models" (*Chapter 004* to *Chapter 068*) presents a wide array of models used by enterprise business architects to illuminate, align, educate, solve problems, draft solutions, highlight structure, and, in the final analysis, facilitate high quality decision-making.

Chapter Number
Model Name
Model Description
Model Element List
Model Element Definitions
Comments on Model and Patterns
Model Patterns

Each chapter introduces a model, outlines the elements of the model, defines the elements of the model, then, as necessary, the chapter provides comments on the model and its various patterns, and, finally, presents the model and its patterns.

Part 3: Catalogs

The third part "Catalogs" (*Chapter 069* to *Chapter 096*) presents catalogs which enterprise business architects require in order to manage information of importance to the effective and efficient management of the enterprise itself. Catalogs manage data about the enterprise, enterprise structure and relationships, performance information, and business architecture function.

Chapter Number
Catalog Name
Catalog Description
Catalog Element List
Catalog Element Definitions

Each chapter in this section introduces a catalog, lists the catalog elements, and, finally, defines each of the catalog elements.

Part 4: Interactions

The fourth and final part "Interactions" (*Chapter 097* to *Chapter 123*) presents the interactions (simple tables which map the relationship between catalogs or between the elements of the same catalog) which enterprise business architects should find useful as they solve problems, make decisions, and communicate with clients.

Chapter Number
Interaction Name
Interaction Description
Key Interaction List
Example Interaction Name
Comments on Example Interaction
Example Interaction Build Diagram
Example Interaction Table

Each chapter of this section will: introduce and describe an interaction; list the related key interactions; identify an example interaction; provide comment on the example interaction, as necessary; show a diagram of the process used to build the example interaction; and, finally, presents a table representing the example interaction.

The interactions section identifies over 400 key interactions. Approximately 125 of these interactions are unique.

CHAPTER 001

What is Enterprise Business Architecture?

To understand the art of enterprise architecture for business architects, we must first understand what architecture is. Fortunately, architecture is a fairly simple concept to grasp. The most useful definition of architecture comes from ISO/IEC 42010: 2007, which defines architecture as "the fundamental organization of a system, embodied in its components, their relationships to each other and the environment, and the principles governing its design, and evolution." The most useful definition of enterprise architecture is based on the ISO architecture definition, and defines enterprise architecture as:

- the organization of the enterprise and its constituent components,
- the component-to-component relationships,
- the component-to-environment relationships,
- the definition of the environment in which the enterprise operates,
- the enterprise principles governing design, and
- the enterprise principles governing change.

What's complicated about that? Not a thing. Our definition of enterprise business architecture is an even briefer and even easier concept to grasp.

Enterprise business architecture
is the business of alignment.

The business of alignment is the business of bringing all the parts of the enterprise into position for optimal enterprise performance. Optimal alignment is achieved when:

- the leader of the enterprise have a clear mission, vision, and strategic goals and objectives for creating an effective and efficient organization;
- all the parts of the enterprise have a shared understanding of the enterprise's strategic goals and objective;
- all the parts of the enterprise are committed to taking individual and shared actions to realize the enterprise's strategic goals and objectives;
- business capabilities are created and calibrated to realize the enterprise's strategic goals and objectives;
- IT capabilities are created and calibrated to support the enterprise's business capabilities; and,
- the execution of strategy leads to the achievement the enterprise's intended strategic outcomes.

Of course, EBA is concerned with the relationships between the technical components of IT architecture and with the design principles regarding integration, interoperability, reuse, agility, usability, convergence, cost, and sustainability which guide the development and maintenance of these components—but that is just half the EBA story.

Here's the other half of the story: The business architect seeks to bring alignment to the relationship between an enterprise's strategic planning, tactical planning, operational planning, enterprise reference architecture, and outcomes. The relationship between IT components and their design requirements are important, but of equal or perhaps greater importance to EBA are the relationships between enterprise components and the strategic goals of the enterprise and, of course, results.

Here's the backstory. The enterprise business architect's focus on alignment isn't derived from the collective wisdom of IT business analysts. The alignment approach to enterprise business architecture is "Deming-driven." William Edwards Deming (1903-1993) was an American business management guru that advocated a transformation in the American style of management; this transformation began with responsible leadership committed to improving quality, teamwork, and productivity—the by-product of which would be decreased costs and improved competitive position. For Deming-driven enterprise business architecture, this means: enterprise business architects are though-leaders and champions of innovation; the important problems of tomorrow are given as much priority as the urgent problems of today; EBA supports the organization's ability to innovate; change happens automatically and chaotically and, in response, enterprise business architects provide leadership to ensure change is a pro-actively managed positive "transformation" and that everyone in the organization understands they have a role to play in making the transformation work.

A common measure of quality is the extent to which product and service outcomes meet strategic expectations. In this sense, quality is the degree of alignment between strategic requirements and enterprise outcomes. In short, from the EBA perspective, *quality* equals *alignment*. We can extend this. If, from the Deming-perspective, *quality* equals *doing the right things*, then a key objective of *alignment* is ensuring that everyone in the organization knows what to do and are doing it, but more than this, the organization itself knows what it should be doing, is doing it, and is continuously evolving itself into an organization that enables its people to do their best work, focusing on quality and productivity innovations and transformations that lead to a healthy organization today and into the future.

Enterprise business architects seek to ensure that the outcomes envisioned in an enterprise's strategic plan closely correlate with the outcomes realized by projects and the programs of the enterprise's organizational units. To do this, enterprise business architects create business context (encoded into enterprise reference architecture) as they align: business strategy with IT risks and opportunities; IT strategy with business strategy; IT capabilities with business capabilities; IT tactical plans with IT strategy; and align change management, project management and operational plans with IT tactical plans.

These alignment points form the fault line of enterprise success. On one side of the line lies prosperity and survival. On the other side, shoddy and shabby performance, downsizing, deteriorating market share, bankruptcy, and dissolution. To the enterprise business architect, these alignments points are the power points of the enterprise and their alignment can lead to greater enterprise effectiveness and efficiency and competitive advantage. The risk of being on the wrong side of this fault line is the risk of having to abandon investments, scrap work, and re-invest and rework— being on the wrong side of the line for too long puts the survival of the enterprise at risk.

To ensure enterprise alignment, there are five key things an enterprise business architect does. The enterprise business architect:

- engages in strategic planning,
- creates EBA assets,
- provides guidance,
- provides governance, and
- conducts evaluations.

Each of these enterprise business architecture functions is examined in detail in Chapter 2.

Why is EBA important?

The answer to the question "why is EBA important?" is the same as the answer to two different but intimately related questions. First: "Why is strategic planning important?" Second: "Why is it important to execute well on the strategic plan?"

Strategy sets the stage for action; EBA does the same. Strategy is a pro-active response to risks and opportunities. EBA is a pro-active management of risks and opportunities. The ROI on strategic planning is the ROI on EBA. In this sense, *EBA is strategy*. Strategic plans are always plans for change and improvement; EBA is always concerned with guiding and governing change and optimising the enterprise's investment in pro-active transformation. While the task of attaching a dollar amount to the ROI of strategic planning and EBA has flummoxed great minds (Deming suggests that the quest to determine ROI on strategic planning is a fool's errand), we intuitively know their value to be priceless—kind of like the ROI on breathing.

A business would always prosper if things rarely changed and if the business always executed its strategy successfully. However, strategy is not always executed well. Things don't always work out as planned. Nothing stays the same. Nothing stands still. A long list of things constantly threaten to foil the enterprise's well laid plans. These things include: the Business-IT gap, the risk of project failure, constant and rapid change, increasing complexity, the need to control costs, the ongoing pressure on IT to contribute to competitive advantage, and strategy confusion. The list is longer than this, but these are good examples of the forces creating misalignment in the modern organization and, consequently, creating the need for enterprise business architecture. As these forces help identify the importance of enterprise business architecture, they deserve closer examination.

First, the problem of the Business-IT gap has been known for several generations and yet there is still a vast chasm between the capabilities businesses need IT to support and the supporting capabilities IT actually delivers. Wherever a Business-IT gap exists, serious misalignment issues exist. The interesting question isn't *if* this gap exists. The interesting question to ask is: "What are we going to do about it?"

Second, projects get launched, but most of them fail to land or crash land. The Standish Group's report "CHOAS Summary 2009" found that 24% of projects were cancelled before usable results were delivered and 44% of projects were late, over budget, or failed to deliver fully functional solutions. Projects are supposed to support strategic outcomes by supporting particular user requirements, but often fail to do this. When projects fail or under perform, enterprise misalignment is the immediate result, and the enterprise risks failing to achieve its strategic goals.

Third, a tsunami of change threatens to make yesterday's business processes obsolete—and that goes double for the IT solutions that support them. Constant change forces the enterprise to evolve and adapt in order to survive. This impacts the enterprise in three important ways. First, change challenges the enterprise to set aside the status quo and re-think how it does business. Second, rapid change is testing the ability of the enterprise to keep up with the change-driven work load and with the requirement to master or contract for new skills. Third, change is expensive and it places an ever increasing burden on organizations to allocate resources to enable change. Wherever the rate of change exceeds an enterprise's ability to comprehend or manage that change or pay for that change, serious alignment issues are sure to follow.

Fourth, in today's enterprise, complexity is a fact of life. We are already on the slippery slope of complexity. The complexity of modern business is growing by orders of magnitude and this complexity is a defining trait of almost every aspect of business life. Supply chains and product distribution chains are becoming tremendously intricate and interdependent. Manufacturing and service delivery are comprised of ever more complex services and processes, subject to increasingly rigorous regulatory and accounting requirements. Customers and stakeholders are more and more demanding. A complex enterprise requires complex sup-porting IT systems and infrastructure. The complexity of enterprise data, application, and technology components are growing exponentially and to manage them IT professionals need to continuously upgrade their skills. There is a high and unrelenting cost to managing complexity. Failing to meet the demands of complexity results in misalignment, but, worse than this, it results in enterprise decline and collapse. A primary objective of EBA is find a way to untangle this complexity and wrap it simplicity.

Fifth, operational costs and new system development costs continue to rise. As these costs go up, the status quo becomes more expensive. These costs climb independently of the upward or downward trends of an organization's budget. It is a general rule of thumb that as operational costs increase, the budget available for new projects decreases and discretional investment decreases. When organizations cannot afford optimal strategy, pro-active transformation becomes first difficult and then, by degrees, impossible.

Sixth, the need for IT to contribute to the enterprise's competitive advantage puts continual pressure on both business and IT to innovate and evolve, but business and IT rarely innovate and evolve at the same rate.

Finally, strategy confusion is an enormous problem in the modern enterprise. If an organization is lucky, five percent of enterprise staff are aware of and understand the organization's strategy.[*] This tells us two things. First, there is a clear and present need to address the problem of strategy confusion. And, second, the old ways of communicating strategy—staff meetings, slick brochures and thick documents written in incomprehensible jargon—are ineffective. In fact, these methods of communicating strategy have added to strategy confusion rather than lessened it.

These and other forces are constantly throwing enterprises out of alignment. When any one of these forces brings change to the enterprise, it is never just one thing that gets changed. When we change any one thing in the enterprise, we quickly discover it is connected to a thousand other things. Even small changes can lead to massive misalignment.

Unfortunately, there are no forces at work to naturally bring an enterprise into alignment. There is no technology that can be bought that can bestow the gifts of alignment upon the enterprise. There are no silver bullets. Alignment doesn't happen by chance—it is the result of intentional effort.

This is why EBA is important, because: EBA is the only enterprise-scoped function dedicated to bringing all the parts of the enterprise into alignment with IT and enterprise strategy.

This is an extraordinarily difficult and complex job, but somebody has got to do it.

---

[*] Robert S. Kaplan and David P. Norton (2001). *The Strategy Focused Organization*. Cambridge, MA: Harvard Business School Press. p. 215.

CHAPTER 002

How does EBA work?

The purpose of alignment is to ensure strategic plans produce results. To bring about enterprise alignment, enterprise business architects:

- engage in five key activities: strategic planning, enterprise business architecture asset creation, guidance, governance, and evaluation;
- use EA frameworks; and,
- apply the principles of EBA to everything they do.

This chapter looks at each of the five key EBA activities, the use of EA frameworks, and the principles of EBA.

Strategic Planning

Enterprise business architects are part of the enterprise strategic planning process.

Enterprise business architects are tuned into emerging technologies and business trends with the potential to shift markets, enable new process automation, increase productivity, and develop competitive advantages. They understand the implication of these emerging technologies and business trends and communicate them to the enterprise's senior leadership in the form of risks and opportunities and recommendations for strategic action. In this way, enterprise business architects help align business strategy with emerging IT opportunities and risks. They regularly analyse the enterprise in general and IT services in detail in order to identify gaps and overlaps—and make recommendations on action to bridge gaps and eliminate unnecessary overlaps. For these reasons, the enterprise business architect should be an integral part of the business strategy development team. However, the work of enterprise business architecture does much more than just help set strategic direction.

The enterprise business architect is a leader in the IT strategy development process and plays a key role in helping IT CxOs translate business strategy into deeply aligned IT strategy. Indeed, enterprise business architects provide the glue that binds strategic and tactical plans with effective execution.

A crucial responsibility of the enterprise business architect is to model and make sense of the enterprise's strategic plan and IT strategy and share these models and this understanding with the EA team and with EBA's clients.

None of this EBA strategic alignment work is 'slam-dunk' easy. In the real world, poorly articulated business strategy contributes as much to the Business-IT gap as anything. When an organization fails to engage in strategic planning or is particularly inept at strategic planning, the business-IT gap is bound to widen. It is no easy task to align IT with a poorly defined business. When a business does not have a strategic plan, the business architect does not sit tight waiting for a strategic plan to materialize. Whether written or unwritten, every organization employs some kind of strategy. When necessary, the business architect engages with the business in order to discover its unwritten strategies and undocumented problems and priorities. This effort is sometimes called *discovery consulting* and can be as subtle as meeting with business leaders over coffee and asking simple questions like: What are your top priorities right now? What are the key challenges you're facing? How are you beating the competition today? (Or, why is the competition winning out?) How are you improving the business? What do you want to do differently? The answers to these questions can reveal enough of the organization's strategic direction for the enterprise business architect to begin aligning IT with the business.

EBA Asset Creation

Through the creation of EBA assets, enterprise business architects contribute to a structured understanding of the enterprise. EBA assets define and clarify opportunities, risks, business strategy and business capabilities, IT strategy and IT capabilities, tactical plans, guidance activity and tools, governance activity and tools, evaluation activity and tools.

Important assets include: models, catalogs, interactions, principles, policy, standards, building blocks, due diligence checklists, architecture decision items, current state assessments, baseline architecture, target architecture, and roadmaps that guide enterprise change from baseline to target architecture. These EBA assets form part of an enterprise reference architecture which allows the enterprise to pro-actively manage business change, technological change, and increasing complexity, and by doing

13

this control costs, increase organizational agility, innovation, and, ultimately, help achieve positive strategic outcomes for the enterprsie. EBA artifacts are, at their core, change and innovation management tools demonstrating to stakeholders:

- the root problem and importance of the solution being considered,
- how the solution will benefit the enterprise and stakeholder,
- how the stakeholder relates to the solution,
- what action the stakeholder needs to take in order to align themselves with the greater enterprise strategy, and
- what actions they need to take in order to contribute to successful enterprise outcomes.

EBA assets provide all other enterprise architects with an understanding of business context so that reasoned architectural decisions can be made. The assets created by the enterprise business architect are used as a starting point for progressive elaboration by data, application, and technology architects; they form the basis for enterprise business architecture engagements; and are the primary problem solving and communication tools of the enterprise business architect.

Guidance

Guidance is a key service provided by enterprise business architects to projects, organizational units, other enterprise architects, and other stakeholders. A great deal of this guidance activity happens in engagements. Each EBA engagement with clients and stakeholders will differ slightly. The enterprise business architect identifies which existing artifacts support these engagements and which new artifacts will be required and at what granularity.

It is by providing guidance that enterprise business architects communicate key information on business strategy, IT strategy, tactical plans, and EBA assets. It is through guidance that the enterprise business architects help ensure IT activity is aligned with the enterprise's strategic goals and objectives. Guidance is not about telling clients what to do; guidance is about providing clients with ways to align their ideas and actions with broader enterprise strategy. Guidance is not about the enterprise architect playing superhero and saving the day. Guidance is about the enterprise architect playing an enabling-role in helping to create an enterprise with a shared sense of mission and strategy.

Governance

The enterprise business architect is required to perform a governance role. At key touchpoints, enterprise business architects review IT activity for compliance with the enterprise reference architecture. A core alignment factor always at the top of the enterprise business architect's mind: Is the project going to deliver a fully functional solution that satisfies the requirements of its users? The goal of this governance activity is to ensure projects, operational units, and strategic and operational outcomes contribute to the enterprise's desired strategic and tactical outcomes.

Evaluation

Enterprise business architects conduct evaluations. They collect and analyse performance and outcome data. They ask questions like: did the project achieve its goals? was the appropriate knowledge transferred from the project to operational staff? did the organizational unit deliver on its tactical objectives? were the desired outcomes achieved? The results of evaluations are used to revise strategies and tactics during new rounds of enterprise planning and to formulate corrective action for in-flight projects and programs.

The Balanced Approach

Enterprise Business Architects and their EA program must balance:

- strategic focus with tactical focus,
- a focus on business with a focus on technology, and
- theory with action.

EA programs can be too strategic, leaving themselves open to charges of being unresponsive to the practical (tactical) needs of their clients. On the other hand, these programs can be too tactical and, as a result, be denounced for not understanding or managing the big picture. And if they're all tactical, the obvious (and myopic) questions arise: "Why is architecture a separate program at all? Why don't we disband them and assign them to the operational units and projects that need help?"

An EA program can be too focused on business issues and, without deep roots in technology and the IT industry, be unable to understand the true value and transformative power of technology. Of course, the opposite focus is trouble too. When too focused on technology, an EA program is complicit in widening the Business-IT gap. The program can be accused of fundamentally misunderstanding the role of IT in the enterprise: IT is a means to a business end, not an end in-and-of itself. Technology must support the business (even when it's transforming the business).

Theory can lead EA programs astray. Too strong a focus on theory can leads to endless and fruitless ivory tower debates (see below: *What's the horrible truth about frameworks*). When it comes to the practical IT challenges faced by the organization and its projects and programs, too much theory can leave the EA program open to accusation of being irrelevant. A wild swing away from theory can be just as problematic: the EA program can be too action oriented. Action is always a good thing, but not if it comes at the cost of *not* laying a good foundation for EA engagements. Before taking action, EA programs must bring useful EA assets to their engagements; useful assets such as principles, a blueprint, a roadmap, best practices, standards, etc. The program doesn't need to stop the presses and figure out all of the EA puzzle before taking action, but all action must have at least enough supporting EA reference architecture to ensure that the action it does take is effective and efficient.

By engaging in the five key activities of enterprise business architecture—strategic planning, enterprise business architecture asset creation, guidance, governance, and evaluation—the enterprise business architect naturally promotes balance in the larger EA program. There are two prerequisites to be met before balance can be found. First and foremost, the business must be understood. Second, the organization's strategy must be understood. Only then can coherent decisions be made on what elements of EA/IT theory are applicable, what tactical (operational/ project/program) plans make sense, and what technologies are sustainable, effective, and efficient. It is of critical importance for enterprise business architects to take a step back from the urgencies of everyday life in the enterprise and ensure there is an ongoing effort to address the tension between the strategic and tactical, the business and the technology, and between theory and action. Many of the tools presented in this book help the business architect do just that.

What's the horrible truth about frameworks?

The horrible truth about enterprise architecture frameworks is this:

Frameworks don't really matter.

What really matters is for enterprise architecture programs to create value—and you don't need a complex enterprise architecture framework to add value to the organization.

Enterprise architecture program success is often threatened by Goldilocks Syndrome: the architecture is either too hot or too cold, which is to say, the program attempts to do too much or does too little. Doing too much is usually the result of pulling an enterprise architecture framework off the shelf and robotically populating it—this is the cookbook approach. Doing too little is often the result of too much debate.

The problem with cookbook frameworks. There is no such thing as an off-the-shelf framework. Yet frameworks are often taken off of the shelf and treated as cookbooks; each part of the framework is followed without question or comment. Enterprise architecture is an extraordinarily complex undertaking and does not lend itself to cookbooks. Enterprise architects cannot be cognitive misers; architects cannot be lazy thinkers; architects must be ready and willing to invest vast amounts of energy and thinking into the form and function of their work. The cookbook approach can yield mountains of documents, but these document rarely yield business value because the framework from which they sprang had little to do with the enterprise in the first place. Accepting a framework holus-bolus invariably leads to massive misalignment. A perfect framework is an unattainable treasure. Whatever framework is selected by an organization, substantial customization is always required.

The problem with framework debates. Many an enterprise architecture program has crashed upon the rock of debate, and sunk. These debates involve architects arguing over the relative merits of enterprise architecture frameworks. Should the debate ever get beyond the framework, the debaters move on to debates over taxonomies, ontologies, appropriate granularity, rules of engagement, *et cetera*. These debates are largely political and destructive and have left many architects sceptical about the value of closely following any of the 'big name' or 'big consultancy' frameworks. When architecture programs turn into debating societies, the first casualty is the program's ability to deliver value to the enterprise. These debates are ended when architects make smart, pragmatic compromises around the form and function of their framework.

Goldilocks Syndrome usually proves fatal to enterprise architecture programs and is one reason why many organizations now use frameworks for inspirational purposes only. To meet the goals and objectives of their organizations, they create custom frameworks based upon their own specific organizational EA requirements.

The Art of Enterprise Architecture for Business Architects bypasses the framework wars and makes an end run around foolish date. Here's how to avoid unproductive debate: pick a framework or develop a framework, and then get down to business. The point of this is to focus on providing value to the organization.

What is really important for business architects and their architecture programs is: understanding the business, understanding business strategy, understanding and communicating how IT strategy aligns with business strategy, developing a value-adding EA framework, creating value-adding enterprise reference architecture artifacts, and communicating, guiding, governing, and evaluating. *The Art of Enterprise Architecture for Business Architects* provides enterprise business architects with the tools necessary to do this.

What are the principles of EBA?

In the very definition of enterprise architecture (as presented in the first paragraph of Chapter 1) a great deal of importance is placed upon the enterprise principles governing design and change. Just how important are principles to enterprise business architects? Here's the straight goods on principles:

Principles are a prerequisite for success.

The goal of EBA principles are to facilitate alignment by guiding and governing enterprise design and change. The primary implication of this is that the principles are considered and applied whenever an enterprise business architect engages in strategy development, EBA asset creation, guidance, governance, and evaluation.

There are eight key principles used by enterprise business architecture to make high quality decisions and to create high impact, value-adding work product. These principles are:

1. **The Client Principle.** Every enterprise exists to provide products and services to its clients. The enterprise and all of its organizational units are accountable to the client and responsible for aligning their capabilities in order to best service the clients— whether directly or indirectly. It doesn't take a business genius to know that the enterprise that forgets the client-first principle is doomed. The enterprise business

architect always keeps the client in mind when engaging in the business of alignment.

2. ***The Alignment Principle.*** The aim of enterprise business architecture is to support the enterprise in achieving its strategic business goals and objectives. To do this business capabilities must be supported by IT capabilities. Radical idea? Not at all. Enterprise decision-making puts precedence upon enterprise goals, objectives, and priorities. This means business strategy should not just be known by everyone in the organization, but everyone in the organization should know what they have to do in order to ensure strategic success. Change happens automatically and much of this change throws the enterprise out of alignment; this means change and innovation management must be one of the enterprise's core competencies and agility a core IT capability. This means that the 'common good' of enterprise alignment may take precedence over a 'best-of-breed' decision favoured by any particular organizational unit. This means an optimal decision for a project may be sub-optimal for the enterprise and users—and the optimal decision for enterprise and user must take precedence. The enterprise business architect always keeps enterprise interests in mind when engaging in the business of alignment.

3. ***The Principled Decision Principle.*** All decisions made by the enterprise business architect should be traceable to a foundational principle—like this one. Without principles, decision-making soon falls into chaos and corruption: symptoms are confused with root causes; inconsistent decisions make a mockery of the planning process; hard work is shunned in favour of expedient and easy paths; important work is abandoned in favour of so-called urgent work; quality becomes impossible to measure; standards are forgotten. No work should be undertaken by the enterprise business architect without first consulting foundational principles. Indeed, principles become a useful checklist for enterprise business architects—a way to perform basic due diligence upon new enterprise initiatives. The enterprise business architect always keeps principles at the top the agenda when engaging in the business of alignment.

4. ***The Sustainability Principle.*** If the enterprise sinks,

everybody in it sinks. The enterprise business architect shares in this responsibility for ensuring the enterprise stays afloat—sustainability is a core enterprise virtue. There are many way to define and measure sustainability. The enterprise business architect is concerned with dimensions of sustainability (like supportability, reliability, robustness, agility, integratability, convergence, and long-term affordability) and uses them to help promote clear and coherent decision-making.

5. ***The Continuity Principle.*** Disruptions threaten all enterprises. It does not require clairvoyance to see that some threats will eventually materialize. Business continuity capacity (the ability to maintain operations or quickly recover operating capacity in the event of a disruption) is something the business architect promotes. As enterprises become more complex and business/ technology interdependencies proliferate, it becomes tremendously important to anticipate and mitigate potential disruptions to operations. Not all services, data components, applications, and technology components are critical; to mitigate costs, a business continuity plan identifies mission critical enterprise elements. In some countries, legislation requires some organizations to put business continuity plans into place. The enterprise business architect helps the enterprise keep calm and carry on by doing four important things. First, to understand the business. Second, to understand the impact of disruption to both clients/stakeholders and to the enterprise itself. Third, to identify and rank disruption risks. And, finally, to formulate a business continuity strategy and plan to keep the business going even when disaster strikes.

6. ***The Legal Principle.*** Every enterprise operates within the context of federal/central, state/province, and city/town/county legislation, regulation, and bylaws. The enterprise must conform to the legal landscape in which it operates. Conformance means the enterprise designs its business to comply with legal requirements and undertakes staff education to ensure they have an appropriate awareness of the legal landscape. Of course, the enterprise is always free to lobby for changes to its legal landscape. When the laws change, the enterprise changes with them. The enterprise business architect

maintains a catalog that lists all the legislation, regulations, and bylaws with which the enterprise must comply and always keeps the legal landscape in mind when reviewing the business of the enterprise.

7. ***The Information Principle.*** Information is the single most important asset an organization possesses. Every decision an organization makes is based upon its information. Many organizations are now 100% dependent on information and information technology. Today survival depends upon the enterprise's ability to efficiently and effectively collect information, store it, analyse it, report on it, and to ensure the right people get the right information at the right time. To do this well, every part of the enterprise must manage and share information. The enterprise business architect promotes appropriate information sharing within the context of information management, privacy, and security best practices.

8. ***The Discovery Principle.*** Actually, it's about two kinds of discovery.

First, the enterprise business architect must have the ability to detect (*discover*) emerging IT and business trends, translate those nascent trends into risk and opportunity messages, and, finally, work with business leaders to translate those risks and opportunities into strategic direction for the enterprise. The enterprise business architect must be able to filter out painful bleeding edge ideas and flow through actionable innovation to business leaders. In doing this, the enterprise business architect is an integral member of the enterprise strategic development team.

Second, when an enterprise business architect goes into an engagement, they often discover that very little of the information they require is consciously 'known' and documented on paper. They may go into strategic planning sessions only to realize no goals or objectives have been documented. They may meet with the business only to realize the business has never documented who their stakeholders are or written down their policies or documented their processes. They may meet with IT managers and project people and discover they don't really know what problem the project is supposed to solve and even less of an idea as to how their work fits with the larger enterprise. The enterprise business architect's response is *not* to throw her or his hands in the air, retreat to the office, and wait for better weather. This missing information is essential to bringing the enterprise into alignment. When the enterprise business architect finds that the information they need is not available, they engage in 'discovery consulting'. This means the enterprise business architect asks questions to discover the undocumented strategy. This means they ask questions to discover the list of stakeholders. This means they ask questions to discover the undocumented steps of a process. This means they bring EA assets into the discussion in order to discover the appropriate links between strategy and project problem solving. It is these discoveries the enterprise business architect documents and communicates to EBA clients and stakeholders. Ultimately, it is these discoveries that bring greater levels of organization and a sense of common purpose to the enterprise.

The enterprise business architect is always ready to discover and document gaps and overlaps in the enterprise information landscape and always on the watch for emerging IT and business trends, risks, and opportunities.

These eight principles are extraordinarily practical. And while they may seem like common sense, most people will have to make changes in how they organize their decision-making priorities and how they approach their day-to-day work tasks. Principles are not a nice-to-have thing: "Principles-driven decision-making" is a required behaviour for enterprise business architects in high-performance organizations.

CHAPTER 003

The Three Key Tools of EBA

The business of enterprise architecture requires tools. The enterprise business architect uses three key tools to help them create alignment and value in the enterprise. These tools are: models, catalogs, and interactions. This chapter explains what these tools are and how they are used.

What is a model?

A model is a graphical representation of something. In the case of enterprise architecture, a model is a graphical representation of the past-present-future structure of the enterprise, an enterprise component, or a problem or issue faced by the enterprise and/or enterprise stakeholder.

The IT industry has mastered data models, application, models, and technology models—but the modern enterprise demands a broader perspective. This is why business models have risen to a position of great importance in today's enterprise.

The purpose of a model is to clarify understanding, facilitate education, aid the diagnosis of problems and formation of solutions, depict the structure of something or some process, and, ultimately, support better decision-making. Models are a "means" to these ends. It should go without saying (but bears repeating again and again) that models are not some kind of ivory-tower "end" in and of themselves, they are a means used to realize high quality enterprise behaviours and decisions. As a rule of thumb, only create models if the models create business value.

A model manages complexity by shrinking, simplifying, and/or abstracting its subject matter. To shrink, simplify, and abstract, enterprise business architects push some features of the subject into the foreground and push some aspects of the subject into the background—or removes some aspects all together. The goal is to create as easily understandable a representation of the subject matter as possible in order to suit a particular purpose.

Each model is made up of several elements. A model pattern is a way of arranging these elements. Different arrangements of elements—patterns—serve different purposes and highlight different aspects of the model. Some patterns provide maximum detail. Some patterns provide only summary detail. Some patterns foreground certain elements and background or remove other elements. Any given model may have one or many possible patterns. The right pattern to use depends on the message the model is intended to deliver. The desired level of detail is, usually, the level of detail necessary to support informed decision-making.

The esteemed statistician George Box once wrote: "All models are wrong. But some are useful." Unfortunately, when it comes to models and model patterns, *what's useful* is a moving target, changing from enterprise to enterprise, from architecture engagement to architecture engagement, audience to audience, and architect to architect. In other words, the ultimate utility of any model or model pattern is highly contingent on the engagement, audience, enterprise, and architect.

Models are often grouped into perspectives. In terms of taxonomy, 'perspective' is a fancy word for 'category'. There are any number of ways to categorize models:

- using TOGAF's architecture development cycle phases;
- using the Zachman framework's rows and columns;
- using the Federal Enterprise Architecture's taxonomy;
- using the enterprise business architecture lifecycle phases described in this book; or,
- using a custom categorization/taxonomy that suits the needs of your particular enterprise.

The good thing about categorizing models is that the categorization provides an easy way for novice enterprise business architects to understand the relationship of various models to enterprise stakeholders, processes, and to other models. The drawback to categorization is that categories cement our understanding of models into certain rigid categories—even though these categories reflect only one of several possible ways to categorize models. Models are more complex and flexible than any one system of categorization or taxonomy can capture or account for.

This book presents models without categorization. It is expected that business architects will become familiar with a large repertoire of models and use them whenever and wherever they deem it appropriate. This approach empowers and encourages business architects to plug these models into whatever EA frameworks they find their organization employing, in whatever ways they find useful.

Modeling standards. There are a lot of standard notations out there for modeling. The models in this book are built upon a simple idea. If your audience needs to be "trained" to understand the embedded meaning of a modeling language, then that is a model your audience will never understand. Remember, the audience for enterprise business architecture is made up of senior business executives, stakeholders of all stripes, and enterprise architects. Fellow architects can be expected to follow simple business diagrams. The business executives and various non-IT stakeholders cannot be expected to follow a standard technical IT diagram. So, to avoid modeling the same thing multiple times, simple line and shape diagrams have been employed. Modeling standards are one thing that can be debated at great length. The operating principle behind keeping models simple (free from embedded intelligence) is this: there is no such thing as a business executive with the time or patience or inclination to sit through a training course (even if it's just ten minutes long) just so they can understand the diagrams produced by their enterprise business architect. Additionally, there are lots of tools out there promising to automate the production of enterprise architecture models— and if these tools make sense to you, use them. In the pages that follow, you'll find a wide variety of models that you can create using simple tools (all the models in this book were created using Microsoft Visio). The idea behind this is that once you've developed your key templates, you can quickly and easily produce all the models and model variations you need. Finally, by keeping models simple and easy to produce using relatively accessible tools, you'll have developed a very agile modelling capability.

What is a catalog?

When many people think of enterprise architecture, they think of pretty pictures. What many people (including many architects) fail to realize is that good architecture programs have a strong information management component. The major tool used by architects to manage information is catalogs.

Catalogs are lists of important information related to a particular subject or enterprise component. Catalogs manage information about the enterprise, its structure and relationships, its environment, information critical to the performance of the enterprise, and information critical to the performance of the enterprise business architecture function.

The most important characteristics of a catalog is that it is a source-of-truth for whatever information it contains. As a source-of-truth, the catalog serves as the enterprise's authoritative and complete listing. For example, the Stakeholder Catalog is the enterprise's authoritative and complete listing of stakeholders.

These 'catalog lists' can be implemented in spreadsheets, databases, or using collaborative tools via intranets or internet websites. Each catalog is simple and unique—they do not have complex schemas and relationships. Each catalog focuses on managing information about just one subject or component.

Good catalog implementations provide a way to search, filter, query, investigate relationships, analyze, and report on the catalogued information.

When you look at the number of catalogs defined in this book, it becomes obvious that this is way too much information for a business architect, or two, to maintain on their own. Equally obvious to a business architect is that they do not have to do it all on their own. Getting operational staff to contribute to enterprise catalogs is in perfect keeping with the enterprise business principle that every part of the enterprise shares the responsibility to manage and share enterprise information. The maintenance of some catalogs can be built into the daily workflow of different operational staff and into the deliverables expected from projects. The opportunities to outsource this work is almost limitless. Here are four examples.

- First, the maintenance of the organizational structure catalog can be embedded into the workflow of the human resources unit.
- Second, the maintenance of the technology component catalog can be integrated into the workflow of the network and server group.
- Third, the performance catalog can be kept current by linking its regular updating to the enterprise's service level agreement function; the business analyst unit (home to the BAs) regularly manage client needs and performance expectations and make ideal candidates for being assigned responsibility to keep the performance catalog up-to-date.
- Fourth, and finally, projects can be required to update the

lessons learned catalog as part of the 'closing' stage of their lifecycle.

Catalogs serve a myriad of purposes, not least of which is as a primary data source for creating and understanding interactions.

What is an interaction?

An interaction is a simple table/matrix/grid which maps the relationship between catalogs or between the elements of the same catalog.

Interactions are used for a wide variety of purposes, such as (but not limited to) identifying:

- dependencies,
- alignment points,
- alignment gaps
- overlaps and waste,
- touchpoints,
- quality issues,
- enterprise or project maturity status,
- design states,
- task progress, and
- the scope (boundaries) of a problem, opportunity, or risk.

Interactions are normally created to serve the problem solving, decision-making, and educational requirements of a particular architecture engagement, rather than as an ivory tower activity undertaken for its own sake.

Some interactions are more important than others. Keeping your finger on the pulse of technological dependencies between applications and business services is something of perennial importance and interest to the enterprise; keeping your finger on the pulse of lessons learned and business profile interactions is not.

What interactions are important? The importance of an interaction depends on the circumstances of the architectural engagement and the particulars of the enterprise. Interactions are only valuable or worthwhile if they shed light on a particular problem, solution, or issue. Only create interactions if they create business value.

Table 1 depicts the Stakeholder – Business Services Interaction. This interaction identifies which business services are used by which stakeholders.

TABLE 1

INTERACTIONS	Business Service Name			
Stakeholder Name	Service 1	Service 2	Service 3	Service N
Stakeholder 1	X	X	X	X
Stakeholder 2			X	
Stakeholder 3	X	X	X	X
Stakeholder N				X

There are four basic steps to mapping an interaction.

- First, create a table. These tables are sometimes called a matrix or grid.
- Second, select the first catalog and one of its elements—list this element down the first column of the table. In Table 1, the selected element is 'stakeholder name'.
- Third, select the second catalog and one of its elements—list the contents of this element across a top row. In Table 1, the selected element from the second catalog is 'business service name'.

The following diagram shows the selection process described in steps two and three.

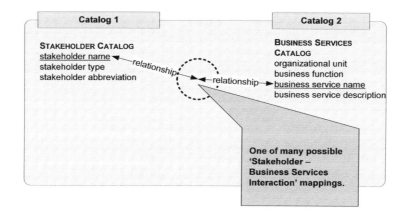

Finally, identify where relationships exist between the listed catalog elements. In Table 1, "X" indicates where a relationship exists between the two catalogs elements.

What's next?

This book explains the *art* of enterprise architecture for enterprise business architects. The *art* were talking about here is immensely practical.

By practicing the art of enterprise architecture, enterprise business architects can:

- demonstrate the value of EA and EBA to the organization;
- create real alignment;
- dramatically reduce strategy confusion;
- create real understanding of the enterprise;
- facilitate high-quality decision-making within the enterprise; and,
- play a crucial role in setting the stage for the enterprise to achieve its strategic goals and objectives.

Enterprise business architects can help bring alignment to the enterprise, but they required the tools to do it. The rest of this book identifies and explains the key tools necessary to create enterprise alignment. Part Two looks at the models. Part Three looks at the catalogs. Part Four looks at the interactions.

As you go through the rest of this book, allow yourself to be challenged by the material, but challenge the material as well. Always keep in mind that there are no cookbooks for any of this; there are no magic formulas or frameworks; master works are not created using the paint-by-number approach. Find ways to apply the ideas and tools you discover—adapt and apply them in your way to your organization. Leverage these ideas and tools to create alignment in your organization. By doing this, the value of enterprise business architecture will be felt at every level of your enterprise.

PART 2

MODELS

CHAPTER 004

Enterprise Business Architecture Lifecycle Model

The Enterprise Business Architecture Lifecycle Model maps the process enterprise business architects use to bring alignment to the enterprise, to create and manage enterprise reference architecture artifacts, and apply enterprise reference architecture artifacts to the development and maintenance of the enterprise. The model answers the question: "What do enterprise business architecture do?"

The Enterprise Business Architecture Lifecycle Model contains the following elements:

- Strategic Planning
- Asset Creation
- Guidance
- Governance
- Evaluation

Strategic Planning. Strategic planning is the process of deliberately documenting the vision, mission, goals and objectives of the enterprise—in both the business and IT realms—in order to ensure the enterprise is healthy, competitive, and possesses or develops the capabilities to fulfil its vision and mission. Strategic plans forecast costs, set timelines, success measures and targets, performance measures and targets, and identify the individuals or parts of the organization responsible for carrying out strategic change.

Asset Creation. Business Architects create enterprise reference architecture assets. The three key types of assets are models, catalogs, and interactions. Other important assets include principles, policy, standards, building blocks, due diligence checklists, architecture decision items, baseline architecture, target architecture, roadmaps, blueprints, and current state assessments.

Guidance. Enterprise architects engage with clients and stakeholders to ensure enterprise alignment—the alignment of tactical plans with strategic plans, and project/program plans with tactical plans. Enterprise reference architecture is the primary tool used to manage engagement and enterprise alignment issues.

Governance. Enterprise business architects review tactical architectural efforts for compliance with the enterprise reference architecture. The goal of this governance activity is to ensure projects, programs, and operational outcomes contribute to the enterprise's desired strategic and tactical outcomes.

Evaluation. Enterprise business architects conduct evaluations to determine if enterprise, project, and program goals were achieved. They ask questions like: did the project deliver a solution that met user needs? did the organizational unit deliver on its tactical objectives? were the strategic outcomes achieved? The results of enterprise business architecture evaluations are used to revise strategies and tactics during new rounds of enterprise planning and to formulate corrective action for in-flight projects and programs.

Pattern 1 lays out the basic elements of the enterprise business architecture lifecycle. It indicates that business architects engage in strategic planning, asset creation, guidance, governance, and evaluation. It also gives examples of what activities can take place at each stage of the lifecycle

Enterprise business architecture is the business of alignment and pattern 2 illustrates exactly what this means. Pattern 2 presents a high-level perspective of the alignment work performed by the enterprise business architect. It maps out how EBA assets are used to enable the alignment efforts of the enterprise business architect. The pattern maps this alignment activity against the backdrop of the enterprise business architecture lifecycle.

Pattern 3 presents the enterprise business architecture lifecycle layered against one possible depiction of the EA value stream. The lifecycle layers indicate which stakeholders (leadership, projects, programs) are involved at each step in the value steam.

Pattern 4 presents the lifecycle as a wheel. In practice, it's not so cut and dry. However, it's a great way to illustrate the lifecycle for business architecture stakeholders.

These four patterns present a good overview of what an enterprise business architect does. The model can also be used to show what an architect has done, is doing, or will do. For example, use pattern 1, label it with the name of a particular unit of work; and, then, list what specific/tactical work is being done at each stage. When business architects do this, they have the potential to operate more efficiently and, when used in this way, the model serves as an easy reference guide to what action needs to be taken in regards to the ongoing enterprise business architecture engagement.

Pattern 5 presents a high-level perspective on the guidance and governance phases of the EBA lifecycle model.

Pattern 6 presents a high-level perspective on the evaluation phase of the EBA lifecycle model.

Pattern 1

BizArch's responsibilities

Strategic Planning	**Plan**	Support development of strategic direction. Support development of strategic plan. Support development of tactical plan.
Asset Creation and Management	**Create**	Develop and Maintain Enterprise Reference Architecture (ERA). Align with strategy. Create new assets. Modify assets. Retire assets.
Guidance	**Guide**	Provide leadership and guidance to the project, program, and operational teams that use the ERA to develop and maintain logical and physical designs and operational assets. Align tactical efforts with strategy.
Governance and Quality Control	**Govern**	At key touchpoints, review tactical architectural efforts for compliance with ERA. Ensure project, program, and operational outcomes align with enterprise's desired strategic and tactical outcomes.
Evaluation and Findings	**Evaluate**	Evaluate the effectiveness and efficiency of enterprise outcomes. Use evaluation results as input for new rounds of strategic planning or for ameliorative action with in-flight programs and projects.

Pattern 2

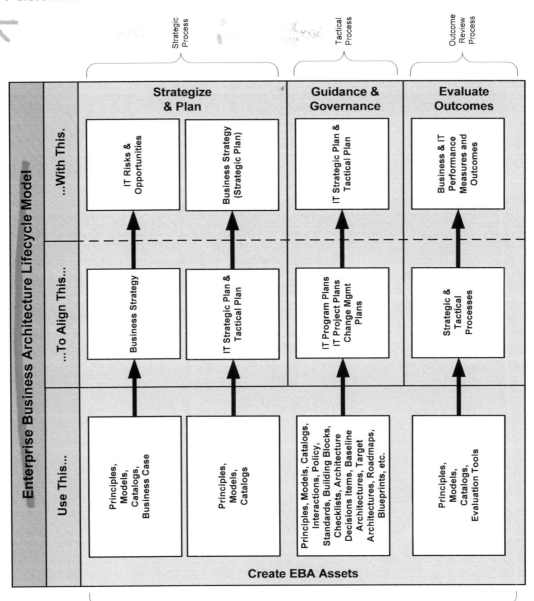

Pattern 3

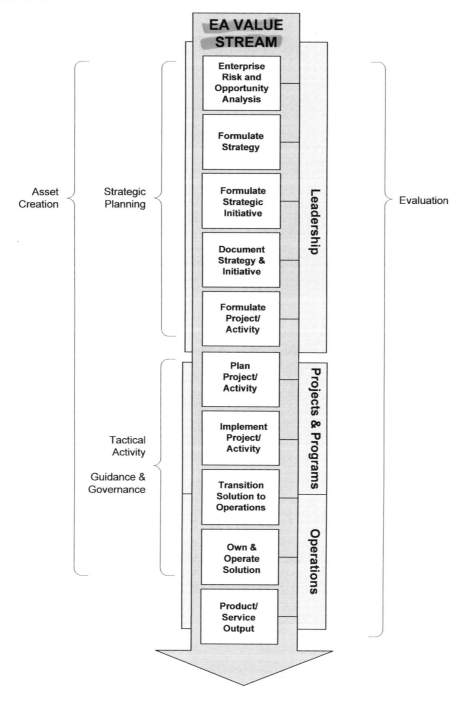

Pattern 4

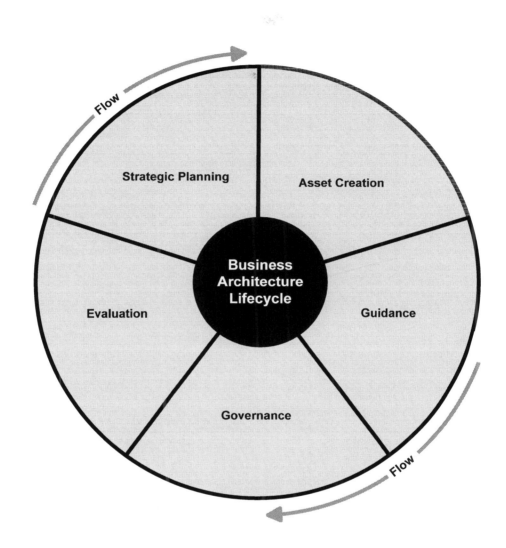

Pattern 5

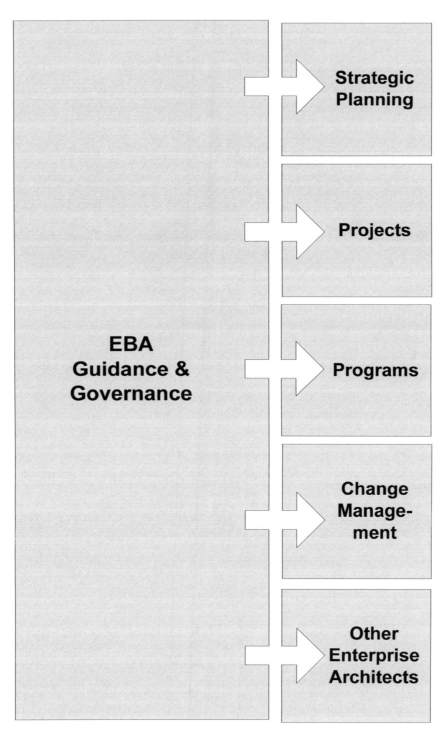

Pattern 6

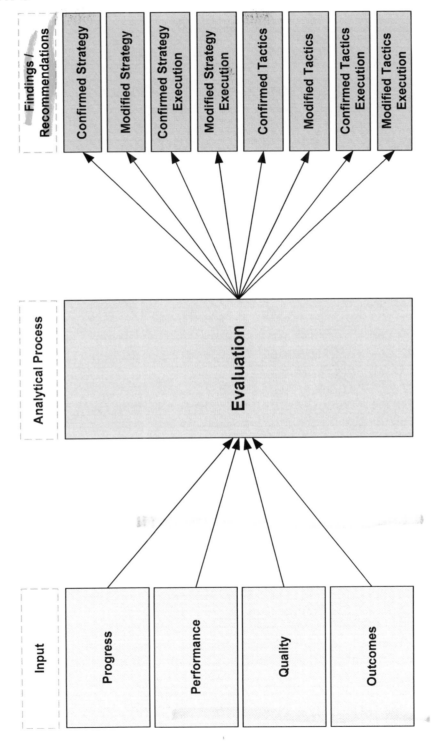

CHAPTER 005

Enterprise Business Architecture and Strategic Planning Lifecycle Touchpoints Model

The Enterprise Business Architecture and Strategic Planning Lifecycle Touchpoints Model documents the business architect's role in the IT strategic planning process.

The Enterprise Business Architecture and Strategic Planning Touchpoints Model contains the following elements:

- IT Strategic Planning Lifecycle Model,
- Business Architecture Touchpoints

IT Strategic Planning Lifecycle Model. The IT Strategic Planning Lifecycle Model is a simplified representation of the IT strategic planning lifecycle. Like the lifecycle itself, the model attempts to answer the following questions for the enterprise: Where are we? Where have we been? Where are we going? How are we going to get there? Are we on the right path? Are we there yet? The reason for asking these questions is to understand the business, how the business needs to change, and to ensure that strategic change plays out as intended.

Business Architecture Touchpoints. The business architecture touchpoints are the interaction points or points of contact between enterprise business architects and their clients. Touchpoints provide clients with guidance, governance, or both.

The IT Strategic Planning Lifecycle Model in patterns 1 and 3 and the Business Planning Lifecycle Model in pattern 4 are based upon the following strategic planning components:

- Current State Analysis
- Mission/Mandate
- Future State Vision
- Goals & Objectives
- Strategic Plan
- Tactical Plan / Action Plan
- Business Plan
- Roadmap
- Due Diligence
- Performance Measures
- Dashboard Tracking & Monitoring
- Success Measures

Current State Analysis. The current state analysis is a process that examines the enterprise and enterprise components and documents a baseline picture of the enterprise. The terms 'baseline' and 'current state' are often used synonymously. The analysis looks at how the industry or jurisdiction is evolving, how the competition is changing, and how the organization's key value streams are changing or need to change. This snapshot of the enterprise is point-in-time specific and identifies important issues, strengths, weaknesses, opportunities, threats, and provides all metrics of relevance to the enterprise's strategic decision-makers.

Mission / Mandate. A mission or mandate statement describes what the business is in existence to do—its *raison d'être*. (This is different from a vision statement which describes a future state target for the business to work towards.) The terms mission and mandate appear to be synonymous—but there is a difference worth noting. A mission is the enterprise's high-level purpose and completes this statement: *The enterprise exists to _____*. A mandate is a duty the enterprise is authorized and/or required to perform. Mandates are often set out in legislation or legally binding contracts. The mission/mandate statement takes the form of a textual description.

Future State Vision. A vision statement describes a future state which the enterprise desires to work towards.

Goals & Objectives. Goals are the targets that, when achieved, will transition the enterprise towards its future state vision. Goals guide enterprise decision-making about the type, scope and priority of all enterprise activity. Objectives are the measurable achievements that, when achieved, will move the enterprise towards the realization of its goals.

Strategic Plan. A strategic plan documents the vision, mission, goals and objectives of the enterprise—in both the business and IT realms—in order to ensure the enterprise is competitive and possesses or develops the capabilities to fulfil its vision and mission. Strategic plans forecast costs, set timelines, success measures and targets, performance measures and targets, and identify the individuals or parts of the organization responsible for carrying out strategic change.

Tactical Plan / Action Plan. The tactical plans or action plans at the strategic level describe how the strategic plan will be implemented at the enterprise level and how the strategy will play out from the perspective of each of the enterprise's organizational units or divisions. The tactical plan identifies initiatives which outline how resources will be marshalled in order to meet strategic goals and objectives. Elements of a strategic level tactical or action plan are sometimes included in the strategic plan document.

Business Plan. An element labelled 'business plan' is not found in any of the strategic planning model patterns. While the business world is perfectly clear on what a strategic plan is, there is much less clarity on what the term business plan means. The term 'business plan' seems to mean whatever anyone wants it to mean. However, there appears to be two very different documents that call themselves 'business plans'. The first of these documents is a marketing tool that explains the nature of the business activity, why the business will be successful, and how success will be achieved; it's used to attract or justify investment in an organization, capability, or project and the document is usually targeted at potential investors or shareholders, or, in the case of government, leaders with the power to allocate budgets. This kind of plan includes an analysis of markets, competitors, products, services, strengths and weaknesses, and risks and contingencies. We're not interested in this type of business plan. We are, however, interested in the second type of 'business plan' document which is used to implement strategy in an organization; it does this by elaborating on how, in the short term, the enterprise plans to organize and expend resources and, then, the document explains how each organizational unit (or line of business) plans to organize and expend resources. This type of business plan outlines steps to achieve the strategy and how to measure progress and performance. This kind of business plan is not an operational-level tactical plan, however, it merely refines strategy by describing how strategy plays out for the organization and how that strategy plays out in the operations of each organizational unit (IT, HR, finance, marketing, R&D, *et cetera*). In this sense, it is a tactical document at the strategic level, not at the operational or project level. Due to this lack of standard meaning, the term 'business plan' in not used in this or any other model.

Roadmap. A roadmap identifies the path the organization will follow as it transitions between a current state and a defined future state. The roadmap usually identifies interim states—phases—that mark progresses between the current and future state. Roadmaps are also called *transition plans* and *migration plans*.

Due Diligence. Prudent oversight of a strategy's implementation requires active due diligence reviews of in-flight work. The purpose of the due diligence is to ensure the in-flight work will meet quality objectives, i.e., that in-flight work will deliver results aligned with the strategic goals and objectives. For an IT system, this means the deliverable meets the needs of its users.

Performance Measures. Performance measures and targets are the qualitative or quantitative metrics used to determine if enterprise components or component resources (people, data, applications, technology, processes) are *performing* their roles appropriately.

Dashboard Tracking & Monitoring. Dashboards are tools used to manage enterprise performance and contain data on key performance indicators. They are used for monitoring purposes: to help align business activity with enterprise strategy.

Success Measures. Success measures and targets are the qualitative or quantitative metric used to determine if enterprise goals and objectives have been achieved.

It is often the Business Architect's job to ask obvious questions, such as the questions outlined above in the IT Strategic Planning Lifecycle Model description. Warning: if your organization has not thought about these obvious questions, be prepared for some uncomfortable moments.

Pattern 1 presents the basic outline of the Enterprise Business Architecture and Strategic Planning Touchpoints Model.

The strategic planning model in pattern 2 and 3 are generic enough to apply to either business or IT planning and can be adapted accordingly.

Pattern 2 is particularly useful for discovery consulting—for those engagements where the information necessary to conduct enterprise business architecture effectively is not yet documented and must be 'discovered'.

Pattern 4 maps interactions between the enterprise business architect and the business strategic planning lifecycle model. The business architect provides "input" to the business strategy, but is not a key crafter of business strategy. The enterprise business architect is a key player in the creation of IT strategy. The exception to this is when IT is being used to drive business change—in this case the business architect is integrally involved, and the "inputs" take on great strategic importance.

Pattern 1

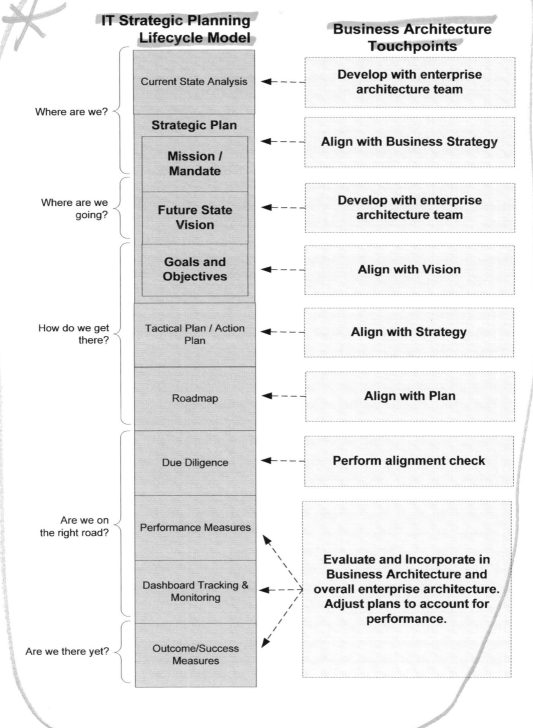

Pattern 2

1. WHERE ARE WE?

2. WHERE ARE WE GOING?

3. HOW DO WE GET THERE?

4. ARE WE ON THE RIGHT ROAD?

5. ARE WE THERE YET?

Pattern 3

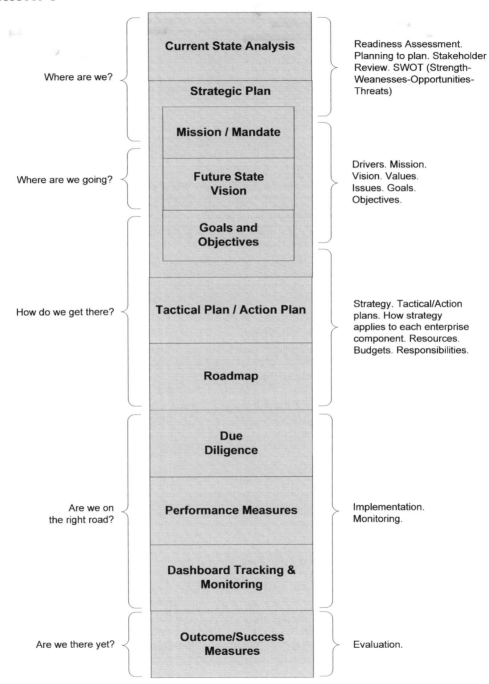

Current State Analysis

Strategic Plan

Mission / Mandate

Future State Vision

Goals and Objectives

Tactical Plan / Action Plan

Roadmap

Due Diligence

Performance Measures

Dashboard Tracking & Monitoring

Outcome/Success Measures

Where are we?

Where are we going?

How do we get there?

Are we on the right road?

Are we there yet?

Readiness Assessment. Planning to plan. Stakeholder Review. SWOT (Strength-Weanesses-Opportunities-Threats)

Drivers. Mission. Vision. Values. Issues. Goals. Objectives.

Strategy. Tactical/Action plans. How strategy applies to each enterprise component. Resources. Budgets. Responsibilities.

Implementation. Monitoring.

Evaluation.

Pattern 4

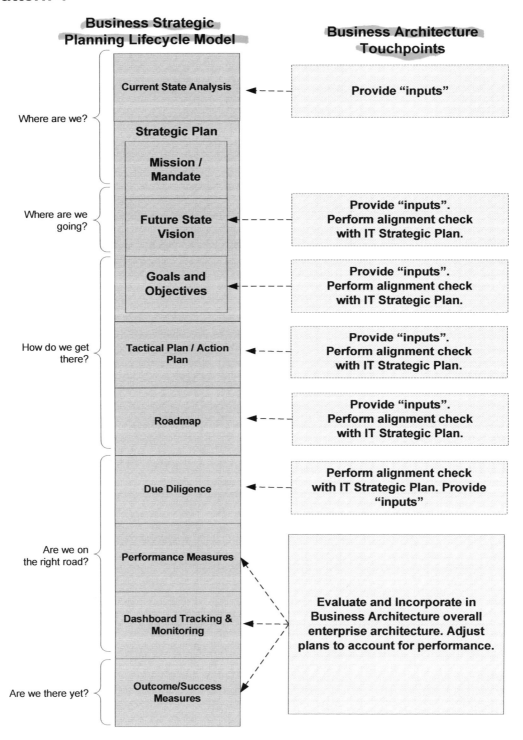

CHAPTER 006

Enterprise Business Architecture and IT Asset Lifecycle Touchpoints Model

The Enterprise Business Architecture and IT Asset Lifecycle Touchpoints Model documents the business architect's role in the IT asset lifecycle. The model explores in detail seven phases of the IT Asset Lifecycle and each phase's relationship with enterprise business architecture.

The Enterprise Business Architecture and IT Asset Lifecycle Touchpoints Model contains the following elements:

- IT Asset Lifecycle
- Business Architecture Touchpoints

IT Asset Lifecycle. The IT asset lifecycle describes the stages through which an IT asset passes over the course of its life within the enterprise, from its first selection and deployment to it final retirement from use.

Business Architecture Touchpoints. The business architecture touchpoints are the interaction points or points of contact between enterprise business architects and their clients. Touchpoints provide clients with guidance, governance, or both.

The IT asset lifecycle contains the following elements:

IT Strategy. The first phase of the IT asset lifecycle begins with IT strategy. In this phase, IT strategy identifies the need for a new IT asset.

IT Plan. In the seconds phase of the lifecycle, an IT plan is created. It identifies the resources necessary to acquire or develop the asset. Aligning the IT plan with IT strategy means the architect ensures resources set out in the tactical plan are used to acquire an asset capable of fulfilling the broader enterprise strategy.

Acquire or Develop. Trial. In the third and fourth phase—acquire or develop and trial—the IT asset is created and its performance refined so that it fits the purposes for which the asset was brought into the enterprise. During these phases, the business architect aligns work on the asset—usually performed by a project—with the IT (tactical) plan, the enterprise reference architecture, and, with the relevant service level requirements. This means the business architect provides guidance and governance services to the project.

Operate. Maintain & Enhance. In the fifth and sixth phase—the operate and the maintain & enhance phases—the new asset is used by its intended users. During this phase, from time to time (usually in conjunction with updates to the reference architecture), the business architect will perform alignment checks of the asset against changing business and IT strategy and plans. The goal of this phase is to ensure quality: that the asset meets users needs and service level objectives.

Decommission. In the final phase the asset is retired. The asset decommissioning is documented in the enterprise reference architecture.

Pattern 1

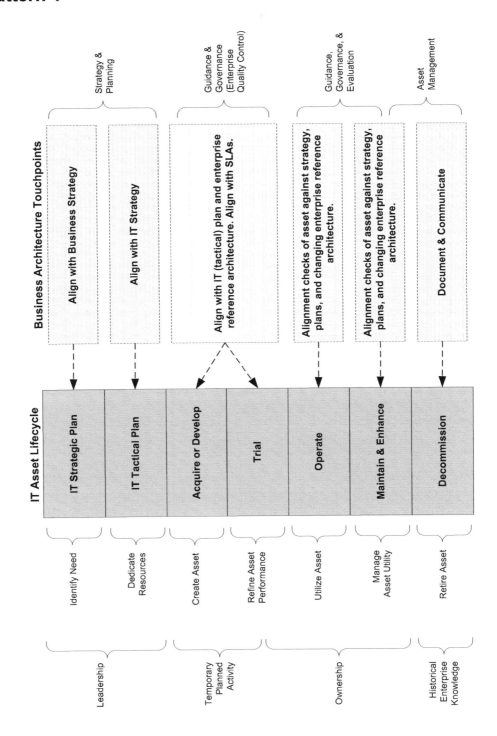

Pattern 2

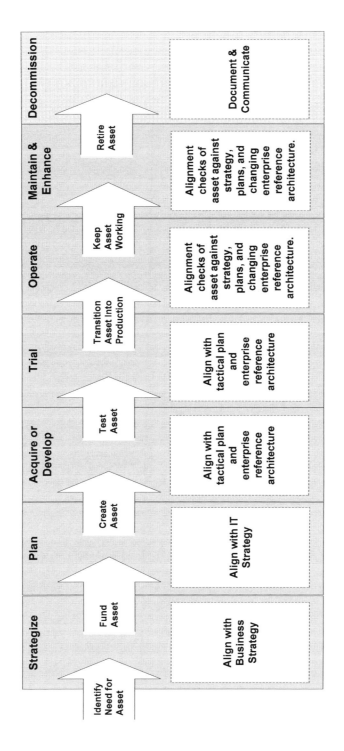

CHAPTER 007

Enterprise Business Architecture and IT Project Touchpoints Model

The Enterprise Business Architecture and IT Project Touchpoints Model documents the business architect's guidance and governance role in the IT project lifecycle.

The Enterprise Business Architecture and IT Project Touchpoints Model contains the following elements:

- IT Project Lifecycle
- Business Architecture Touchpoints

IT Project Lifecycle. The IT Project Lifecycle describes the stages through which an IT project passes from its first inception to it final closing.

Business Architecture Touchpoints. The business architecture touchpoints are the interaction points or points of contact between enterprise business architects and their clients. Touchpoints provide clients with guidance, governance, or both.

The IT project lifecycle model contains the following elements:

Initiation. During the initiation phase of the IT project lifecycle the project concept is confirmed. The concept is not developed during the initiation phase, it is an input from the

IT tactical plan. The business architect ensures the project concept aligns with both the IT tactical plan and the enterprise reference architecture. There should be a gated approval (go or no-go) provided by the business architect at the end of this phase.

Planning. In the second phase—planning—the IT project lifecycle confirms the project scope and develops a project plan. The business architect works with the project to ensure project scope and plans align with the IT tactical plan and enterprise reference architecture. There should be a gated approval at the end of this phase.

Design. The design phase begins the process to create the project deliverables. The design work delineates the shape of the new enterprise IT asset through either a buy or build process. The business architect works with the project to ensure the design aligns with the IT tactical plan and enterprise reference architecture. There should be a gated approval at the end of this phase.

Buy Track. Build Track. Between the design and test phase there are two possible tracks: the buy track and the build track. While these tracks are underway, the business architect stays informed of progress. The buy track procures the asset—often as a commercial off the shelf asset—and then configures and, possibly, customizes it for the enterprise. The build track sees the asset built first as a prototype and if the prototype is successful, the full system is then developed.

Test. The purpose of the test phase is to ensure the developed asset works as planned. The business architect works with the project to ensure the design aligns with the IT tactical plan, enterprise reference architecture, and service level agreements. There should be a gated approval at the end of this phase.

Deploy The deploy phase sees the asset transitioned from the test environment to the operational environment. The business architect may perform an evaluation on the new asset at this time. There should be a gated approval at the end of this phase.

Closing. The closing phase wraps up the project. During this phase the project supplies enterprise architecture programs with relevant work product, which is then archived in the enterprise architecture repository.

Quality matters. A perennial challenge with projects is that at any stage in-scope requirements and solution functionality can be de-scoped—declared 'out-of-scope'. This is one of the primary ways that project deliverables get out of alignment with the needs of the users and the needs of the enterprise. Projects de-scope to stay on budget, to stick to their timelines, and to keep their resource consumption on plan. Couple this with the project manager's understanding of quality: to PMs quality often seems to be the business of minimizing software defects or, in fact, staying on time and on budget. Of course, this notion of quality is not the kind of quality the enterprise needs to keep its eye on.

The big question for business architects to ask is: "Is the project on quality?" By 'quality' the enterprise business architect means two closely related things. First, does the project solution meet user needs? Second, is the project scoped appropriately so that it delivers true utility to the enterprise? If a project de-scopes an important requirement—such as the software perform a key function—then the utility of the delivered system is compromised and the ability of the enterprise to fulfil its goals and objectives is compromised. In the context of scope, alignment should be reviewed at every checkpoint / approval gate.

Pattern 1

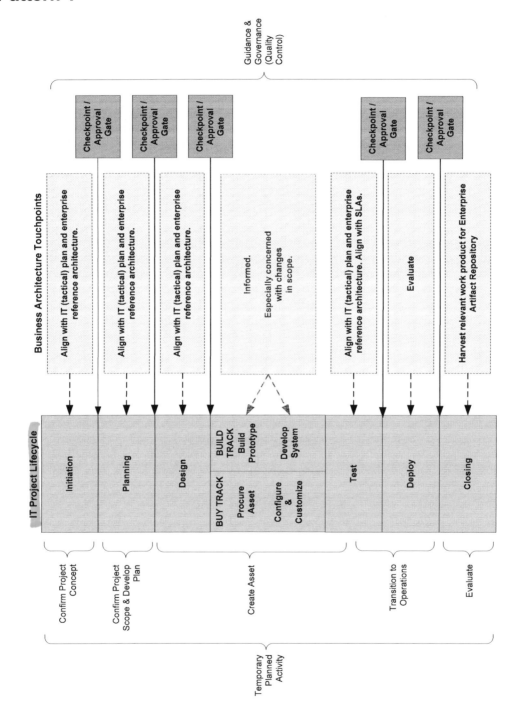

Chapter 008

Enterprise Business Architecture Alignment Assurance Model

The Enterprise Business Architecture Alignment Model shows the links between business strategy, IT strategy, IT tactical planning, operational and project planning, and the enterprise's physical IT structure. This model helps clarify the relationship between strategy, business capabilities, IT capabilities, and supporting resources.

The Enterprise Business Architecture Alignment Model contains the following elements:

- Business Strategy
- IT Strategy
- IT Tactical Plan
- Operational & Project Plans
- Business Structure
- IT Structure

Business Strategy. Strategy is the means used by the enterprise to pursue its mission or mandate. Business strategy is defined by the vision, goals and objectives of the enterprise in order to ensure the enterprise is competitive and possesses or develops the capabilities to fulfil its mission or mandate. This strategy forecasts costs, sets timelines, identifies resources, and identifies the individuals or parts of the organization responsible for carrying out strategic change.

IT Strategy. IT strategy is defined by IT specific definitions of vision, mission, goals, and objectives. IT strategy is crafted to support the business capabilities necessary to fulfil business strategy.

IT Tactical Plan. The IT tactical plan describes "how" the IT strategy will be executed. If we think of strategy as a *diagnosis*, then the tactical plan is the *treatment plan*. The IT tactical plan breaks down the actionable steps for transforming the IT strategy into reality.

Operational & Project Plans. Operational plans and project plans are tactical-level plans, however, they provide more detail than found in an enterprise's tactical plan. These plans are a further refinement of the enterprise's tactical plan. An operational plan sets out the details of "how" operational objectives are going to be met. The operational plan breaks down the actionable steps necessary for meeting their operational objectives. A project plan sets out the detail of "how" the project objectives are going to be realized. The project plan breaks down the actionable steps that must be taken in order for the project deliverables to be operationalized.

Business Structure. Business structure refers to the organizational form of the enterprise, the relationship between organizational units, business functions, business services, and business processes. Business structure gives form to the functions of a business capability.

IT Structure. IT structure refers to a particular collection of IT enterprise assets that are put in place to support a particular business structure. The core elements of IT structure are: data, application, technology, and infrastructure. IT structures give form to the functions of an IT capability.

The model is intended to trace the relationship between actual elements of strategy, plans, and capabilities. Pattern 2 extends the relationship to people and skills. Pattern 4 traces the relationship to the underlying data, application, technology and infrastructure components. The model makes it clear that there are many alignment points in the enterprise: plans align with business and IT capabilities, business and IT capabilities align with physical IT infrastructure, and business and IT capabilities and IT structure require the enterprise to align people and skills. Each alignment point offers a unique perspective from which to examine alignment.

To make this model come alive, put specifics in place of the labels. In place of 'business strategy' insert a business goal or objective. In place of 'IT strategy', insert a goal or objective. In place of 'IT tactical plan', insert an actual planned activity. In place of 'operational and project plans', insert an actual planned outcome/deliverable. If also considering capabilities, relate each strategy element to an aspect of the desired capability.

Filling in this model creates a storyline. For example: To address *Business Strategy Item X*, IT strategy added *IT Strategy Item Y*. The implementation steps for *IT Strategy Item Y* are *actions A, B, and C* from the IT tactical plan. The operational and project plan *actions M, N, and O* are related to tactical *actions A, B, and C*. In this way complex relationships can be traced and validated and a high-level strategic-tactical gap analysis can be performed.

Pattern 5 represents the relationship between the actual plans. The pattern visually depicts the following three-step narrative: First, the IT strategic plans implement the enterprise strategic plan. Second, the IT tactical plans implement IT strategic plans. Finally, operational IT unit plans, IT project plans, and change management plans implement the IT tactical plan.

Pattern 1

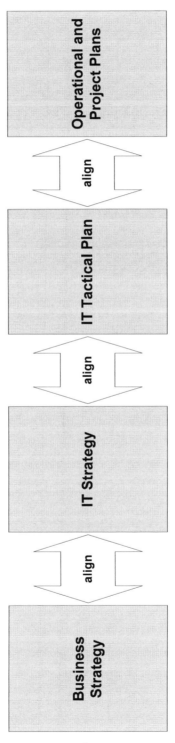

Pattern 2

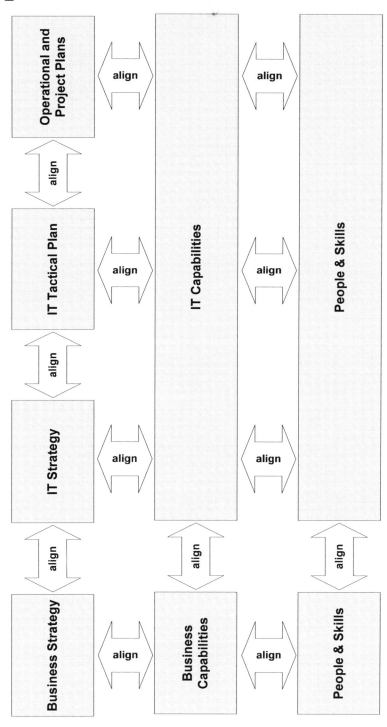

Pattern 3

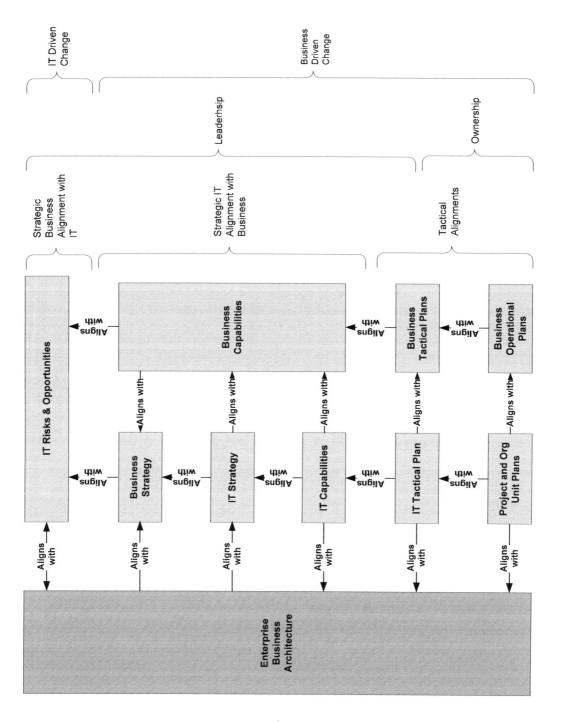

Pattern 4

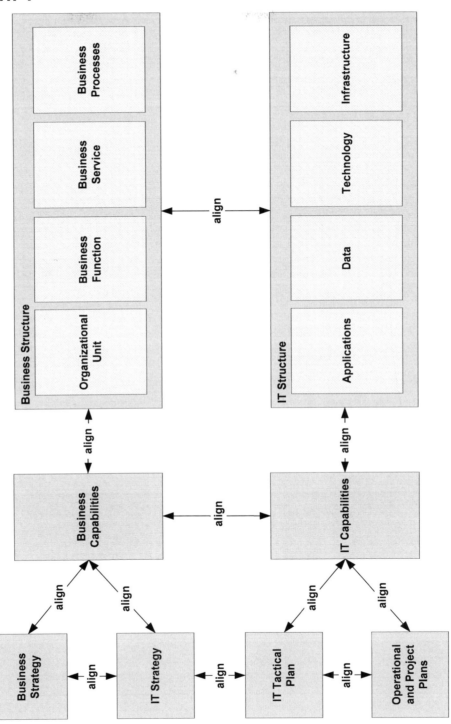

Pattern 5

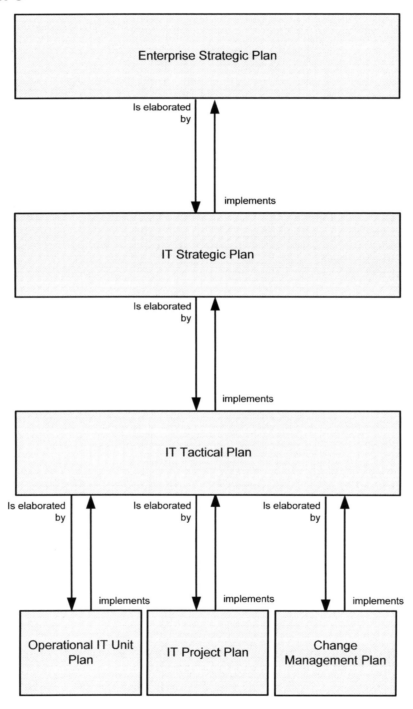

CHAPTER 009

Enterprise Mission/Mandate Model

The Enterprise Mission/Mandate Model documents the enterprise's mission/mandate statement and identifies the mission/mandate objectives embedded in the statement. Mission and mandate statements are usually made up of long prose sentences; translating them into a series of short, clear mission/mandate objectives makes communicating the mission/mandate easier and makes tracking strategic alignment with the enterprise's mission/mandate a straightforward exercise.

The Enterprise Strategic Plan Model contains the following elements:

- Mission/Mandate Statement
- Mission/Mandate Objective
- Source

Mission/Mandate Statement. A mission or mandate statement describes what the business is in existence to do— its *raison d'être.* (This is different from a vision statement which describes a future state target for the business to work towards.) The terms mission and mandate appear to be synonyms—but there is a difference worth noting. A mission is the enterprise's high-level purpose and completes this statement: *The enterprise exists to _____.* A mandate is a duty the enterprise is authorized and/or required to perform. Mandates are often set out in legislation or legally binding contracts. The mission/mandate statement is a textual description of the mission or mandate.

Mission/Mandate Objective. A mission/mandate objective is a statement about something the enterprise wishes to achieve. Mission/mandate objectives are embedded in almost all mission/mandate statements. This element of the model is created by parsing the mission/mandate statement and identifying each of the embedded mission/mandate objectives.

Source. This element of the model identifies the document from which the mission/mandate statement is quoted.

Pattern 1 presents the standard mission/mandate statement model. The following page shows *Pattern 1 Example*, which presents pattern 1 filled in with data from a fictional company.

Pattern 2 presents a summary list of mission/mandate objectives.

Pattern 3 is particularly useful for discovery consulting—for those engagements where the information necessary to conduct enterprise business architecture effectively is not yet documented and must be 'discovered'. Mandate/mission statements are usually documented, so, when this case, pattern 3 can serve as a worksheet for parsing the statement into objective statements.

Pattern 1

MISSION/MANDATE STATEMENT MODEL
for [NAME OF ENTERPRISE]

Mission/Mandate Statement

1 Mission/Mandate Objective	6 Mission/Mandate Objective
2 Mission/Mandate Objective	7 Mission/Mandate Objective
3 Mission/Mandate Objective	8 Mission/Mandate Objective
4 Mission/Mandate Objective	9 Mission/Mandate Objective
5 Mission/Mandate Objective	10 Mission/Mandate Objective

Source of Mandate Statement

Pattern 1 Example

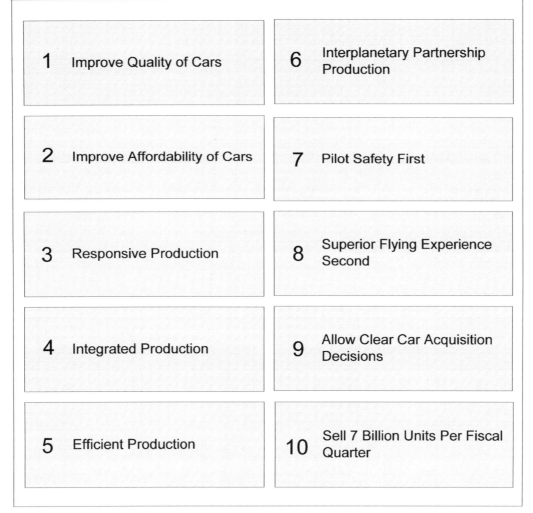

MISSION STATEMENT MODEL
for MAKE-BELIEVE MOTORS INC

Make-Believe Motors strives to produce the highest quality and most affordable line of flying cars in the galaxy Through leadership, innovation and interplanetary partnership, Make-Believe Motors is dedicated to achieving a responsive, integrated and efficient partner-based production system that puts pilot safety first, and enables pilots to achieve a superior flying experience and make a superior flying car acquisition decision. Make-Believe Motors will sell 7 billion cars per fiscal quarter.

1	Improve Quality of Cars	6	Interplanetary Partnership Production
2	Improve Affordability of Cars	7	Pilot Safety First
3	Responsive Production	8	Superior Flying Experience Second
4	Integrated Production	9	Allow Clear Car Acquisition Decisions
5	Efficient Production	10	Sell 7 Billion Units Per Fiscal Quarter

Source of Mandate Statement: MBM Strategic Plan for 2310-11.

Pattern 2

ENTERPRISE MISSION

Mission/Mandate Objective 1
Mission/Mandate Objective 2
Mission/Mandate Objective 3
Mission/Mandate Objective 4
Mission/Mandate Objective 5
Mission/Mandate Objective 6
Mission/Mandate Objective 7
Mission/Mandate Objective 8
Mission/Mandate Objective 9
Mission/Mandate Objective 10

Pattern 3

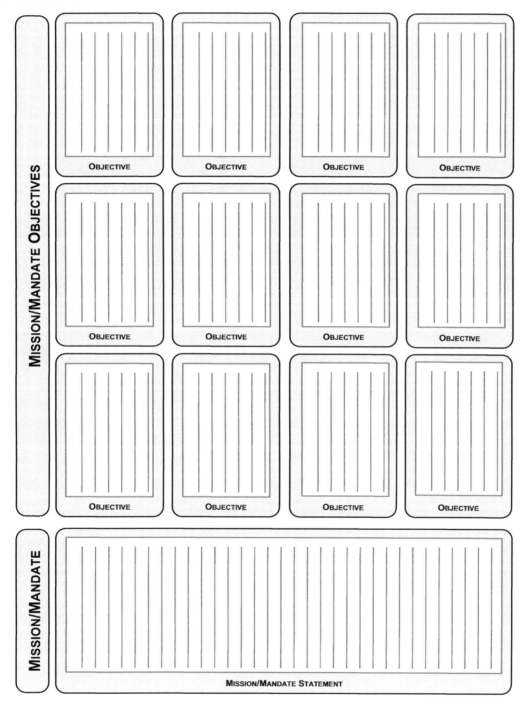

CHAPTER 010

Enterprise Strategic Plan Model

The Enterprise Strategic Plan Model documents the key elements of the enterprise's strategic plan. It can also be used to model the IT strategic plan. The purpose of the model is to translate the enterprise strategic plan into something easily understood by the clients and stakeholders of the enterprise business architect. Strategic plans need to be translated for many reasons: the plans are often filled with obscure business jargon, warm fuzzy statements or scary statements, oceans of charts and tables, and pictures of people either smiling or grimacing at the camera. In short, the enterprise business architect uses this model to strip away the pyrotechnics of the presentation, the fluff and puffery, the distracting detail, and the nice-to-know and focuses attention on the need-to-know aspects of the plan.

The model is particularly useful to the enterprise business architecture because the model identifies the crucial baseline alignment data necessary to promote alignment within the enterprise.

The Enterprise Strategic Plan Model contains the following elements:

- Mission / Mandate
- Business Drivers
- Vision Statement
- Goals
- Objectives
- Measures of Success
- Responsible Unit(s)
- New Capability
- New Data
- New Application

- New Technology
- New People/Roles/Skills
- Budget Allocation
- Other Resources

Mission / Mandate. A mission or mandate statement describes what the business is in existence to do—its *raison d'être*. (This is different from a vision statement which describes a future state target for the business to work towards.) The terms mission and mandate appear to be synonyms—but there is a difference worth noting. A mission is the enterprise's high-level purpose and completes this statement: *The enterprise exists to _____.* A mandate is a duty the enterprise is authorized and/or required to perform. Mandates are often set out in legislation or legally binding contracts. The mission/mandate statement takes the form of a textual description.

Business Drivers. Business drivers are the events and situations which motivate the business to take particular actions.

Vision Statement. A vision statement describes a future state which the enterprise desires to work towards.

Goals. Goals are the targets that, when achieved, will transition the enterprise towards its future state vision. Goals guide enterprise decision-making about the type, scope and priority of all enterprise activity.

Objectives. Objectives are the measurable achievements that, when achieved, will move the enterprise towards the realization of its goals.

Measures of Success. Success measures and targets are the qualitative or quantitative metric used to determine if enterprise goals and objectives have been achieved.

Responsible Unit(s). This element identifies who in the enterprise is responsible for the success of a specific goal and/or objective. A responsible unit may be an organizational unit, business function, business service, or project team.

New Capability. If the strategic plan requires a new enterprise capability to be developed, this element identifies that new capability. Business capabilities are made up of organizational units and people, business functions, business services and processes. IT capabilities are made up of data and information components, application components, and technology components.

New Data. If the strategic plan requires a new enterprise data component to be developed, this element identifies that new component.

New Application. If the strategic plan requires a new enterprise application component to be developed, this element identifies that new application component.

New Technology. If the strategic plan requires a new enterprise technology component to be developed, this element identifies that new technology component

New People/Roles/Skills. If the strategic plan requires new roles, new people, or new skills, this element identifies those roles, people, and/or skills.

Budget Allocation. Change is never free. This element identifies the budget allocation necessary to implement the goals and objectives of the strategic plan.

Other Resources. To implement goals and objectives, sometimes resources need to be added or borrowed, such as office space (for certain durations), secondments, special equipment borrowed from other parts of the organization. This element identifies all of the other known resources required to carry out the goals and objectives of the strategic plan.

Pattern 1 presents an overview of the strategic plan's mission/mandate and its vision, goals, and objectives.

Pattern 2 focuses on presenting the strategic plan's vision and goals.

Pattern 3 presents a more complex view of the strategic plan, incorporating the mission/mandate, business drivers, vision statement, goals, and objectives.

Pattern 4 presents a simplified version of the strategic plan, incorporating the mission/mandate, business drivers, vision statement, goals, objectives, and measures of success.

Pattern 5 presents the strategic plan's vision, goals, and objectives in a simplified format. This pattern is useful for presenting complex lists of goals and objectives.

Pattern 6 focuses attention on one goal at a time and one objective. This pattern identifies important information from the strategic plan; this information may include: a measure of success, responsible unit(s), new capability, new data, new application, new technology, new people, roles, skills, budget allocation, and other resources.

Like pattern 6, pattern 7 focuses attention on one goal at a time. However, unlike pattern 6, pattern 7 looks at *all* of the goal's related objectives. For each objective—when appropriate—this pattern identifies important information from the strategic plan, such as: a measure of success, responsible unit(s), new capability, new data, new application, new technology, new people/roles/skills, budget allocation, and other resources. Pattern 7 is particularly useful for communicating the complex details of the strategic plan in a simple and straightforward way and for checking the completeness of the strategic plan.

Pattern 1

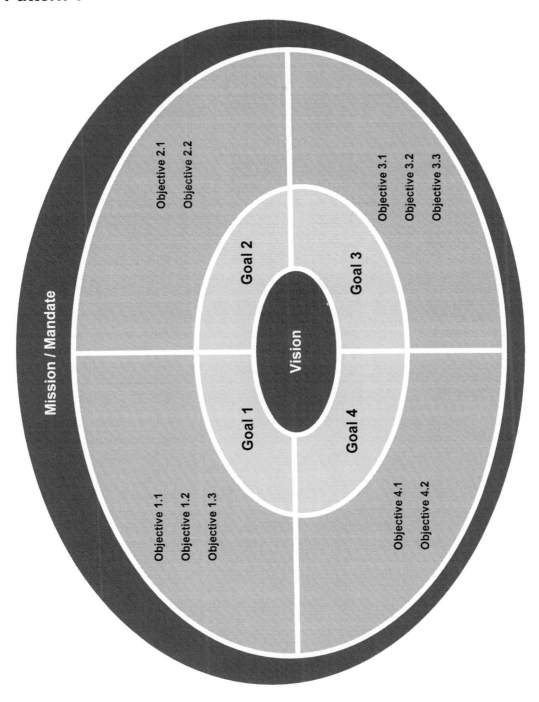

Pattern 2

ENTERPRISE STRATEGIC PLAN

Vision
Goal 1
Goal 2
Goal 3
Goal 4
Goal 5
Goal 6
Goal 7
Goal 8
Goal 9
Goal 10

Pattern 3

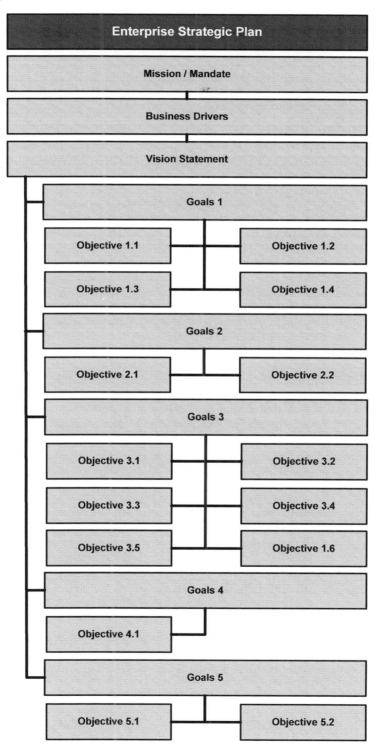

Pattern 4

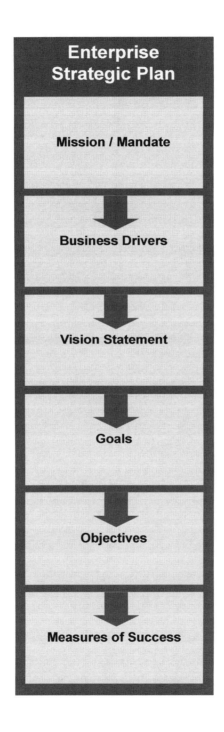

Pattern 5

ENTERPRISE STRATEGIC PLAN

Vision

GOAL 1				
Objective 1.1	Objective 1.2	Objective 1.3	Objective 1.4	Objective 1.5
GOAL 2				
Objective 2.1	Objective 2.2	Objective 2.3	Objective 2.4	Objective 2.5
GOAL 3				
Objective 3.1	Objective 3.2	Objective 3.3	Objective 3.4	Objective 3.5
GOAL 4				
Objective 4.1	Objective 4.2	Objective 4.3	Objective 4.4	Objective 4.5
GOAL 5				
Objective 5.1	Objective 5.2	Objective 5.3	Objective 5.4	Objective 5.5

Pattern 6

GOAL 1
Objective 1.1
Measure of Success
Responsible Unit(s)
New Capability
New Data
New Application
New Technology
New People/Roles/Skills
Budget Allocation
Other Resources

Pattern 7

GOAL 1				
Objective 1.1	Objective 1.2	Objective 1.3	Objective 1.4	Objective 1.5
Measure of Success	Measure of Success	Measure of Success	Measure of Success	Measure of Success
Responsible Unit(s)	Responsible Unit(s)	Responsible Units(s)	Responsible Unit(s)	Responsible Unit(s)
New Capability	New Capability	New Capability	New Capability	New Capability
New Data	New Data	New Data	New Data	New Data
New Application	New Application	New Application	New Application	New Application
New Technology	New Technology	New Technology	New Technology	New Technology
New People/Roles/ Skills	New People/Roles/ Skills	New People/Roles/ Skills	New People/Roles/ Skills	New People/Roles/ Skills
Budget Allocation	Budget Allocation	Budget Allocation	Budget Allocation	Budget Allocation
Other Resources	Other Resources	Other Resources	Other Resources	Other Resources

CHAPTER 011

IT Tactical Plan Model

The IT Tactical Plan Model documents the key elements of an IT department's tactical plan. The purpose of the model it to translate the tactical plan into something easily understood by the clients and stakeholders of the enterprise business architect. This model is often created first and used to guide the drafting of the IT Tactical Plan. A key use of this model is to focus attention on the primary initiatives of the IT department.

The IT Tactical Plan Model contains the following elements:

- IT Tactical Plan
- Tactical Initiative
- Tactical (Initiative) Goal
- Tactical (Initiative) Objective
- Tactical (Initiative) Performance Measure
- Tactical Activity (Project or Program)

Tactical Plan. The tactical plan describes how the strategic IT plan will be implemented and how the IT strategy will play out for each IT organizational unit. The tactical plan identifies tactical initiatives that align with strategic goals and articulates tactical goals, objectives, performance measures, and identifies tactical activity (which takes the form of either project activity or program activity).

Tactical Initiative. An initiative is a unit of work to be undertaken as part of the tactical plan. Each initiative has its own set of tactical goals, tactical objectives, performance measures, and tactical activities (or actions) which take the form of project work or program (unit) work.

Tactical (Initiative) *Goals.* Tactical Goals are the targets that, when met, will result in the enterprise achieving the aims of the tactical initiative.

Tactical (Initiative) *Objectives.* Tactical Objectives are the measurable achievements that, when achieved, will move the enterprise towards the realization of its tactical goals.

Tactical (Initiative) Performance Measures. Tactical performance measures are the qualitative or quantitative metrics used to determine if a tactical initiative's goals and objectives have been met/accomplished.

Tactical Activity. The fulfillment of a strategic activity requires work—tactical activity—to be performed. This tactical activity usually takes place within one of two contexts. The first context: a project. A project is a temporary planned activity undertaken to fulfill the specific requirements of a tactical activity. The second context: a program. A program is an organizational unit responsible for a particular business function and they often participate in tactical activity related to their business function.

Pattern 1 depicts the IT Tactical Plan as a hierarchy under which initiatives, goals, and objectives are situated.

Pattern 2 presents a summary of an IT Tactical Plan's initiatives.

Pattern 3 is a simple view of tactical plan relationships. It traces the link from a single tactical initiative to the related goal, to objective, to performance measure, and to tactical activity.

Pattern 4 shows a detailed view of an initiative and its goals, the goal and several objectives, a performance measure related to each objective, and related tactical activity.

Pattern 1

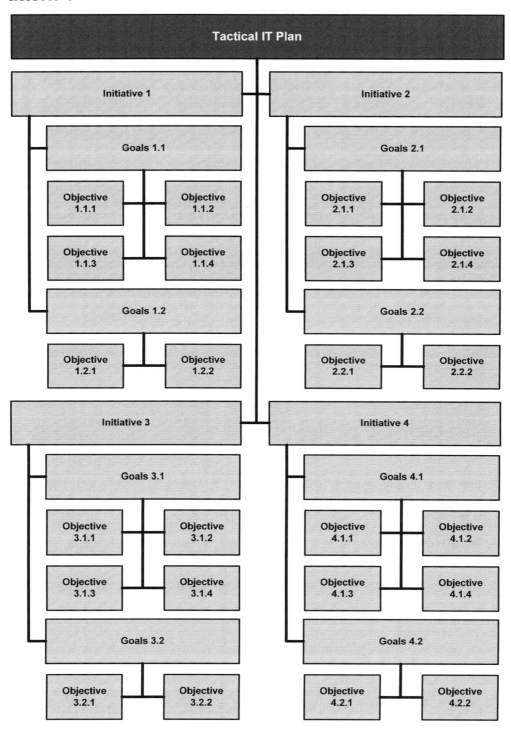

Pattern 2

TACTICAL IT PLAN

Initiative 1
Initiative 2
Initiative 3
Initiative 4
Initiative 5
Initiative 6
Initiative 7
Initiative 8
Initiative 9
Initiative 10

Pattern 3

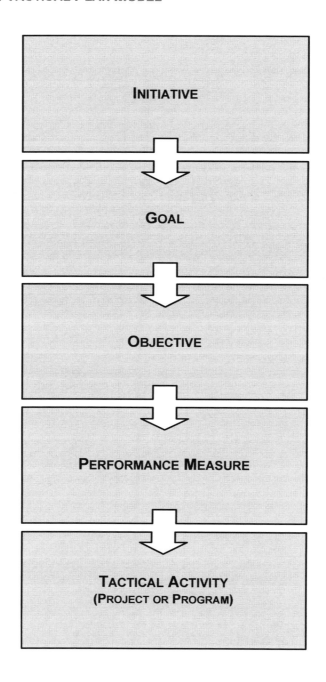

Pattern 4

TACTICAL IT PLAN

Initiative 1

GOAL 1

Objective 1.1	Objective 1.2	Objective 1.3	Objective 1.4	Objective 1.5
Performance Measure 1.1	Performance Measure 1.2	Performance Measure 1.3	Performance Measure 1.4	Performance Measure 1.5

TACTICAL ACTIVITY (PROJECT OR PROGRAM)

Initiative 2

GOAL 2

Objective 2.1	Objective 2.2	Objective 2.3	Objective 2.4	Objective 2.5
Performance Measure 2.1	Performance Measure 2.2	Performance Measure 2.3	Performance Measure 2.4	Performance Measure 2.5

TACTICAL ACTIVITY (PROJECT OR PROGRAM)

Initiative 3

GOAL 3

Objective 3.1	Objective 3.2	Objective 3.3	Objective 3.4	Objective 3.5
Performance Measure 3.1	Performance Measure 3.2	Performance Measure 3.3	Performance Measure 3.4	Performance Measure 3.5

TACTICAL ACTIVITY (PROJECT OR PROGRAM)

CHAPTER 012

Enterprise Mission/Mandate Alignment Model

The Enterprise Mission/Mandate Alignment Model is used to document the alignment between the enterprise mission/mandate and mission/mandate objectives and the enterprise vision and strategic goals.

The Enterprise Mission/Mandate Alignment Model contains the following elements:

- Enterprise Mission/Mandate Statement
- Enterprise Mission/Mandate Objectives
- Enterprise Vision
- Enterprise Strategic Goals

Mission/Mandate Statement. A mission or mandate statement describes what the business is in existence to do—its *raison d'être.* (This is different from a vision statement which describes a future state target for the business to work towards.) The terms mission and mandate appear to be synonymous—but there is a difference worth noting. A mission is the enterprise's high-level purpose and completes this statement: *The enterprise exists to _____ .* A mandate is a duty the enterprise is authorized and/or required to perform. Mandates are often set out in legislation or legally binding contracts. The mission/mandate statement is a textual description of the mission or mandate.

Enterprise Mission/Mandate Objectives. A mission/mandate objective is a statement about something the enterprise wishes to achieve. Mission/mandate objectives are embedded in almost all mission/mandate statements and are identified by parsing the mission/ mandate statement.

Enterprise Vision. An enterprise vision statement describes a future state which the enterprise desires to work towards.

Enterprise Strategic Goals. Enterprise Strategic Goals are the targets that, when achieved, will transition the enterprise towards its future state vision. Enterprise goals guide enterprise decision-making about the type, scope and priority of all enterprise activity. Objectives are the measurable achievements that, when achieved, will move the enterprise towards the realization of its goals.

Pattern 1 identifies the core relationship between the enterprise mission/mandate and mission/mandate objectives and the enterprise vision and strategic goals.

Pattern 2 presents a direct mapping of strategic goals to mission/mandate objectives.

Pattern 3 presents a map of mission/mandate objectives and strategic goals where there are multiple relationships between the objectives and goals. In this pattern there is a gap. One of the reasons we create models and map relationships is to discover gaps in enterprise efforts. Pattern 3 reveals that for Mission/Mandate Objective 4 there is no associated strategic activity. This may be because: the enterprise does not need to change anything about how it performs activity related to Mission/ Mandate Objective 4; or, this is actually a gap and strategic activity needs to be planned for Mission/Mandate Objective 4.

Pattern 1

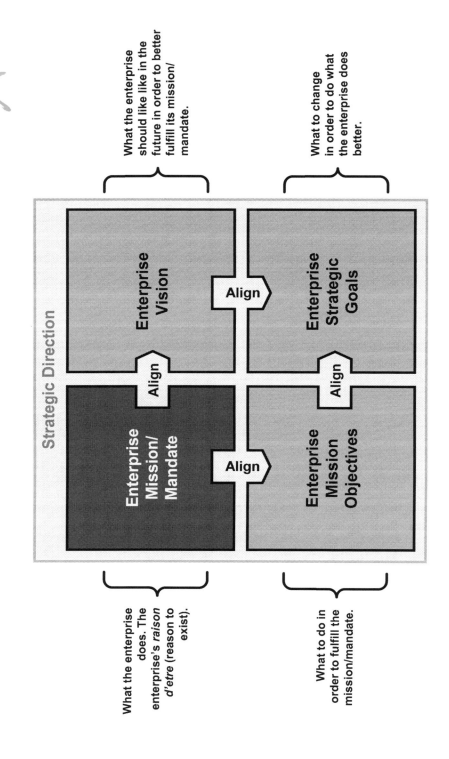

Pattern 2

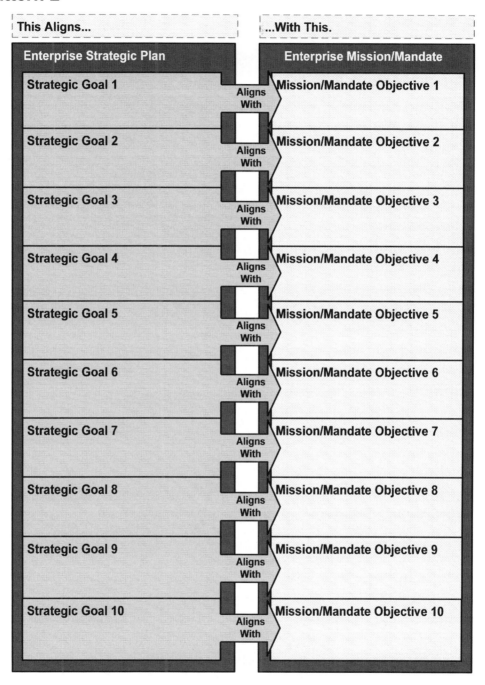

This Aligns...

...With This.

Enterprise Strategic Plan		Enterprise Mission/Mandate
Strategic Goal 1	Aligns With	Mission/Mandate Objective 1
Strategic Goal 2	Aligns With	Mission/Mandate Objective 2
Strategic Goal 3	Aligns With	Mission/Mandate Objective 3
Strategic Goal 4	Aligns With	Mission/Mandate Objective 4
Strategic Goal 5	Aligns With	Mission/Mandate Objective 5
Strategic Goal 6	Aligns With	Mission/Mandate Objective 6
Strategic Goal 7	Aligns With	Mission/Mandate Objective 7
Strategic Goal 8	Aligns With	Mission/Mandate Objective 8
Strategic Goal 9	Aligns With	Mission/Mandate Objective 9
Strategic Goal 10	Aligns With	Mission/Mandate Objective 10

Pattern 3

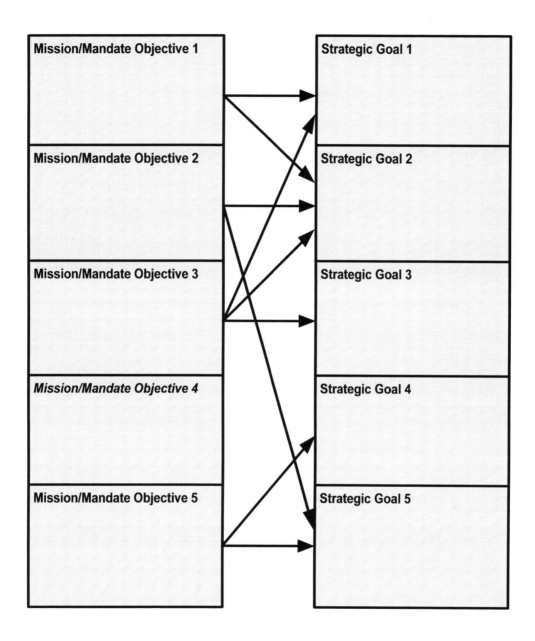

CHAPTER 013

Enterprise Strategy and IT Opportunities & Risks Alignment Model

The ultimate role of IT in the enterprise is to support the business. However, sometimes IT transforms the business. When IT transforms the business of the enterprise, that transformation often begins with the identification of an IT opportunity or risk. The Strategy and IT Opportunities & Risks Alignment Model identifies IT opportunities and risks, traces the impact of the risk on the element of enterprise strategy, and, finally, identifies any possible impact of the opportunity/risk on the mission/mandate or vision of the enterprise.

The Enterprise Strategy and IT Opportunities & Risks Alignment Model contains the following elements:

- Mission/Mandate Statement
- IT Opportunity Statement
- IT Risk Statement
- Vision Statement
- Goal
- Objective
- Measures of Success
- Organizational Unit
- Business Function
- Business Service
- Policy
- New Capability
- Data Component

- Application/System Component
- Technology Component
- New People/Roles/Skills
- Budget Allocation
- Other Resources

Mission / Mandate. A mission or mandate statement describes what the business is in existence to do—its *raison d'être.* (This is different from a vision statement which describes a future state target for the business to work towards.) The terms mission and mandate appear to be synonymous—but there is a difference worth noting. A mission is the enterprise's high-level purpose and completes this statement: *The enterprise exists to _____.* A mandate is a duty the enterprise is authorized and/or required to perform. Mandates are often set out in legislation or legally binding contracts. The mission/mandate statement takes the form of a textual description.

IT Opportunity Statement. Information technology presents the enterprise with ways to do business differently—sometimes in dramatically different ways. The IT opportunity statement articulates to the enterprise how IT can enable improved enterprise performance.

IT Risk Statement. Information technology presents the enterprise with important ways to improve the delivery of its goods and services, however, IT also presents the enterprise with risks. Those risk need to be mitigated. When major IT risk arises, the IT risk statement articulates to the enterprise what the IT risk is and what the enterprise needs to do to mitigate that risk.

Vision Statement. A vision statement describes a future state which the enterprise desires to work towards.

Goals. Goals are the targets that, when achieved, will transition the enterprise towards its future state vision. Goals guide enterprise decision-making about the type, scope and priority of all enterprise activity.

Objectives. Objectives are the measurable achievements that, when achieved, will move the enterprise towards the realization of its goals.

Measures of Success. Success measures and targets are the qualitative or quantitative metric used to determine if enterprise goals and objectives have been achieved.

Organizational Unit. The enterprise is defined by an organizational hierarchy. Below the enterprise top level in the hierarchy is the organizational unit level. Each organizational units usually correspond with a high-level enterprise capability.

Business Function. A business function is a collection of business activities and services, usually organized as a sub-unit of an organizational unit.

Business Service. A business service is a collection of business processes that, together, deliver a particular service. Business services are owned and operated by a responsible organizational unit.

Policy. Policies are formal organizational rules used to mandate quality requirements, delineate roles and responsibilities, show where decision-making authority lies, to support consistent and efficient decision-making, to promote or discourage certain organizational behaviours, to articulate performance goals for people and technology, and to set out critical operational rules around each of the enterprise's key functions, services, and processes.

New Capability. A capability is the ability to do something. When the strategic plan requires the enterprise to do something it is currently unable to do, it must develop the capability to do that *something* new. This element of the model identifies new capabilities required to fulfil the strategic plan. Business capabilities are made up of organizational units and people, business functions, business services and processes. IT capabilities are made up of data and information components, application components, and technology components.

Data Component. If the strategic plan requires a new enterprise data component to be developed, this element identifies that new component.

Application/System Component. If the strategic plan requires a new enterprise application component to be developed, this element identifies that new application component.

Technology Component. If the strategic plan requires a new enterprise technology component to be developed, this element identifies that new technology component

New People/Roles/Skills. If the strategic plan requires new roles, new people, or new skills, this element identifies those roles, people, and/or skills.

Budget Allocation. Change is never free. This element identifies the budget allocated to implement the goals and objectives of the strategic plan.

Other Resources. To implement goals and objectives, sometimes resources need to be added or borrowed, such as office space (for certain durations), secondments, special equipment borrowed from other parts of the organization. This element identifies all of the other known resources required to carry out the goals and objectives of the strategic plan.

Pattern 1 presents an IT opportunity statement and traces its impact on enterprise mission/mandate objectives and its impact on the mission/mandate statement, if any.

Pattern 2 presents an IT risk statement and traces its impact on enterprise mission/mandate objectives and its impact on the mission/mandate statement, if any.

Pattern 3 presents an IT opportunity statement and traces its impact on the enterprise strategic plan and its impact on the vision statement, if any.

Pattern 4 presents an IT risk statement and traces its impact on the enterprise strategic plan and its impact on the vision statement, if any.

Pattern 1

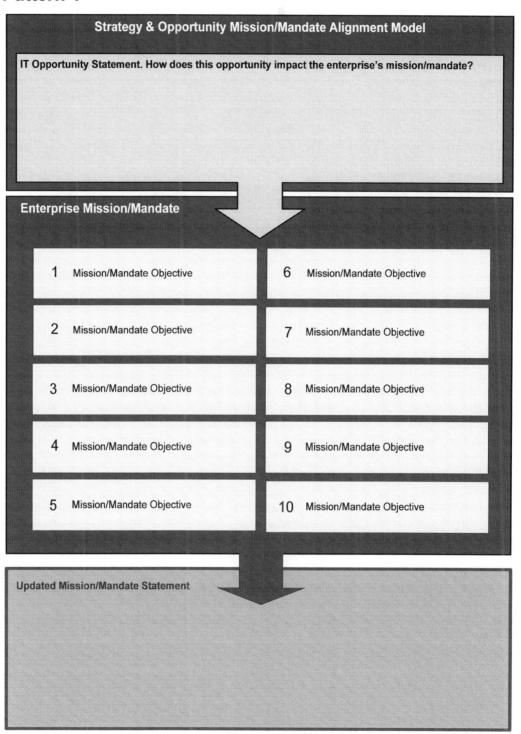

Pattern 2

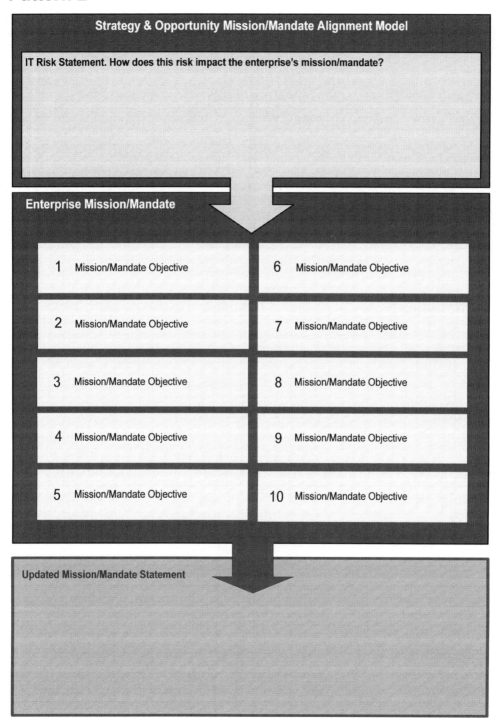

Pattern 3

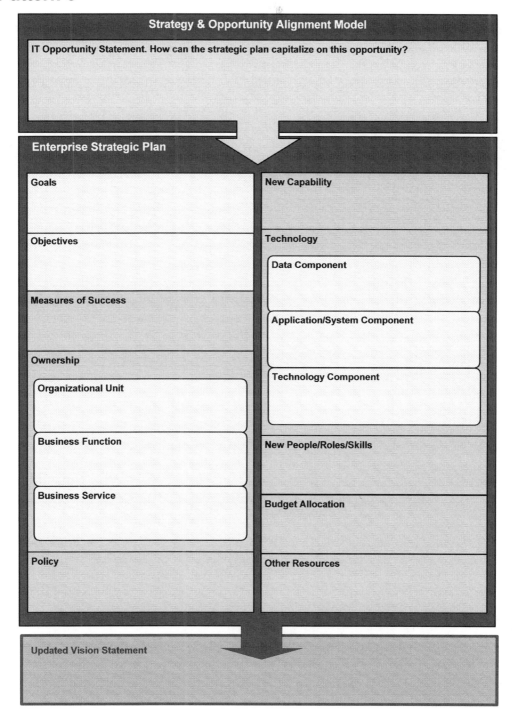

Pattern 4

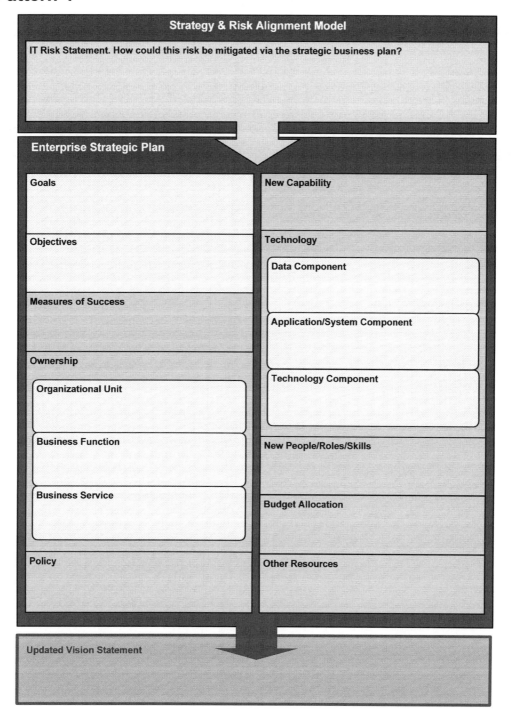

CHAPTER 014

Enterprise Strategic Plan and IT Strategic Plan Alignment Model

The Enterprise Strategic Plan and IT Strategic Plan Alignment Model documents the relationship between the strategic plans of the IT department/organization and the greater enterprise.

The Enterprise Strategic Plan and IT Strategic Plan Alignment Model contains the following elements:

- Enterprise Strategic Plan
- IT Strategic Plan
- Goal
- Objective
- Performance Measure
- Organizational Unit
- Business Function

Enterprise Strategic Plan. An enterprise strategic plan documents the vision, mission, goals and objectives of the enterprise—in both the business and IT realms—in order to ensure the enterprise is competitive and possesses or develops the capabilities to fulfil its vision and mission. Strategic plans forecast costs, set timelines, success measures and targets, performance measures and targets, and identify the individuals or parts of the organization responsible for carrying out strategic change.

IT Strategic Plan. An IT strategic plan sets out a vision, mission, goals and objectives for the enterprise's IT department—this vision, mission, goals and objectives of the IT department are tightly coupled with those of the enterprise. The purpose of the IT strategic plan is to outline *how* the IT department will support the enterprise strategic plan. The goals and objectives of the IT strategic plan should map to the goals and objectives of the enterprise strategic plan. Goals have owners and the ownership of a goal identified in the enterprise strategic plan should be the same owner of the related goal in the IT strategic plan.

Goals. Goals are the targets that, when achieved, will transition the enterprise towards the future state vision expressed in the strategic plan.

Objectives. Objectives are the measurable achievements that, when achieved, will move the organization towards the realization of its goals.

Performance Measures. Performance measures and targets are the qualitative or quantitative metrics used to determine if enterprise components or component resources (people, data, applications, technology, processes) are *performing* their roles appropriately.

Organizational Unit. The enterprise is defined by an organizational hierarchy. Below the enterprise top level in the hierarchy is the organizational unit level. Each organizational units usually correspond with a high-level enterprise capability.

Business Function. A business function is a collection of business activities and services, usually organized as a sub-unit of an organizational unit.

Pattern 1 identifies the key alignment points between the enterprise strategic plan and the IT strategic plan.

Pattern 2 documents the one-to-one alignment of IT strategic goals with enterprise strategic goals.

Pattern 3 is particularly useful for discovery consulting—for those engagements where the information necessary to conduct enterprise business architecture effectively is not yet documented and must be 'discovered'.

Patterns 4 and 5 illustrate strategic mapping scenarios where strategic goals and tactical goals do net necessarily map one-to-one.

Pattern 4 identifies a scenario where a tactical goal helps satisfy more than one strategic goal.

Pattern 5 identifies a scenario where a strategic goal is satisfied by more than one tactical goal.

Pattern 1

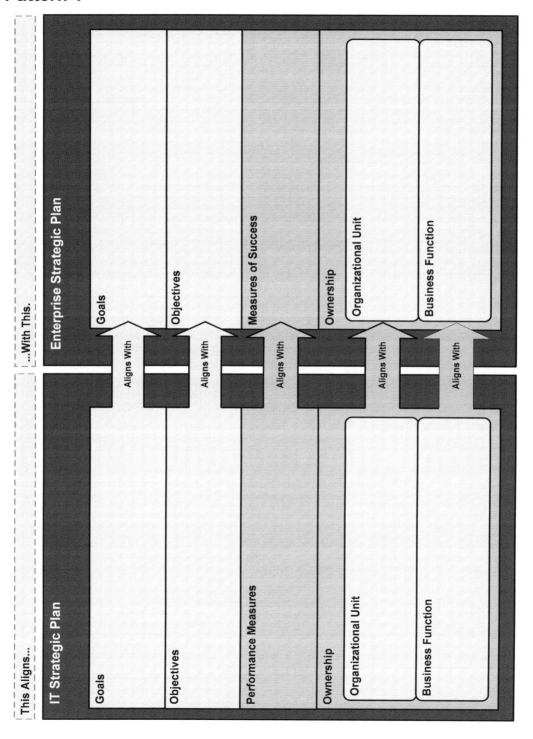

Pattern 2

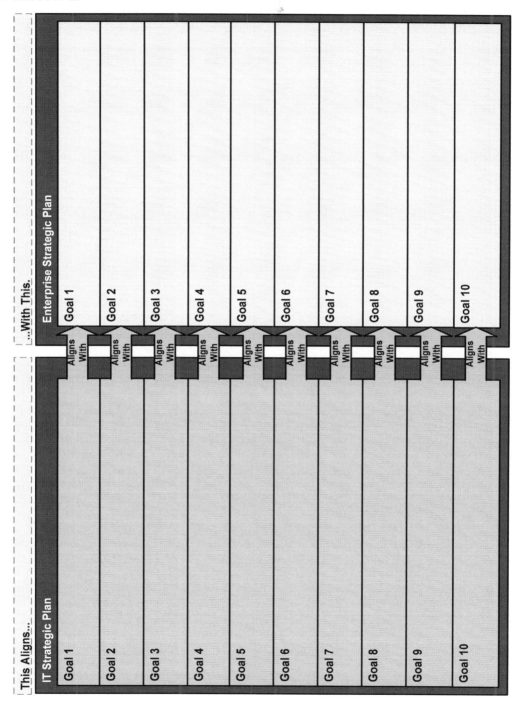

Pattern 3

Enterprise Strategic Plan:

IT STRATEGIC PLAN:

GOAL 1

Enterprise Goal

IT Goal

GOAL 2

Enterprise Goal

IT Goal

GOAL 3

Enterprise Goal

IT Goal

GOAL 4

Enterprise Goal

IT Goal

GOAL 5

Enterprise Goal

IT Goal

Pattern 4

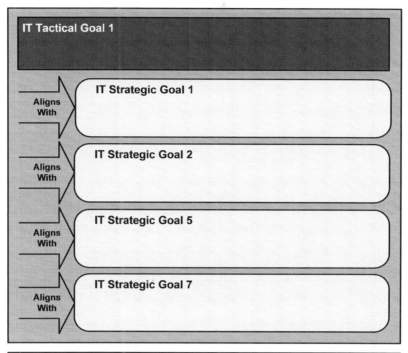

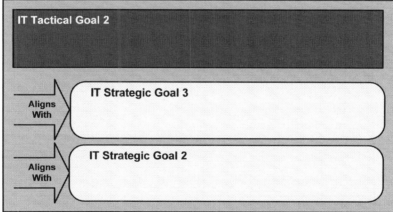

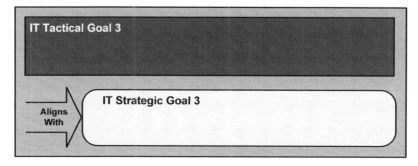

Pattern 5

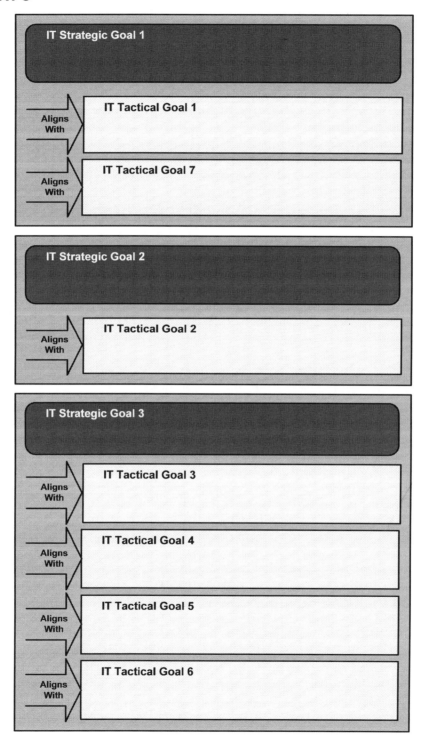

CHAPTER 015

Business and IT Capability Alignment Model

An enterprise lives or dies by its ability to align its capabilities with its strategic direction. The purpose of the Business and IT Capability Alignment Model is to document the relationship between strategy, business capabilities, and supporting/enabling IT capabilities.

The Business and IT Capability Alignment Model contains the following elements:

- Strategic Plan
- Business Capability
- IT Capability

Strategic Plan. A strategic plan documents the vision, mission, goals and objectives of the enterprise—in both the business and IT realms—in order to ensure the enterprise is competitive and possesses or develops the capabilities to fulfil its vision and mission. Strategic plans forecast costs, set timelines, success measures and targets, performance measures and targets, and identify the individuals or parts of the organization responsible for carrying out strategic change.

Business Capability. A business capability is an organizational ability to perform a particular business function or group of business functions. Business capabilities are made up of organizational units and people, business functions, business services and processes.

IT Capability. An IT capability is an ability of information technology to enable one or more corresponding business capabilities. IT capabilities are made up of data and information components, application components, and technology components.

Pattern 1 sets out the basic shape of the Business and IT Capability Alignment Model

Pattern 2 elaborates on pattern 1 by introducing hierarchy to the model and by identifying and inter-relating the composing elements of the strategic plan with business capabilities and IT capabilities. Pattern 2 includes outcome measures for strategy and performance measures for business and IT capabilities.

Pattern 3 is used to document all the key elements related to enterprise capability and offers a more granular picture of the relationships between composing elements and their performance. Pattern 3 is particularly useful for discovery consulting—for those engagements where the information necessary to conduct enterprise business architecture effectively is not yet documented and must be 'discovered'.

The business architect often uses this model to quickly diagnose gaps in strategic-capabilities alignment and, then, take corrective action.

Pattern 1

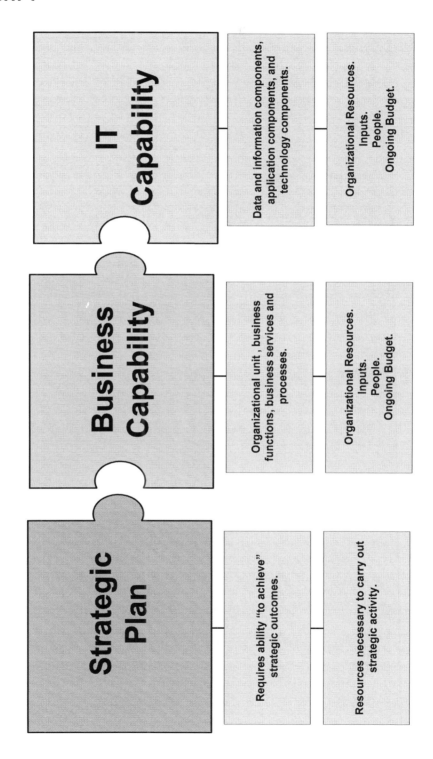

Pattern 2

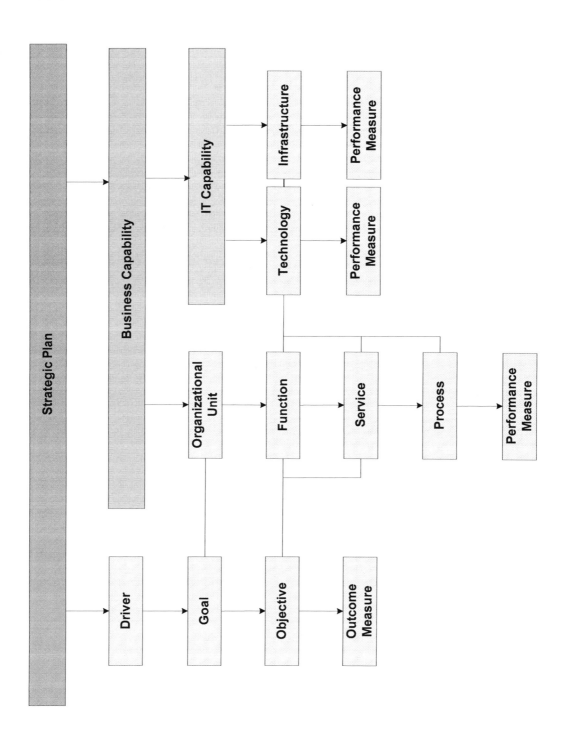

Pattern 3

CAPABILITY NAME		
CAPABILITY DESCRIPTION		

Motivation

GOAL	PERFOMANCE
OBJECTIVE	PERFOMANCE

Business Capability

ORGANIZATIONAL UNIT	PERFOMANCE
BUSINESS FUNCTION	PERFOMANCE
BUSINESS SERVICES	PERFOMANCE
PROCESS 1	PERFOMANCE
PROCESS 2	PERFOMANCE
PROCESS 3	PERFOMANCE
PROCESS N	PERFOMANCE

Information Technology Capability

PRIMARY SUPPORTING TECHNOLOGY 1	PERFOMANCE
PRIMARY SUPPORTING TECHNOLOGY 2	PERFOMANCE
PRIMARY SUPPORTING TECHNOLOGY 3	PERFOMANCE
PRIMARY SUPPORTING TECHNOLOGY N	PERFOMANCE
INFRASTRUCTURE	

CHAPTER 016

IT Strategic Plan and IT Tactical Plan Alignment Model

The IT Strategic Plan and IT Tactical Plan Alignment Model identifies the alignment points between the strategic and tactical plans of the IT department.

The Strategic Plan and IT Tactical Plan Alignment Model contains the following elements:

- IT Strategic Plan
- IT Tactical Plan
- Tactical Initiative
- IT Strategic Goal
- Enterprise Strategic Goal

IT Strategic Plan. An IT strategic plan sets out a vision, mission, goals and objectives for the enterprise's IT department—this vision, mission, goals and objectives of the IT department are tightly coupled with those of the enterprise. The purpose of the IT strategic plan is to outline *how* the IT department will support the enterprise strategic plan. The goals and objectives of the IT strategic plan should map to the goals and objectives of the enterprise strategic plan. Goals have owners and the ownership of a goal identified in the enterprise strategic plan should be the same owner of the related goal in the IT strategic plan.

IT Tactical Plan. The IT tactical plan describes how the strategic IT plan will be implemented and how the IT strategy will play out for each IT organizational unit. The tactical plan identifies tactical initiatives that align with strategic goals and articulates tactical goals, objectives, performance measures, and identifies tactical activity (which takes the form of either project activity or program activity).

Tactical Initiative. An initiative is a unit of work to be undertaken as part of the tactical plan. Each initiative has its own set of tactical goals, tactical objectives, performance measures, and tactical activities (sometimes referred to as tactical actions) which take the form of project work or program work.

IT Strategic Goals. IT strategic goals are the targets that, when met, will result in the enterprise achieving the aims of the IT strategic plan and realizing the vision of the IT strategic plan. IT strategic goals guide decision-making about the type, scope, and priority of all IT activity.

Enterprise Strategic Goals. Enterprise strategic goals are the targets that, when achieved, will transition the business of the enterprise towards its future state vision. Enterprise strategic goals guide enterprise decision-making about the type, scope and priority of all enterprise activity.

Pattern 1 depicts the alignment points between IT strategic goals and the tactical initiatives that align with these goals.

Pattern 2 elaborates upon pattern 1 by identifying the tactical initiative and IT strategic goal relationship and their link to enterprise strategic goals.

The link between goals and actual initiative-based work is a traditional break-point for Business-IT alignment and it is this fact that makes this model and patterns 1 and 2 of particular interest to the enterprise business architect. The creation of this alignment model should be a simple task; if it isn't, red flags should be raised regarding the quality of enterprise alignment.

Pattern 3 relates IT Strategic Goals to multiple, aligned Tactical Initiatives.

Patterns 3 and 4 illustrate a strategic mapping scenarios where IT strategic goals and IT tactical initiatives do not necessarily map one-to-one.

Pattern 3 identifies a scenario where an IT strategic goal is addressed by more than one tactical initiative.

Pattern 4 identifies a scenario where a tactical initiative addresses more than one strategic goal.

Patterns 1, 3, and 4 can be easily adapted to illustrate the relationship between Enterprise Business Goals and multiple aligned tactical business initiatives.

Pattern 1

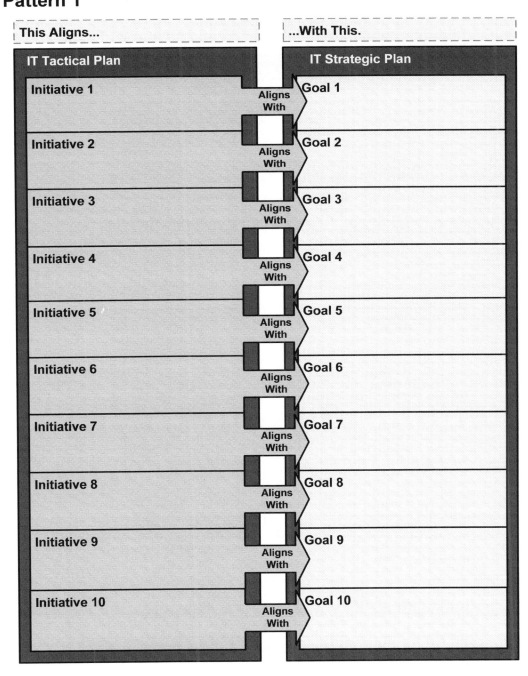

Pattern 2

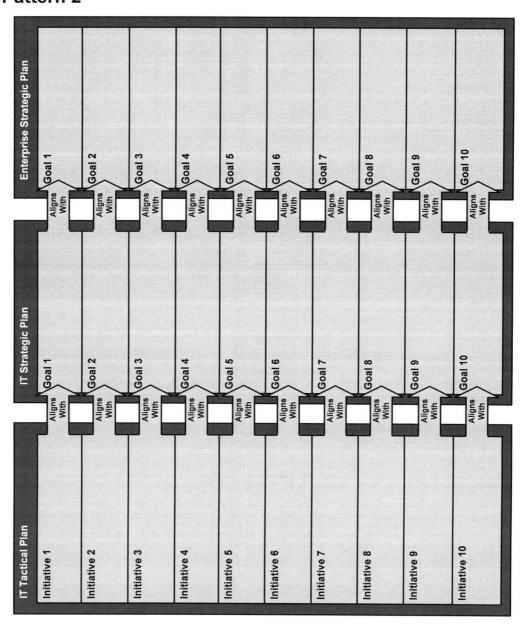

Pattern 3

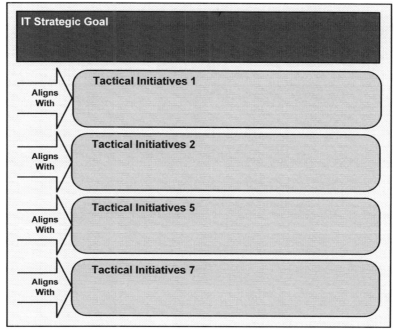

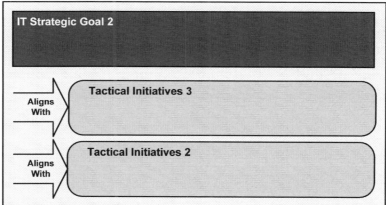

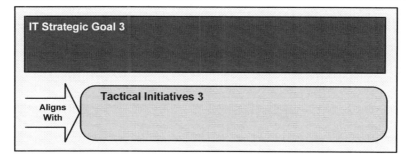

Pattern 4

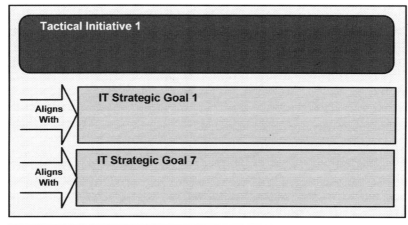

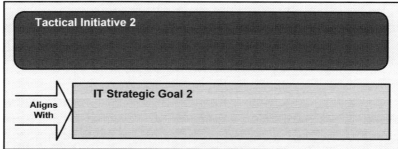

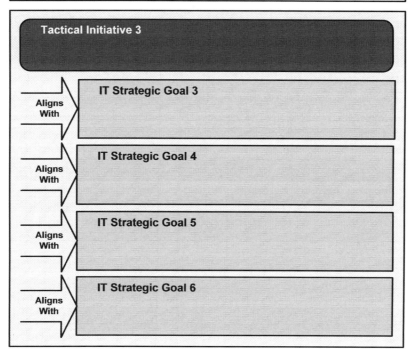

CHAPTER 017

Project/Program Alignment Model

The Project/Program Alignment Model demonstrates the aligning relationships between a project/program and the planning efforts that initiated the project/program.

The Project/Program Alignment Model contains the following elements:

- Enterprise Strategic Goal
- IT Strategic Goal
- IT Tactical Goal
- IT Tactical Initiative
- IT Tactical Activity
- IT Project/Program Activity
- Project/Program

Enterprise Strategic Goals. Enterprise strategic goals are the targets that, when achieved, will transition the business of the enterprise towards its future state vision. Enterprise strategic goals guide enterprise decision-making about the type, scope and priority of all enterprise activity.

IT Strategic Goals. IT strategic goals are the targets that, when met, will result in the enterprise achieving the aims of the IT strategic plan and realizing the vision of the IT strategic plan. IT strategic goals guide decision-making about the type, scope, and priority of all IT activity.

Tactical Goals. Tactical Goals are the targets that, when met, will result in the enterprise achieving the aims of the tactical initiative.

Tactical Initiative. An initiative is a unit of work to be undertaken as part of the tactical plan. Each initiative has its own set of tactical goals, tactical objectives, performance measures, and tactical activities (sometime referred to as actions) which take the form of project work or program work.

Tactical Activity. The fulfillment of a tactical initiative requires work—tactical activity—to be performed. This tactical activity usually takes place within one of two contexts: a project or a program.

IT Project/Program Activity. IT Project Activity and Program Activity are synonyms for *tactical activity.*

Project/Program. A project is a temporary planned activity undertaken to fulfill the specific requirements of a tactical activity. The second context: a program. A program is an organizational unit responsible for a particular business function and they often participate in tactical activity related to their business function.

Pattern 1 identifies the essential relationships between elements of this model.

Pattern 2 identifies the key alignment points for project/program activity: the link between the project/program and the tactical initiative that defined the project/program.

Pattern 3 elaborates on pattern 2 by including an additional link between the tactical initiative and the IT strategic goal which the initiative is intended to fulfill.

Pattern 4 presents a complex table of relationships demonstrating—at a glance—the alignment (or misalignment) of:

- all ongoing project/program activity with the related tactical (initiative) goal,
- the tactical (initiative) goal with the related tactical initiative,
- the tactical initiative with the related IT strategic goal, and
- the IT strategic goal with the related Enterprise strategic goal.

Pattern 1

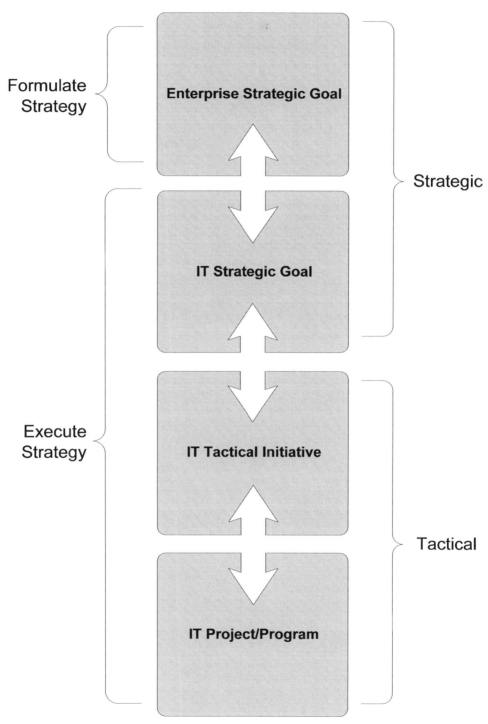

Pattern 2

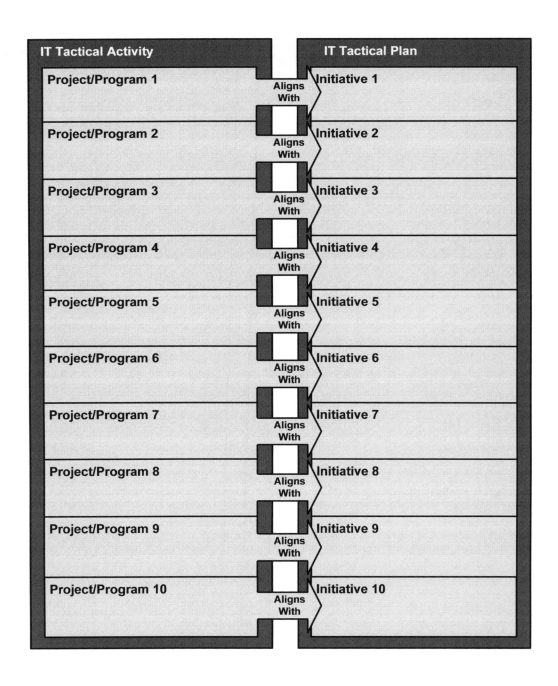

Pattern 3

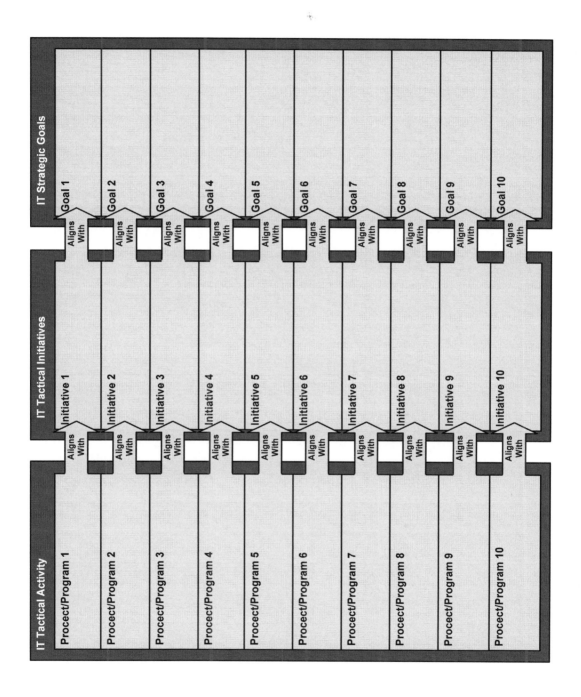

Pattern 4

PROJECTS / PROGRAMS	ALIGNED TACTICAL (INITIATIVE) GOALS	ALIGNED IT TACTICAL INITIATIVES	ALIGNED IT STRATEGIC GOALS	ALIGNED ENTERPRISE STRATEGIC GOALS
Project/Program 1	Aligned Tactical (Initiative) Goal	Aligned IT Tactical Initiative	Aligned IT Strategic Goal	Aligned Enterprise Strategic Goal
Project/Program 2	Aligned Tactical (Initiative) Goal	Aligned IT Tactical Initiative	Aligned IT Strategic Goal	Aligned Enterprise Strategic Goal
Project/Program 3	Aligned Tactical (Initiative) Goal	Aligned IT Tactical Initiative	Aligned IT Strategic Goal	Aligned Enterprise Strategic Goal
Project/Program 4	Aligned Tactical (Initiative) Goal	Aligned IT Tactical Initiative	Aligned IT Strategic Goal	Aligned Enterprise Strategic Goal
Project/Program 5	Aligned Tactical (Initiative) Goal	Aligned IT Tactical Initiative	Aligned IT Strategic Goal	Aligned Enterprise Strategic Goal
Project/Program 6	Aligned Tactical (Initiative) Goal	Aligned IT Tactical Initiative	Aligned IT Strategic Goal	Aligned Enterprise Strategic Goal
Project/Program 7	Aligned Tactical (Initiative) Goal	Aligned IT Tactical Initiative	Aligned IT Strategic Goal	Aligned Enterprise Strategic Goal
Project/Program 8	Aligned Tactical (Initiative) Goal	Aligned IT Tactical Initiative	Aligned IT Strategic Goal	Aligned Enterprise Strategic Goal

CHAPTER 018

Principles-Decision Alignment Model

The Principles-Decision Alignment Model documents the practical application of principles to decision-making.

The Principles-Decision Alignment Model contains the following elements:

- Issue
- Business Architecture Principle
- Implication
- Recommendation / Decision
- Rationale

Issue. In general, an issue is a problem that requires a decision. In this case, it is an issue that requires a response from an enterprise business architect.

Business Architecture Principle. A principle is a basic underlying assumption used to guide and govern decision-making. In this model, an enterprise business architecture principle is put forward for consideration.

Implications. The key implication to consider in this model is the impact of any given business architecture principle on the solution to the issue at hand. What are the consequences of applying the business architecture principle to the issue?

Recommendation / Decision. What decision or recommendation did the enterprise business architect make in regards to this issue? This element of the model documents the business architect's opinion/recommendation on how the issue/decision is impacted by the principle and, often comes in the form of a do/do not, shall/shall not, or should/should not statement.

Rationale. A rationale is an underlying reason for something. What is the rationale—the underlying reason—or justification for this decision?

Pattern 1 shows the linear relationship between an issue (the problem), principle (the constraint), the implication (the analysis), the decision / recommendation, and the rationale (the justification).

Pattern 2 illustrates the relationship between a recommendation and the related issue, business architecture principle, implications of the principle for the issue, and rationale for the recommendation.

Pattern 3 shows the relationship between an issue/decision item, multiple business architecture principles, and a comprehensive recommendation.

Pattern 4 is particularly useful for discovery consulting—for those engagements where the information necessary to conduct enterprise business architecture effectively is not yet documented and must be 'discovered'.

Pattern 1

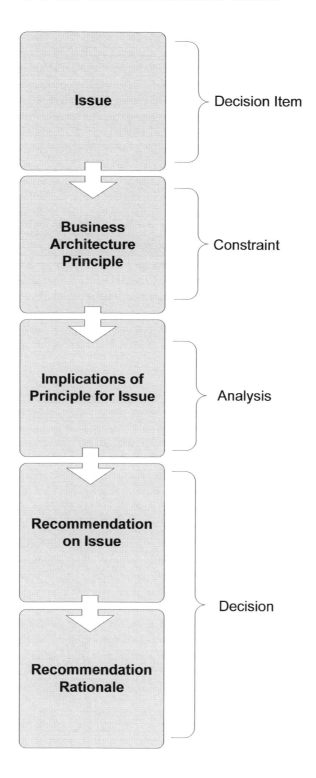

Pattern 2

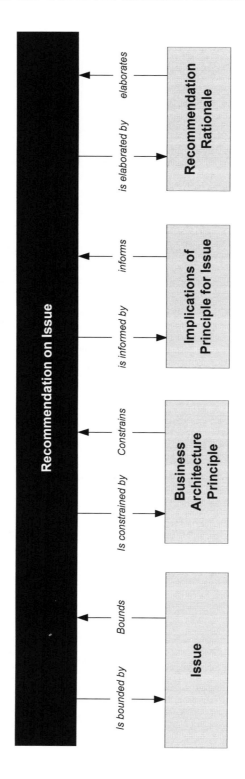

Pattern 3

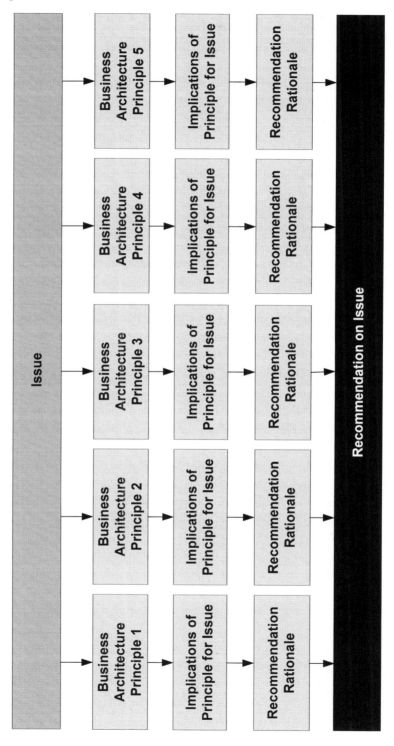

Pattern 4

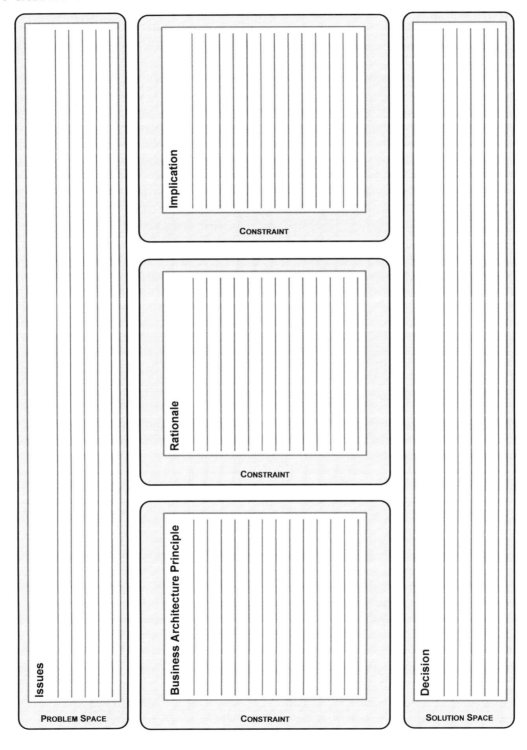

CHAPTER 019

Strategic Goals and Enterprise Elements Alignment Model

The Strategic Goals and Enterprise Elements Alignment Model illustrates the relationship between strategic goals and service delivery and is used to facilitate planning, tracking, and evaluation activities.

The Strategic Goals and Enterprise Elements Alignment Model contains the following elements:

- Strategic Goal
- Organizational Unit
- Business Functions And Services
- Enterprise Element

Strategic Goals. Strategic Goals are the targets that, when achieved, will transition the enterprise towards its future state vision. Strategic goals guide enterprise decision-making about the type, scope and priority of all enterprise activities.

Organizational Unit. The enterprise is defined by an organizational hierarchy. Below the enterprise top level in the hierarchy is the organizational unit level. Each organizational units usually correspond with a high-level enterprise capability.

Business Functions and Services. A business function is a collection of business activities and services, usually organized as a sub-unit of an organizational unit. A business service is a collection of business processes that, together, deliver a particular service. Business services are owned and operated by a responsible organizational unit.

Enterprise Element. Enterprises are made of many things. We call the bigger things *components*. We call the smaller things *elements*. For the purposes of the strategic alignment model, the following things can be considered enterprise elements: standards, performance measures, applications, date components, technology components, etc.

The Strategic Goals and Enterprise Elements Alignment Model illustrates the relationship between business vision, goals, organizational units, business services and selected elements of the enterprise. Together the elements 'business functions and services' and 'enterprise elements' define a 'service delivery' viewpoint.

The Strategic Goals and Enterprise Elements Alignment Model illustrates the relationships between strategic planning and tactical implementations and traces the link between leadership, ownership, service delivery, and supporting IT.

The strategic alignment model is used to document and demonstrate the link between:

- strategic - tactical thinking;
- leadership - ownership - service delivery; and
- goal, organizations, and services

and enterprise elements like:

- standards;
- performance;
- technical components; and
- systems.

The ultimate purpose of this model is to help senior business leaders understand the link between their decisions and various elements found in the IT world and the link between those various IT elements and service delivery.

Pattern 1 identifies the key elements of the model.

Pattern 2 and pattern 4 are particularly useful for discovery consulting—for those engagements where the information necessary to conduct enterprise business architecture effectively is not yet documented and must be 'discovered'.

Pattern 3 elaborates on the model by identifying the vision to which the strategic goal is aligned.

Pattern 1

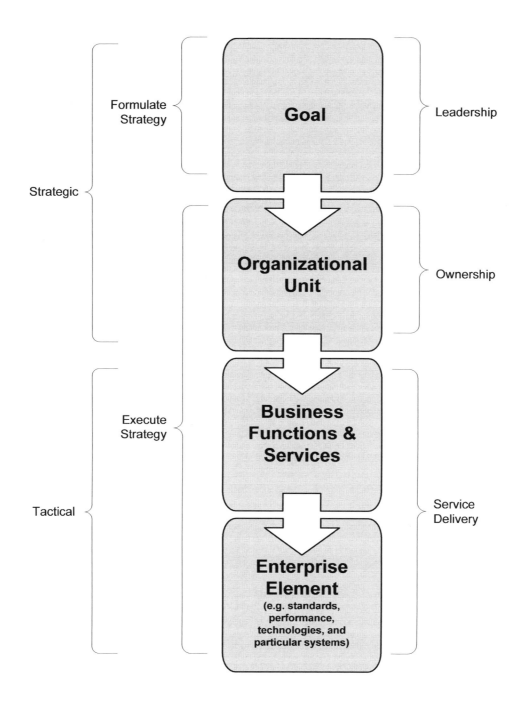

Pattern 2

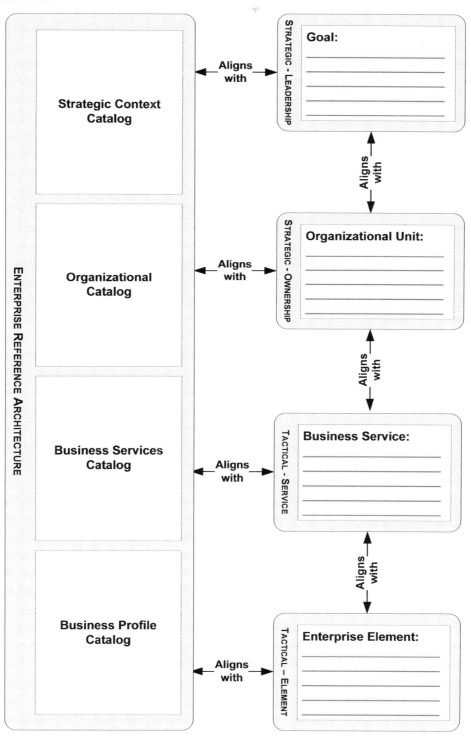

Pattern 3

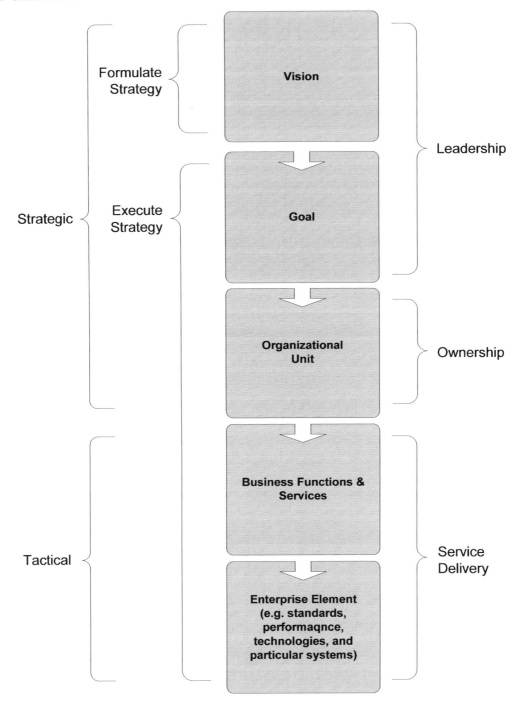

Pattern 4

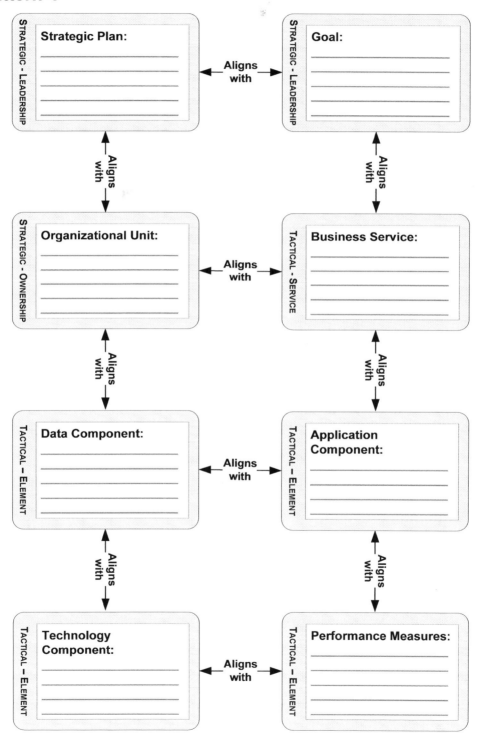

CHAPTER 020

Performance Alignment Model

The Performance Alignment Model defines the relationship between performance and business services, objectives, and goals.

The Performance Alignment Model contains the following elements:

- Goal
- Objective
- Service
- Service Performance

Goals. Goals are the strategic targets that, when achieved, will transition the enterprise towards its future state vision. Goals guide enterprise decision-making about the type, scope and priority of all enterprise activity.

Objectives. Objectives are the measurable achievements that, when achieved, will move the enterprise towards the realization of its goals. What are the organizational unit's objectives?

Service. A service may refer to a business service or a technological service. A business service is a collection of business processes that, together, deliver a particular service. A technological service is one or more technologies that integrate and interoperate in order to perform a particular service—sometimes serving multiple components (as in service oriented architectures)—usually exposed to the enterprise via an API or UDDI interface. IT services support business services either directly or indirectly.

Service Performance. A performance measure is a way to

assess the effectiveness of business functions, business services, and business processes. Services are usually expected to meet certain performance requirements as articulated in a service contract. Performance requirements are expressed in terms of service levels. Service Performance involves an examination of actual performance against contracted service levels.

The Performance Alignment Model defines the role a service plays in fulfilling business strategy. The model can be used to illustrate the relationship between strategic planning and the effectiveness of strategic execution and the model can be used to trace the link between, leadership, service delivery and the performance of that service.

Pattern 1 is used to illustrate linear relationships between strategic goals and objectives and the tactical services and service performance measures.

Pattern 2 elaborates on the basic elements of the performance alignment model by examining a single goal and multiple objectives. For each objective, this pattern traces the aligned service, service measure, the actual observed performance and presents a performance score—and indication if the performance was poor, fair, good, or excellent.

Pattern 3 extends this model by including an indication of expected vs. actual performance and is particularly useful for discovery consulting—for those engagements where the information necessary to conduct enterprise business architecture effectively is not yet documented and must be 'discovered'.

Pattern 4 explores the relationship between strategic planning, the service delivery implementation of that strategy, and the strategic outcomes achieved through this delivery of service.

Pattern 5 elaborates on the performance alignment model by relating service performance results to the accomplishment of strategic outcomes. The pattern examines the enterprise's full complement of strategic goals, their relationship to the services through which the goals are accomplished, to the measures of service performance and actual observed performance, and relates observed performance to the accomplishment of strategic outcomes. The goals in pattern 5 may be enterprise (business) strategic goals or IT strategic goals.

Pattern 1

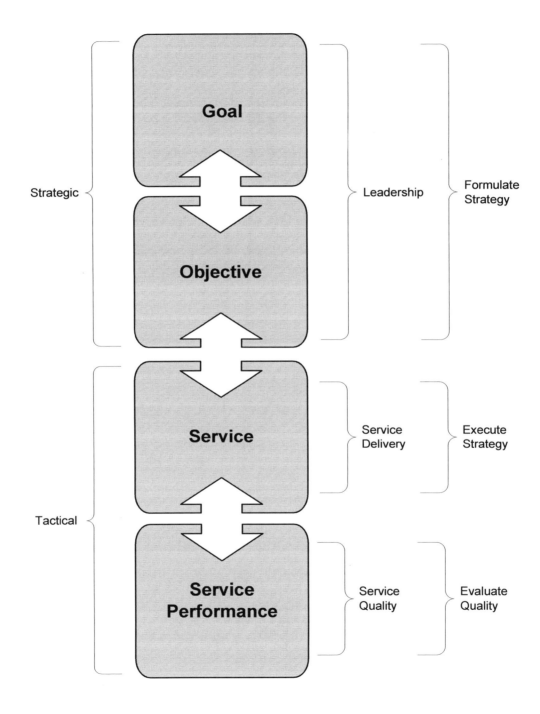

Pattern 2

Goal 1		Objective 1.1		Objective 1.2		Objective 1.3		Objective 1.4		Objective 1.5	
		Service		Service		Service		Service		Service	
		Service Measure		Service Measure		Service Measure		Service Measure		Service Measure	
		Actual Observed Performance		Actual Observed Performance		Actual Observed Performance		Actual Observed Performance		Actual Observed Performance	
		Performance Score		Performance Score		Performance Score		Performance Score		Performance Score	

Pattern 3

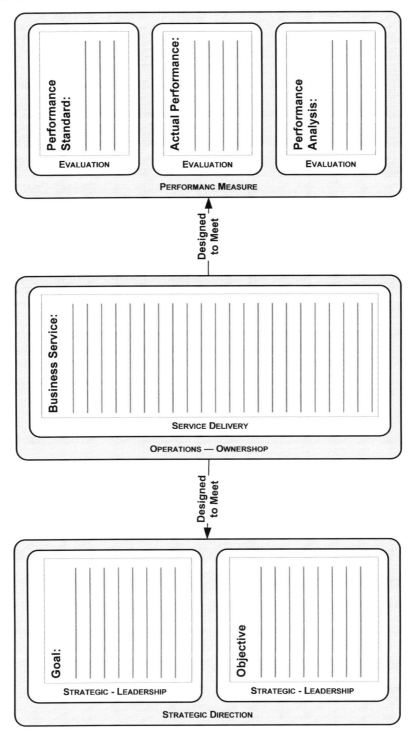

Pattern 4

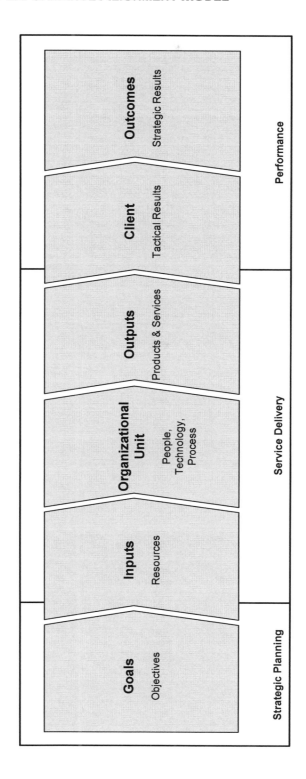

Pattern 5

	Service	Service Measure	Observed Service Performance	Strategic Outcome
Goal 1				
Goal 2				
Goal 3				
Goal 4				
Goal 5				
Goal 6				
Goal 7				
Goal 8				
Goal 9				
Goal 10				

148

CHAPTER 021

Change Management Alignment Model

The Change Management Alignment Model identifies the high-level components of a change management plan.

The Change Management Alignment Model contains the following elements:

- Impacted Area
- Change
- Importance
- People

Impacted Area. The impacted area defines where in the enterprise the change is occurring. The impacted area can be identified by one or more of the following enterprise elements: organizational structure, business function, business service, business process.

Change. The 'change' element in the model is a textual description of the change, identifying the 'what' and 'when' of the change. The change statement may also identify what is 'good' about the change.

Importance. The 'importance' element describes 'why' the change is important and identifies exactly 'why' the change must occur. There are often stakeholders who only support change when they understand the risk of not changing. One way to communicate 'importance' is to highlight the consequences of failure.

People. The 'people' element identifies 'who' the change impacts, both in terms of roles and actors.

The model allows the scope of a change in the enterprise to be understood within the context of various enterprise dimensions, such as: organizational structure, functional structure, service structure, and process structure .

The key areas of change management mapped in this model are: the impacted area; the change itself; a measure of the importance of changing; and an outline of who is impacted by the change and how they are impacted.

If a major change initiative is underway in the enterprise and this simple model cannot be easily filled in, there's an urgent gap (or two) to be filled in the initiative's change management strategy.

Pattern 2 is particularly useful for discovery consulting—for those engagements where the information necessary to conduct enterprise business architecture effectively is not yet documented and must be 'discovered'.

Once the model is completed and the change understood, the next challenge is to communicate this information. See: Socialization-Communication Model.

Strategic plans are always a plan for organizational change and improvement. The Change Management Alignment Model is an excellent strategic tool to help identify and communicate how that strategy will play out for the enterprise's operational units and staff. Pattern 4 can be used to understand how strategic goals play out in impacted areas and with impacted people.

Pattern 1

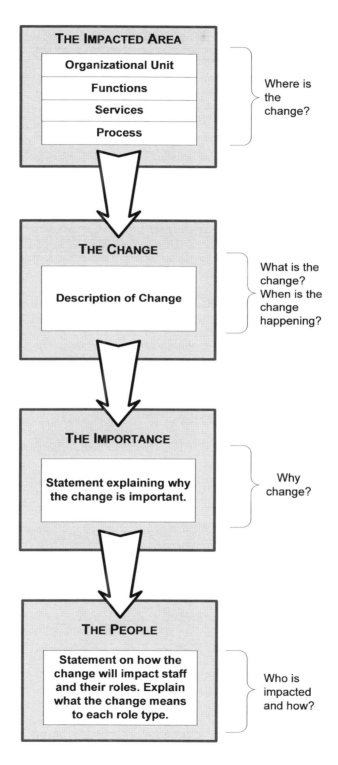

Pattern 2

IMPACTED AREA

Where is the change?

Organizational Unit:

Function:

Service:

Process

Resouces:

THE DELTA

What is the change and when is it happening?

Describe the Change:

IMPORTANCE

Why change?

Explain Importance of Change:

PEOPLE

Who is impacted, how, and what is expected of them?

Explain What Change Means for Each Organization Role:

Pattern 3

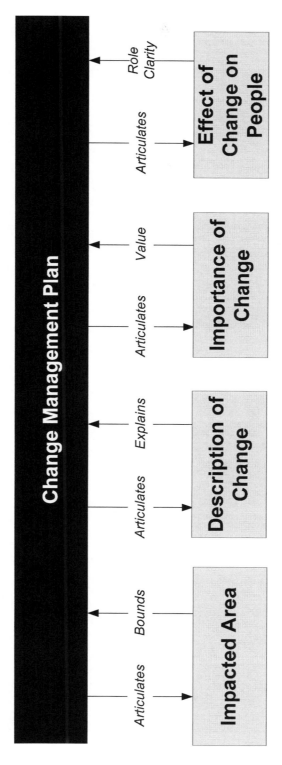

Pattern 4

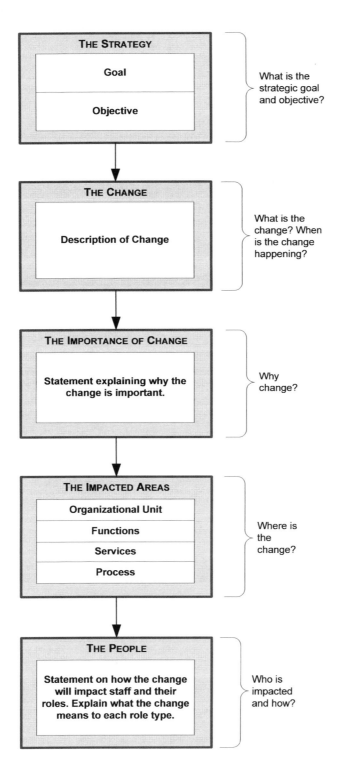

CHAPTER 022

Risk Alignment Model

The Risk Alignment Model illustrates the relationship between risk and the enterprise's response to that risk.

The Risk Alignment Model contains the following elements:

- Risk
- Goal
- Objective
- Organizational Unit
- Business Service
- Policy
- Procedure/Process
- Data
- Application
- Infrastructure

Risk. A risk is any event or crisis with the potential to disrupt the operations of the enterprise. A good risk statement identifies the risk, describes the nature of the risk, the likelihood of the risk occurring, and describes the potential impacts on the enterprise of failing to mitigate the risk.

Goals. Goals are the strategic targets that, when achieved, will transition the enterprise towards its future state vision. Goals guide enterprise decision-making about the type, scope and priority of all enterprise activity.

Objectives. Objectives are the measurable achievements that, when achieved, will move the enterprise towards the realization of its goals.

Organizational Unit. The enterprise is defined by a functional hierarchy. Below the enterprise top level in the hierarchy is the organizational unit level. Each organizational unit maps to a high-level enterprise capability.

Business Service. A business service is a collection of business processes that, together, perform a particular service. Business services are owned and operated by a responsible organizational unit.

Policy. Policies are formal organizational rules used to mandate quality requirements, delineate roles and responsibilities, show where decision-making authority lies, to support consistent and efficient decision-making, to promote or discourage certain organizational behaviours, to articulate performance goals for people and technology, and to set out critical operational rules around each of the enterprise's key functions, services, and processes.

Procedure/Process Name. A procedure or process is a series of actions and tasks taken in order to achieve the objective of the process.

Data. Data components are containers for computerized information. In certain circumstances, data may be stored in paper files.

Application. Applications are software programs designed to fulfill specific tasks.

Infrastructure. Data and applications run on infrastructure, which is hardware and software that enable the operation of enterprise systems.

Enterprises must deal with risks to their profits, budget, timelines, overall success, security, privacy, service levels, etc. Any of these risks—these types of risks—can be modeled using the Risk Alignment Model.

The model is used to map risk mitigation at the leadership, ownership, activity, or technology levels—or at any combination of these levels. Contrariwise, the model can be used to highlight gaps in risk mitigation efforts. At the leadership level, strategic planning outlines what is to be done to mitigate the risk. At the ownership level, organizational structure indicates who is responsible for mitigating the risk. At the service delivery level, policy, procedures, and process indicate how the risk will be mitigated. At the technology level, the data, application, and infrastructure required to support the risk mitigation activity are indicated.

Pattern 2 is particularly useful for discovery consulting—for those engagements where the information necessary to conduct enterprise business architecture effectively is not yet documented and must be 'discovered'.

Pattern 1

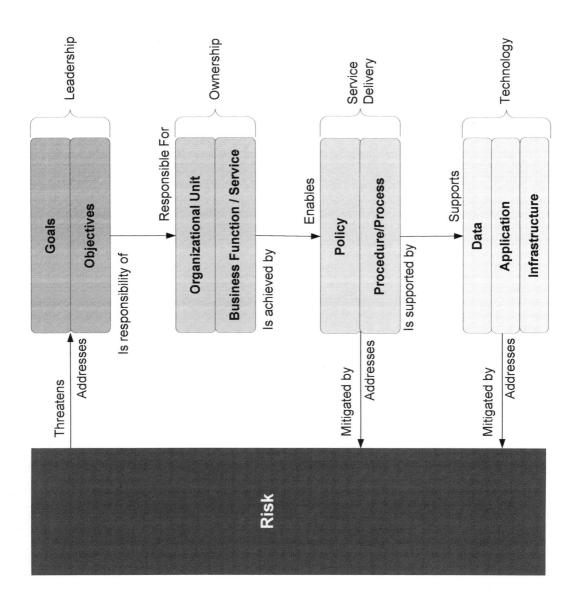

Pattern 2

RISK:

LEADERSHIP — **Risk Threatened Goals:**	**LEADERSHIP** — **Risk Threatened Objective:**
OWNERSHIP — **Organizational Unit:**	**OWNERSHIP** — **Business Service:**
SERVICE DELIVERY — **Risk Mitigated by Policy:**	**SERVICE DELIVERY** — **Risk Mitigated by Procedure/Process:**
COMPONENT — **Risk Mitigated by Data:**	**COMPONENT** — **Risk Mitigated by Application:**
COMPONENT — **Risk Mitigated by Technology:**	**COMPONENT** — **Risk Mitigated by Security:**

CHAPTER 023

Business Services Design Alignment Model

The Business Services Design Alignment Model illustrates the relationship between the business architect's business service description and its elaboration into more detailed data architectures, application architectures, and technology architectures.

To make sense of this model, it is necessary to define the following terms: *component, conceptual architecture, logical architecture,* and *physical architecture.* The Business Services Design Alignment Model differentiates between three standard architectural design states: conceptual, logical, and physical. The difference between conceptual, logical, and physical states is like mother's milk to the enterprise business architect, however, it may seem a strange brew to the business architect's various clients. Here, then, are some important definitions.

> *Component.* Anything can be considered a component if it is one part of a larger whole. An arm is a component of the human body. The navy is a component of the armed services. Servers are a technological component of an enterprise. A database may be considered a component of the enterprise as well as a component of a particular solution.

> *Conceptual Architecture.* Conceptual architecture decomposes a system or solution into its essential components, defines the purpose of each conceptual component, and outlines the key relationships between the conceptual components. Conceptual architecture avoids complicating detail whenever possible and is abstract by design (in order to avoid unnecessary detail). The primary purpose of conceptual architecture is to communicate the

high-level purpose and function of its subject system and lay the ground work for elaboration via logical architecture and, subsequently, physical architecture. Finally, in doing this, the conceptual architecture focuses on high-level functional requirements.

Logical Architecture. Logical architecture is a detailed specification for a system and its interactions. This level of architecture provides exacting detail — including definitions and standards — for components, interfaces, and informational flows. The logical architecture elaborates in detail both functional and non-functional requirements. Logical architecture also explains how the system will be constructed.

Physical Architecture. Elaborating on the logical architecture, the physical architecture takes each component and interface and maps it to a selected technology. Logical architecture identifies and defines components, interfaces and information flows; it identifies a data layer and its components, a business layers and its components, and a user interface layer and its interfaces; but the logical architecture does not define the physical details like how many servers a data layer requires and how many servers a given component will be installed on, or what interfaces will be located where on the network, or the specific pipes information will flow through—this is the job of the physical architecture. For this reason, physical architecture is sometimes referred to as deployment architecture. There is usually a one-to-one relationship between physical data components and operationalized data components—which are, confusingly, often referred to as physical (existing) components or physical assets.

With this understanding of components and conceptual, logical and physical architecture, we can now examine the elements of the business services design alignment model.

The business service design alignment contains the following elements:

- Business Service Description
- Conceptual Data Component
- Logical Data Component

- Physical Data Component
- Conceptual Application Component
- Logical Application Component
- Physical Application Component
- Conceptual Technological Component
- Logical Technological Component
- Physical Technological Component

Business Service Description. A business service is a collection of business processes that, together, deliver a particular service. Business services are owned and operated by a responsible organizational unit. Business services are supported by technological services, which are composed of data, application, and technology components that are integrated and interoperate in order to support the business activity.

Conceptual Data Component. In conceptual architecture, conceptual data components are identified and named, their purpose defined, and their key interactions identified.

Logical Data Component. In logical architecture, logical data components are defined in exacting detail. The result of this is a comprehensive specification for the building of the component.

Physical Data Component. In physical architecture, the logical architecture is elaborated upon with the detail necessary to successfully deploy the architecture. This includes identifying the technologies to be used for each component and where in the network and in conjunction with what other deployed technologies the new data component will be deployed. There is usually a one-to-one relationship between physical data components and operationalized data components—which are, confusingly, often referred to as physical (existing) components or physical assets.

Conceptual Application Component. In conceptual architecture, conceptual applications components are identified and named, their purpose defined, and key interactions identified.

Logical Application Component. In logical architecture, logical application components are defined in exacting detail. The result of this is a comprehensive specification for the building of the application.

Physical Application Component. In physical architecture, the logical architecture is elaborated upon with the detail necessary to successfully deploy the architecture. This includes identifying the technologies to be used for each component and where in the network and in conjunction with what other deployed technologies the new application component will be deployed. There is usually a one-to-one relationship between physical application components and operationalized application components—which are, confusingly, often referred to as physical (existing) components or physical assets.

Conceptual Technology Component. In conceptual architecture, conceptual technological components are identified and named, their purpose defined, and key interactions identified.

Logical Technology Component. In logical architecture, logical technology components are defined in exacting detail. The result of this is a comprehensive specification for the building of the application.

Physical Technology Component. In physical architecture, the logical architecture is elaborated upon with the detail necessary to successfully deploy the architecture. This includes identifying the technologies to be used for each component and where in the network and in conjunction with what other deployed technologies the new technology component will be deployed. There is usually a one-to-one relationship between physical technology components and operationalized technology components—which are, confusingly, often referred to as physical (existing) components or physical assets.

Elaboration of this model takes the form of designs for conceptual components, logical components, and physical components.

This model may be elaborated with additional information, such as, the name of the responsible enterprise architects, the project-level solution architect responsible for delivering component designs, when each component is due to be delivered, or which documents contain the designs.

Pattern 2 is particularly useful for discovery consulting—for those engagements where the information necessary to conduct enterprise business architecture effectively is not yet documented and must be 'discovered'.

Some technologists may wonder where infrastructure and security components fit into the model. The term technology component—as used in this and all the models presented in this book—includes infrastructure and security components.

Pattern 1

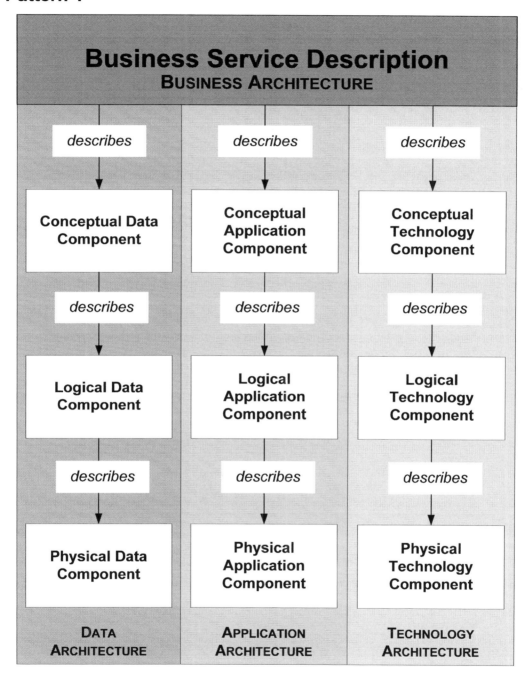

Pattern 2

TECHNOLOGY ARCHITECTURE

Conceptual Technology Component Name:

CONCEPTUAL

Logical Technology Component Name:

LOGICAL

Physical Technology Component Name:

PHYSICAL

APPLICATION ARCHITECTURE

Conceptual Application Component Name:

CONCEPTUAL

Logical Application Component Name:

LOGICAL

Physical Application Component Name:

PHYSICAL

DATA ARCHITECTURE

Conceptual Data Component Name:

CONCEPTUAL

Conceptual Data Component Name:

LOGICAL

Physical Data Component Name:

PHYSICAL

BUSINESS SERVICE

Business Service Description:

BUSINESS REFERENCE ARCHITECTURE

Pattern 3

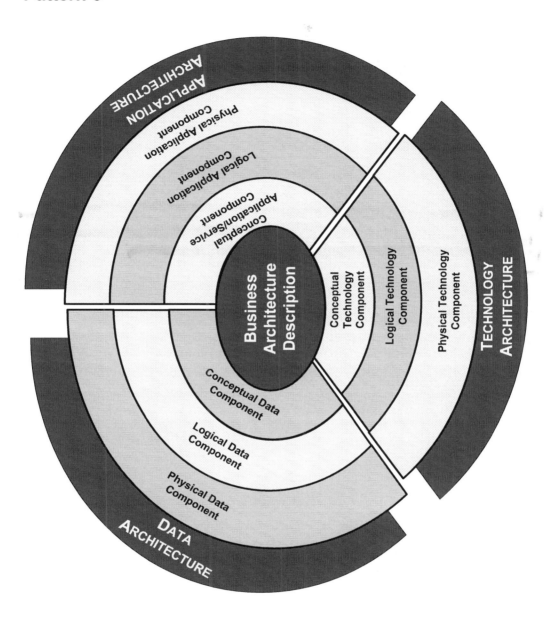

CHAPTER 024

Business Architecture Policy Model

Policies are a business architect's best-friend because policies document the guidelines, rules, procedures, and best practices of the enterprise and when these things are documented . . . life becomes easier.

Policy serves many complimentary purposes: to mandate quality requirements, to delineate roles and responsibilities, to show where decision-making authority lies, to support consistent and efficient decision-making, to promote or discourage certain organizational behaviours, to articulate performance goals for people and technology, and to set out critical operational rules around each of the enterprise's key functions. Ultimately, policies are used to ensure the likelihood that an enterprise achieves its goals and objectives.

Like any function in the enterprise, business architecture has its own policy set.

The purpose of the Business Architecture Policy Model is to document a policy framework for enterpriser business architecture policies. This model is derived from the Enterprise Business Architecture Lifecycle Model.

The Business Architecture Policy Model contains the following elements:

- Planning Policy
- ERA Asset and Work Product Policy
- Client Engagement Policy
- Governance & Quality Policy
- Evaluation Policy

Planning Policy. Policy which guides and governs all aspects of the enterprise business architect's planning activities.

ERA Asset and Work Product Policy. Policy which guides and governs all aspects of the enterprise business architect's creation of ERA assets and management of work product.

Client Engagement Policy. Policy which guides and governs all aspects of the enterprise business architect's engagements with clients.

Governance and Quality Policy. Policy which guides and governs all aspects of the enterprise business architect's governance activities and quality control activities.

Evaluation Policy. Policy which guides and governs all aspects of the enterprise business architect's evaluation activity.

Implementing a full framework of policies is an extraordinarily time consuming effort. There is a risk in having too many policies: when an enterprise's policy catalog is as thick as a phone book there's the chance that these policies will be perceived as barriers to success and, as a result, be ignored. To maximize the effectiveness of policies, implement as many as necessary but not one more than that.

Pattern 1

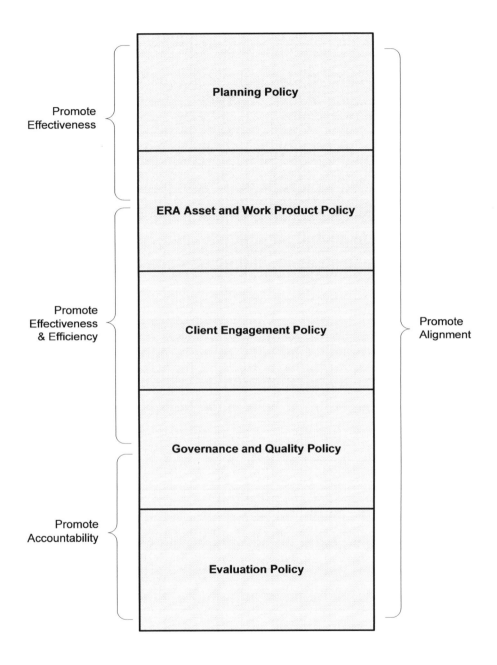

Pattern 2

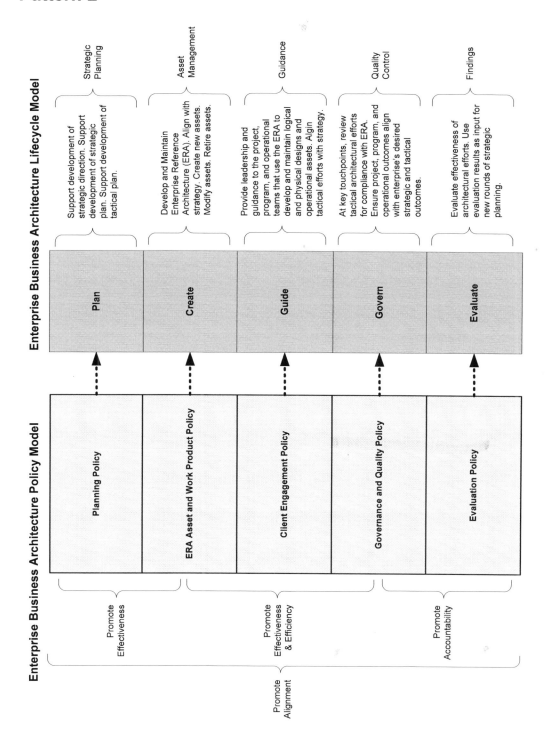

CHAPTER 025

Business Architecture Engagement Model

The Business Architecture Engagement Model maps the four key areas of project/program engagement for the business architect. The model serves as a point of understanding between the business architect and the program/project being engaged.

The Business Architecture Engagement Model contains the following elements:

- Engagement Package
- Motivation Package
- Scoping Package
- Model Package

Engagement Package. The engagement package sets out the key process elements of the business architect's engagement. In short, it describes what the engagement will look like and the human resources involved. The engagement package will usually include an engagement description, a statement on enterprise business architecture's support commitment to the engagement and any possible constraints on that support, the identification of guidance and governance touchpoints, and, if the engagement requires approvals from the enterprise business architect that could potentially delay the project, these 'blocking approvals' are identified.

Motivation Package. The motivation package sets out the key motivational elements necessary to bring the target project/program into deep alignment with the enterprise. This package inventories known planning elements, such as the relevant business strategy's goals and objectives, the aligned IT goals and objectives, the aligned goals and objectives from the IT tactical plan, a 'problem statement' which the project is addressing, and, finally, the goals and objectives of the project.

Scoping Package. The scoping package sets out the key elements necessary to shape the unit of work being undertaken by the project or program. The goal is to shape a work package for the project/program that yield deliverables that seamlessly fit into the enterprise at the strategic, tactical, and operational levels. The elements of the scoping package usually include:

- business architecture principles,
- a future state concept statement,
- the identification of the primary client (the 'user' whom the project deliverable must satisfy),
- the identification of stakeholders—the people and organizations— impacted by the planned activity,
- the identification of key technologies, a change and/or innovation management plan, a budget plan, the relevant business architecture standards and business common core requirements, service level requirements, and constraints.

Model Package. The model package identifies what models the business architect will bring to the table during the engagement. Most major engagements will include an Enterprise Context Model, a Gap Model, a roadmap state model, and several other models selected based on the needs of the project or enterprise activity.

Pattern 1 identifies the key components of the Business Architecture Engagement Model. Pattern 2 elaborates on the first pattern and provides detailed elements of each of the key components.

Pattern 1

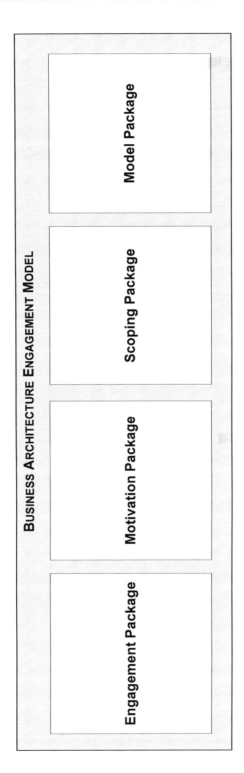

Pattern 2

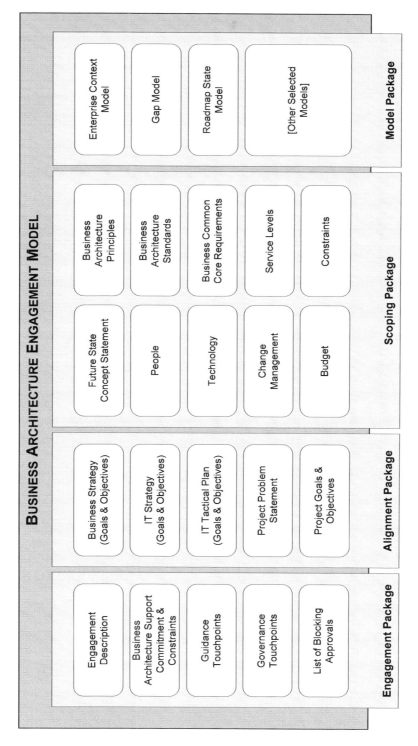

CHAPTER 026

Performance Management Model

The Performance Management Model documents the key elements of the enterprise's approach to managing performance within the enterprise.

The Performance Management Model contains the following elements:

- Performance Management Plan
- Performance Data Management Plan
- Tactical Performance Indicators
- Strategic Outcomes Indicators
- Data Collection
- Data Storage
- Data Analysis
- Performance Monitoring
- Performance Dashboard
- Performance Reporting

Performance Management Plan. The Performance Management plan identifies all the elements necessary for an enterprise to manage the performance of existing enterprise components and new investments. This plan looks at performance of ongoing activities and the outcome of completed activities. This includes identifying a Performance Data Management Plan and the processes of performance monitoring (which includes initiating corrections to in-flight strategy and tactics) which may span all enterprise activities. The Performance Management Plan may identify both tactical performance indicators and indicators of strategic outcomes.

Performance Data Management Plan. Data is a key resource for performance management. The performance data management plan identifies how data will be collected, stored, and analyzed.

Data Collection. This element of the model identifies the data that needs to be captured for performance monitoring.

Data Storage. This element of the model identified how the collected data will be stored for secondary use purposes. As part of the data management plan, this element identifies the data component required and puts it into context of the overall information solution.

Data Analysis. This element of the model identifies how data will be processed for performance monitoring via performance reporting and a performance dashboard.

Performance Monitoring. Performance monitoring is the process of reviewing performance data, determining the quality of performance, and formulating action if performance does not meet enterprise performance requirements. Key performance indicators are identified in the Performance Management Plan and evaluated during the activity of 'performance monitoring'.

Performance Dashboard. The performance dashboard is a tool used to continuously monitor the quality of performance by presenting the current status of tactical performance indicators and strategic outcome indicators. Dashboards usually report summary information for quick and easy consumption and usually report up-to-date current state information.

Performance Reporting. Performance reporting presents both summary and detailed information on performance indicators and strategic outcome indicators. The term 'reporting' is used here in its widest sense. A report may be a static document, a custom dataset, a balanced scorecard, a chart, an online user-manipulated business intelligence tool, a dashboard data widget, etc.

Patterns 1 and 2 both present an overview of performance planning and monitoring. Pattern 1 shows the high-level plan elements. Pattern 2 shows a more detailed perspective, tracing the relationship between the elements of the model, from the definition of an indicator to its data source, to data storage, analysis, dashboard and reporting.

Pattern 1

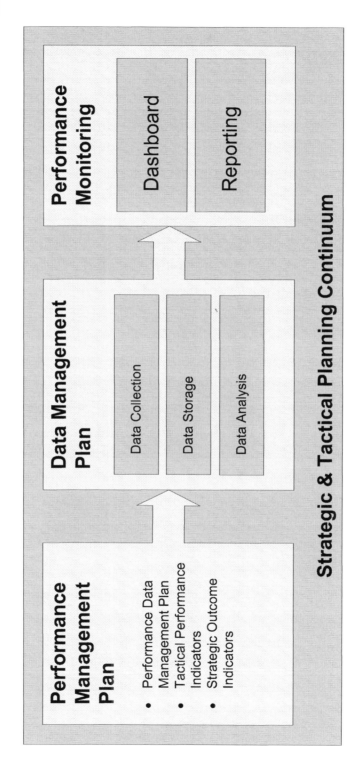

Pattern 2

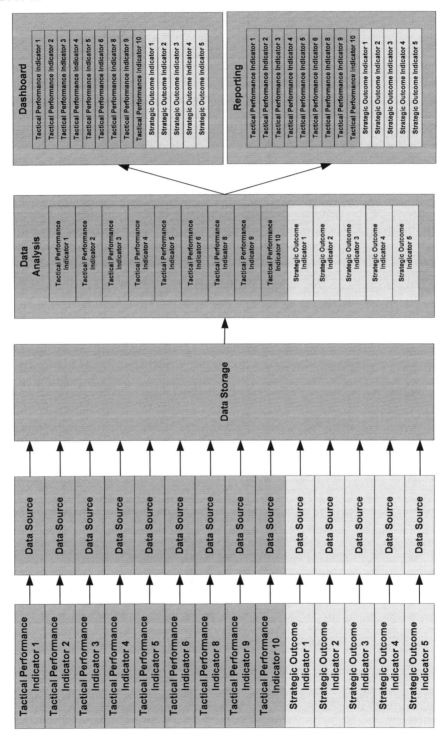

CHAPTER 027

Enterprise Maturity Model

The Enterprise Maturity Model identifies the status of the enterprise as a functioning integrated entity.

The Enterprise Maturity Model contains the following elements:

- Function Driven
- Enterprise Driven

Function Driven. The term 'function driven' refers to an enterprise in which each function is developed in isolation from each other function resulting in business islands, silos, and stovepipes.

Enterprise Driven. The term 'enterprise driven' refers to an enterprise in which each function is developed in consideration of common core elements which may serve multiple functions across the enterprise, regardless of the boundaries between organizational units and business functions and business services. SOA (service oriented architecture) and SOE (service oriented enterprise) are both examples of the 'enterprise driven' approach. The hallmarks of the enterprise driven organization are: standardized technology and common infrastructure; standard information/data and applications; standardized common services and processes; and, plug and play business and technology services.

Pattern 1 shows the path of an old 'function driven' enterprise composed of 'non-reusable components' as it moves towards an 'enterprise drive' approach that involves standardization and reusable components. The inset in pattern 1 shows the path of increasing maturity.

The path to enterprise maturity passes through the enterprise architecture objectives of interoperability, integration, and alignment.

Pattern 1 shows standardization taking place in the areas of 'technology & common infrastructure', 'information/data and applications', and 'services and processes'. The level of standardization can be fine-tuned when elaborating this model. For example, standardization can be expanded to reflect standardization goals in the areas of integration, interoperability, sustainability, etc.

Reaching maturity takes the concerted effort of the entire organization. Some planned or ongoing enterprise work contributes to the overall effort, while some are a step backwards.

Pattern 2 illustrates where different projects or ongoing services fit in the enterprise's maturity model. If a project is important and a major step backwards in terms of maturity, this pattern highlights the issue and invites careful reconsideration.

Pattern 1

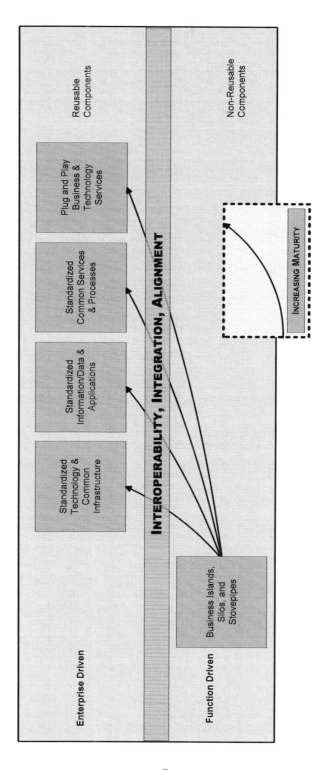

Pattern 2

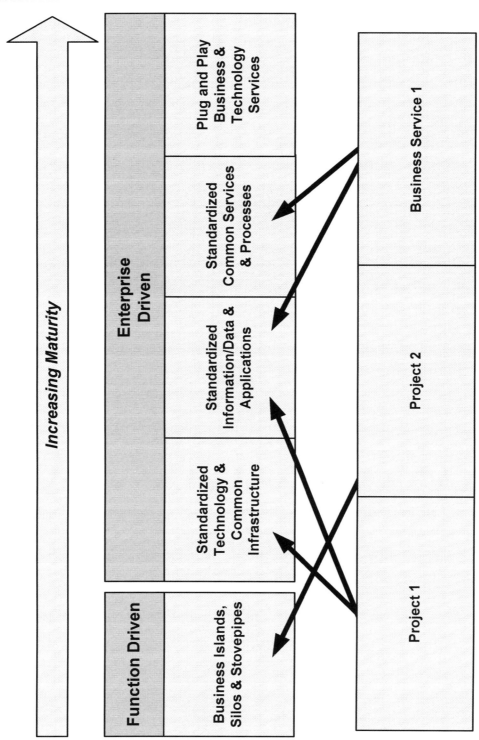

CHAPTER 028

Enterprise Model

A practical and useful definition of enterprise architecture comes from ISO/IEC 42010: 2007, which defines architecture as "...the fundamental organization of a system, embodied in its components, their relationships to each other and the environment...." In keeping with this definition, the Enterprise Model does three important things. First, it depicts the enterprise as a single solution—as one large system. Second, it provides a high-level overview of the key components that, together, make up the greater enterprise. Third, the layout of the model indicates the general relationships between the enterprise components and their environment. The goal of the Enterprise Model is to paint the big picture and communicate an idea of the enterprise as a system in and of itself.

The Enterprise Model contains the following elements:

- Technology Components
- Data Components
- Applications/System Components
- Business Services
- Common Services
- Inputs
- Outputs

Technology Components. A technological component of the enterprise is a component which supports the operation of other application, data, and technology components. In this model, a technology component may perform a very specific function or represent a type of technology product. The term technology component includes infrastructure and security components.

Data Components. A data component of the enterprise is an existing enterprise data asset. Data components are usually managed by an application and supported by multiple technology components. Some data components are manage via loosely coupled services like those available via web services or message brokers.

Application/System Components. An application component is an operationalized application or system that supports a specific business service and its various business processes. Applications are used to access and manage specific data components and depend on the support of specific technology components. An application will always have human users directly accessing it via some type of user/client interface—a data or technology component may not.

Business Service. A business service is a collection of business processes that, together, deliver a particular service to enterprise clients. Business services are owned and operated by a responsible organizational unit. Business services are supported by technological services, which are composed of data, application, and technology components that are integrated and interoperate in order to support the business activity.

Common Services. A common service is a type of technology component that is shared by multiple application, data, and technology components. Common services are often designed using SOA methods and support basic services such as messaging, security, and administrative functions.

Inputs. The input element of the Enterprise Model can be used to indicate interfaces to business suppliers, the systems feeding the enterprise crucial information, etc.

Outputs. The output element of the Enterprise Model can be used to indicate client or stakeholder (consumer) information interfaces and the output of products and services.

The Enterprise Model may depict current state, future state, or various interim states.

The Enterprise Model can be elaborated upon by listing the key things that make up each of the enterprise elements. For example, the common services element may list security services, privacy service, employee or client authorization services, etc. The data element may include a listing of the enterprise's crucial data holdings.

Whether your enterprise is n-tier, 3-tier, flat, or something entirely unique, the goal of the Enterprise Model remains the same, namely, to put all the key pieces of the puzzle onto one page.

Pattern 1 presents the full conceptual Enterprise Model. It contains embedded meanings, suggesting how the components should be group and arranged.

Pattern 2 shows a simplified view of the Enterprise Model presented in pattern 1.

Pattern 3 shows a very simple view of the enterprise-as-solution, from internal, to connecting services, to external entities.

Pattern 4 presents the full conceptual Enterprise Model without any embedded meaning. This presents the core components of the enterprise-as-solution, without getting bogged down in side conversations about how the pieces of the puzzle should be arranged and connected.

Pattern 4 shows a simplified view of the Enterprise Model presented in pattern 4.

Pattern 5 shows a very simple view of the enterprise-as-solution, from internal, to connecting services, to external entities.

Pattern 1

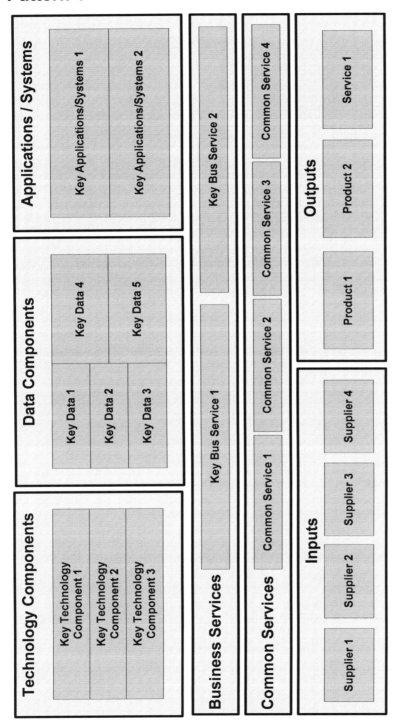

Pattern 2

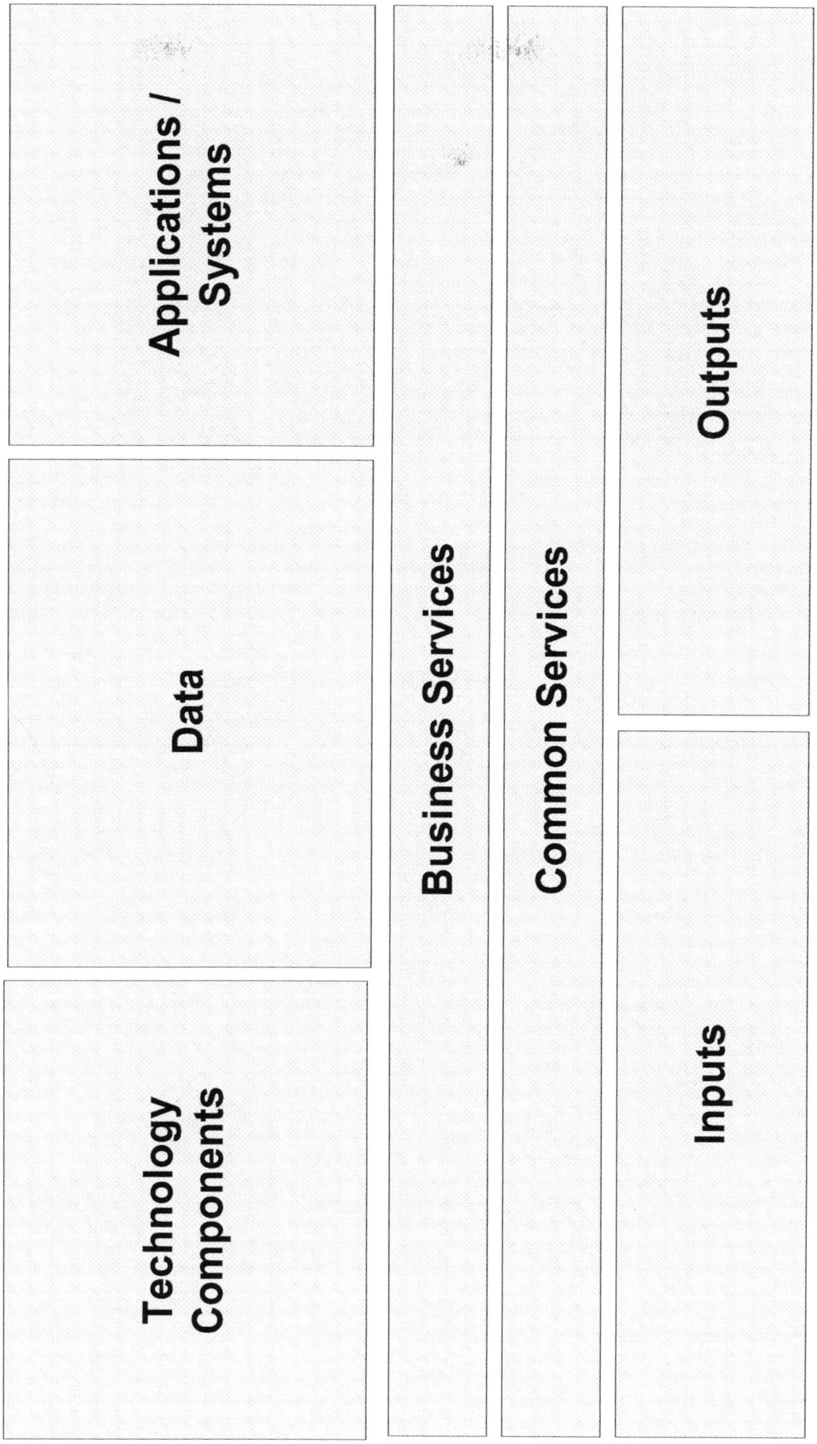

Applications / Systems

Data

Technology Components

Business Services

Common Services

Outputs

Inputs

Pattern 3

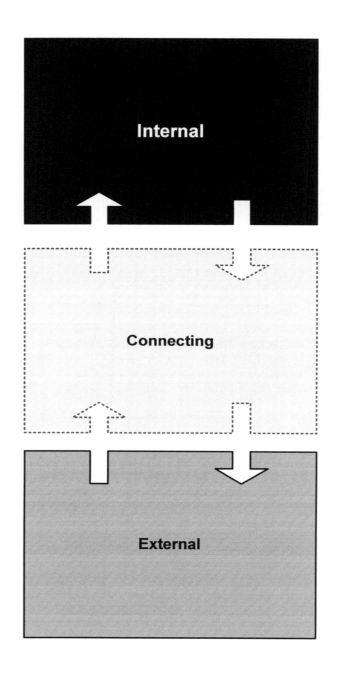

Pattern 4

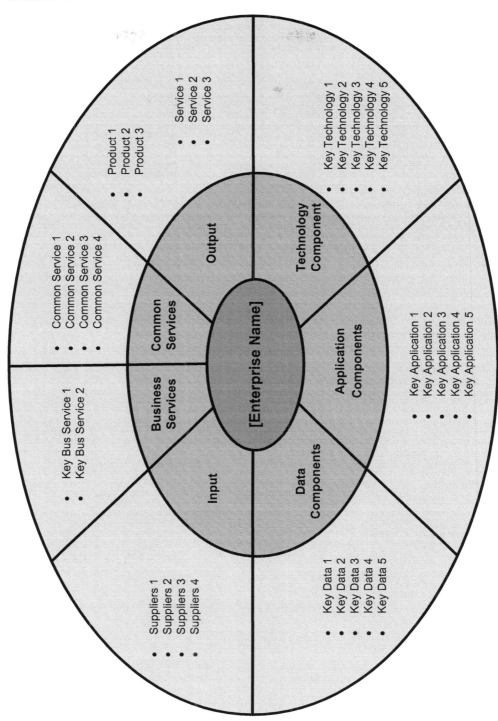

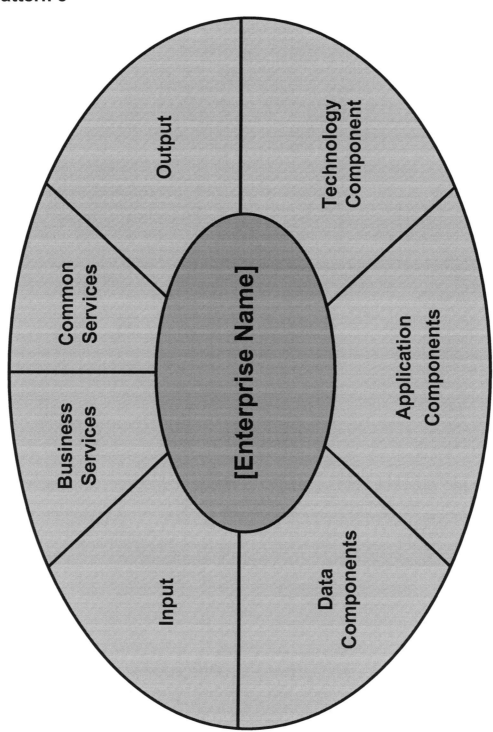

Pattern 6

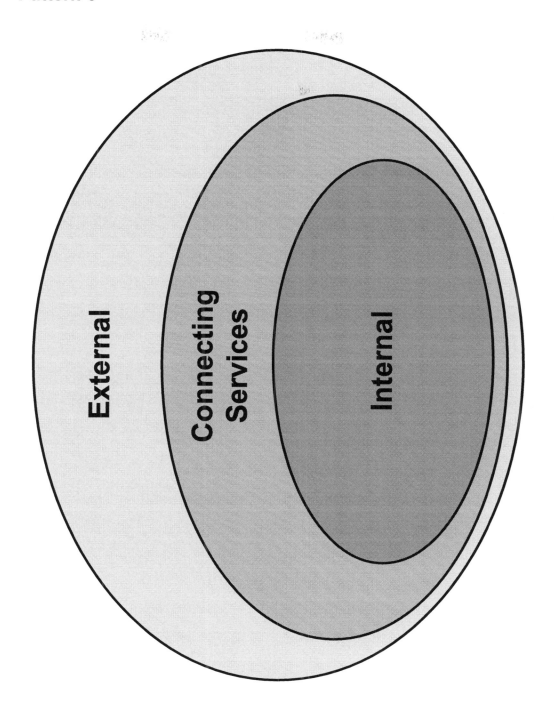

CHAPTER 029

Enterprise Context Model

An Enterprise Context Model starts with the Enterprise Model and layers on new enterprise elements, showing how each new element fits within the context of the enterprise.

The Enterprise Context Model contains the following elements:

- Enterprise Model
- Solution Context Statements

Enterprise Model. The Enterprise Model depicts the enterprise as a single solution and provides a high-level overview of the key enterprise components: technology, data, applications & web services, business services, common services, inputs (data, resources, etc), and outputs (products and services).

Solution Context Statements. Solution context statements add environmental detail to our understanding of the proposed solution. These statements are usually provided inside a call-out box which points to the component of the Enterprise Model which is being elaborating upon. The statements may add any type of information to the Enterprise Model.

The primary purpose of the Enterprise Context Model is to define how new IT initiatives and projects fit into the enterprise and helps project and program teams understand the cross-enterprise dependencies related to their activity.

In this example, context is set for a new business service, its data component, and the related output service.

Each new element has a solution context statement associated with it to explain what the new element is.

The Enterprise Context Model may show the enterprise current state, future state, or any transition state in between.

One of the takeaways from this model is that *any model* can be augmented by the use of color to highlight certain aspects of the model or by the use of callout boxes to provide additional information on model elements that are new, old, changing, broken, under performing, grouped, and so on.

Pattern 1

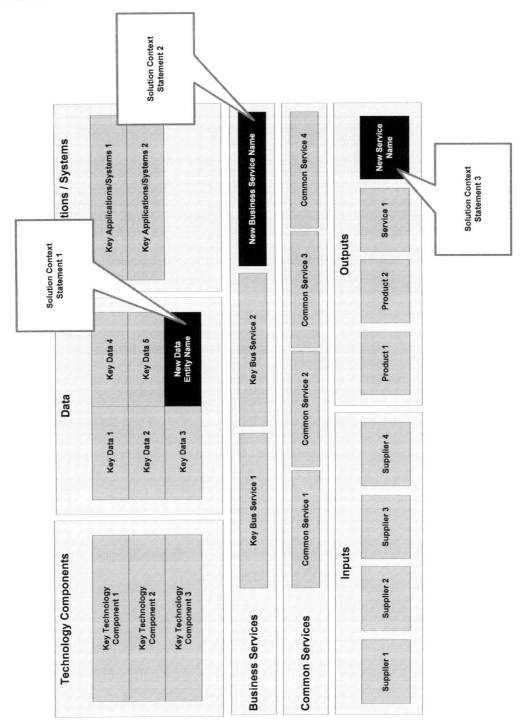

Pattern 2

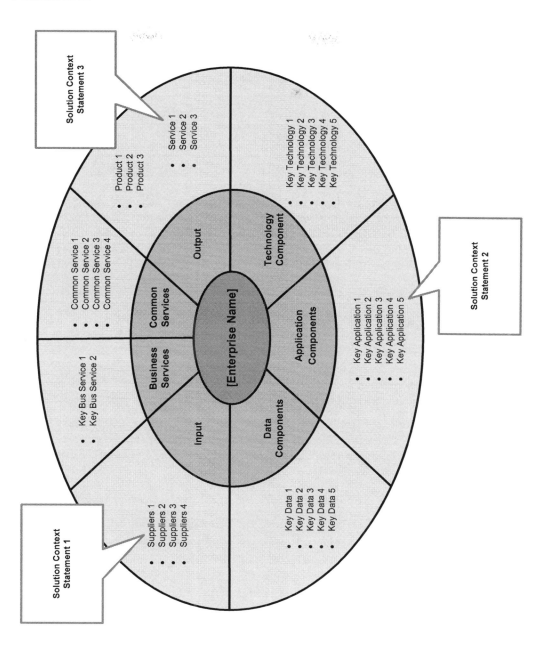

CHAPTER 030

Enterprise Roadmap State Model

The Enterprise Roadmap State Model is based upon the Enterprise Model (future state) and illustrates the roadmap the enterprise will follow as it transitions from current to future state.

The Enterprise Roadmap State Model contains the following elements:

- Enterprise Model
- Color Key Code
- Phase

Enterprise Model. The Enterprise Model depicts the enterprise as a single solution and provides a high-level overview of the key enterprise components: technology, data, applications & web services, business services, common services, inputs (data, resources, etc), and outputs (products and services).

Color Key Code. A color key code is a textual list of Enterprise Model elements where each element is assigned a particular color and the corresponding element in the Enterprise Model is assigned the same color.

Phase. It is extraordinarily rare that an enterprise can transition from a current state to a future state in one giant step. This is because most changes to an enterprise are complex and require a complex, coordinated planning effort across one or more years. Therefore, the work to transition an enterprise from current to future state usually requires several distinct phases. These phases break down the work of transformation into a phased sequence of manageable projects and tasks.

Using a key and color coding, the model illustrates which enterprise elements will be implemented during which phases of the migration from current to future state. Any number of interim states may be indicated.

Pattern 2 shows breakout detail from the Enterprise Roadmap State Model and usually provides more detail than is available in the parent model.

Pattern 3 illustrates a consolidation path that takes an enterprise from five disparate systems to two consolidated systems.

Pattern 4 depicts a three-phase IT roadmap that spans twelve business quarters. This pattern elaborates on the Enterprise Roadmap State Model by slotting enterprise components/elements into a timeline and by including other enterprise elements, such as business continuity and an integrated training program.

In EA terminology, the term 'roadmap' is a synonym for 'migration plan', 'evolution plan', and 'transition plan'.

Pattern 1

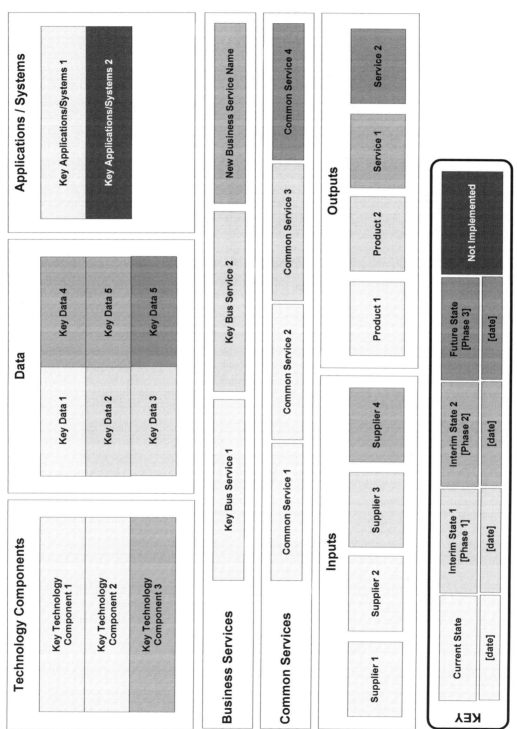

Pattern 2

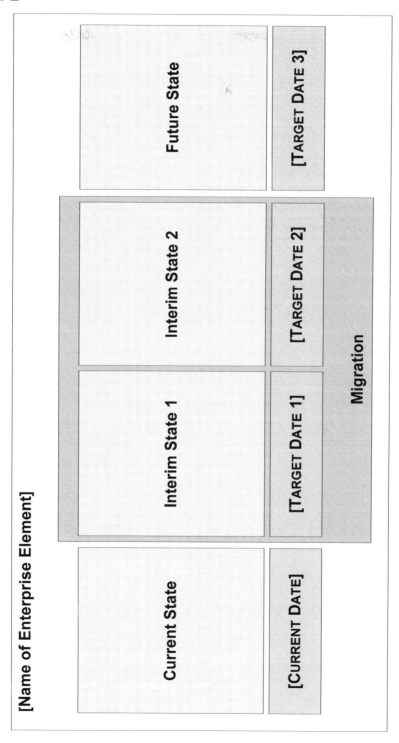

Pattern 3

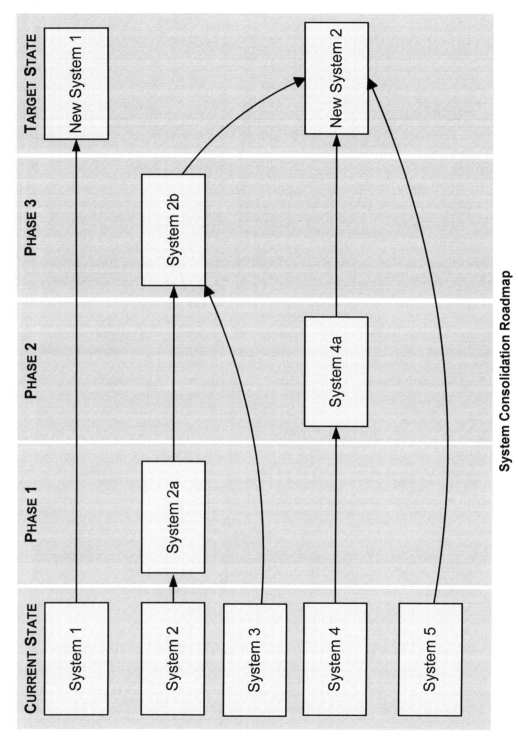

System Consolidation Roadmap

Pattern 4

Service	Phase 1				Phase 2				Phase 3			
	2010-11			2011-12				2012-13				2013-14
	Q2	Q3	Q4	Q1	Q2	Q3	Q4	Q1	Q2	Q3	Q4	Q1
Technology Components	Infrastructure Component 1	Infrastructure Component 2			Infrastructure Component 3					Infrastructure Component 4		
Data Components		Data Component 1		Data Component 2			Data Component 3		Data Component 4		Data Component 5, 6	
Application Components		Application 1	Application 2	Application 3			Application 4	Application 5	Application 6, 7, 8		Upgrade Applications 2, 6, 8	
Business Services		Business Service 1		Business Service 2		Business Services 3, 4		Business Service 5		Business Service 5		
Common Services	Common Services 1, 2, 3				Common Service 4					Common Service 5		
Inputs	Supplier 1, 2	Supplier 3, 4, 5, 6			Supplier 7			Supplier 8, 9				
Outputs				Product 1 Service 1, 2		Product 2	Product 3 Service 3		Service 4	Product 4, 5, 6, 7		Service 5
Business Continuity	Data Center 2.0 Re-Design		Data Center 2.0 Buy & Build		Data Center 2.0 Test	Data Center 2.0 Launch		Expansion Buy & Build	Expand Data Center	Data Center Test	Expansion Launch	
Capable People Program	Training Programs 1, 2, 3		Training Program 4	Training Program 5	Training Program 6	Training Program 7		Training Program 8, 9, 10, 11		Training Program 12, 13	Training Program 14	Training Program 15

CHAPTER 031

Enterprise Component Model

The Enterprise Component Model is used to elaborate on the components found in the Enterprise Model.

The Enterprise Component Model contains the following elements:

- Component
- Service
- Process
- Process Description

Component. Any thing can be considered a component if it is one part of a larger whole. An arm is a component of the human body. The navy is a component of the armed services. Servers are a technological component of an enterprise. A database may be considered a component of the enterprise, but also a component of a particular solution.

Service. A service may refer to a business service or a technological service. A business service is a collection of business processes that, together, deliver a particular service. A technological service is one or more technologies that integrate and interoperate in order to perform a particular service—sometimes serving multiple components (as in service oriented architectures), and are usually exposed to the enterprise via an API or UDDI interface.

Process. A process is a series of actions and tasks performed in order to achieve the objective of a service.

Process Description. This element of the model is a textual description of the process.

In some ways, the component model appears similar to a Functional Decomposition Model. However, the construction of a component does not necessarily reflect the tight coupling found in hierarchical relationships.

The constituent services and process of a component may be 'common/shared/reused' services or processes. In this sense, the component model is analogous to the concept of an EA building block.

The elements found in the Enterprise Component Model (represented as services in all three patterns presented here) can be elaborated upon as a group or individually. The elements inside the Enterprise Component Model should reflect the appropriate elements for any given enterprise and architectural engagement.

Pattern 1 elaborates on an enterprise component as a group of services and processes. This pattern provides significantly more detail than is seen in the parent 'Enterprise Model'.

Patterns 2 and 3 elaborate on component elements—processes, in this case.

Pattern 1

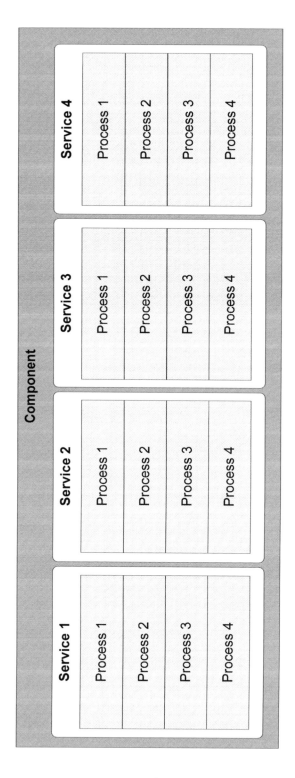

Pattern 2

Component 1: Service 1	
Process 1	Description
Process 2	Description
Process 3	Description
Process 4	Description

Pattern 3

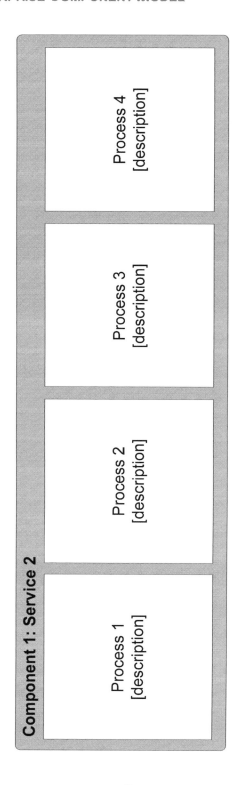

Component 1: Service 2

Process 1 [description]

Process 2 [description]

Process 3 [description]

Process 4 [description]

CHAPTER 032

Perspective Model

The Perspective Model is used to create a view of the enterprise or a particular solution which reflects just those elements of relevance to a particular point-of-view (POV).

The Perspective Model contains the following elements:

- Perspective Owner
- In-Sight Elements
- Out-of-sight Elements
- Relationship Lines

Perspective Owner. The perspective owner's view of the enterprise is depicted in the Perspective Model. The perspective owner may be a person (stakeholder, client, domain architect, *et cetera*) or thing (enterprise entity, application, database, technology, *et cetera*).

In-Sight Elements. The in-sight elements are those components of the enterprise that the perspective owner interacts with.

Out-of-sight Elements. The out-of-sight elements are those enterprise components which support the function of the in-sight elements, but which the perspective owner does not directly interact with.

Relationship Lines. In the first pattern, relationship lines connect elements from the perspective owner's interface with supporting components in the Enterprise Model.

Pattern 1 uses the Enterprise Model as a reference point for the selected perspective. (The Enterprise Model is just an example; any appropriate model may be used.) From the perspective owner's POV, a client portal perspective is shown. The perspective may belong to a person (stakeholder, client, domain architect, *et cetera*) or thing (enterprise entity, application, database, technology, *et cetera*). The relationship lines are drawn between the Enterprise Model and the 'perspective' to show which elements in the Enterprise Model relate directly to the perspective.

In pattern 2, the first set of elements are visible to the POV and usually provide direct value to the perspective's owner. The second set of elements are 'out-of-sight' of the perspective's owner, but provide secondary or supporting value to the in-sight elements.

There are other views of the enterprise that this model does not and cannot capture, such as the data perspective, the application perspective, the technology perspective, the security perspective, the infrastructure perspective, the integration perspective, and so on. Some of these perspectives are touched on in this book. However, these other perspective fall squarely into the domain of other architects on the EA team and it is these team members who will elaborate on these important perspectives.

Pattern 1

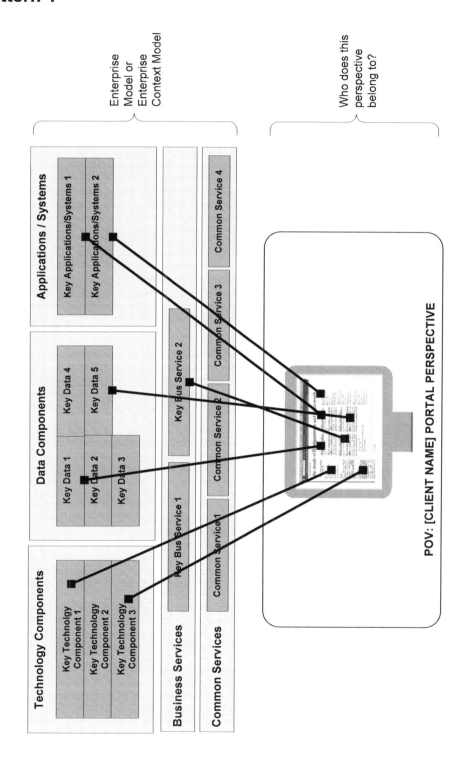

Pattern 2

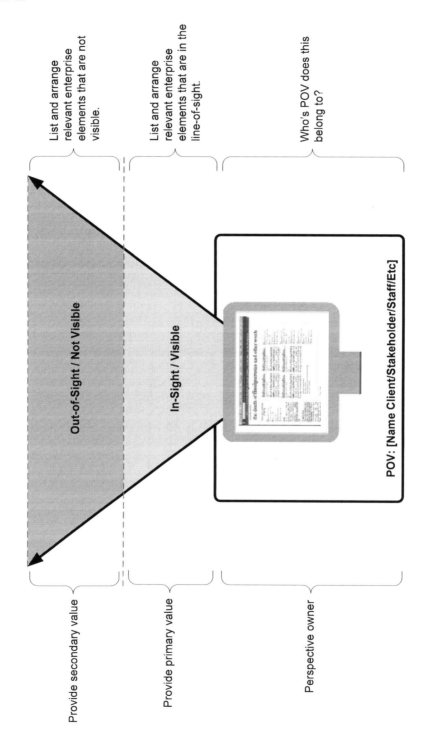

List and arrange relevant enterprise elements that are not visible.

List and arrange relevant enterprise elements that are in the line-of-sight.

Who's POV does this belong to?

Out-of-Sight / Not Visible

In-Sight / Visible

POV: [Name Client/Stakeholder/Staff/Etc]

Provide secondary value

Provide primary value

Perspective owner

CHAPTER 033

Service Level Agreement Model

The Service Level Agreement Model maps the 'service level' interdependencies between services and can be used to indicate the total 'SLA commitment' or 'load' placed upon any given service.

The Service Level Agreement Model contains the following elements:

- Service
- Contract
- Service Measure
- Service Operations
- Service Measurement
- Governance
- Action
- Capacity Metric
- Total SLA Load
- SLA Profile
- SLA Delivered
- SLA Dependency

Service. A service may refer to a business service or a technological service. A business service is a collection of business processes that, together, deliver a particular service. A technological service is one or more technologies that integrate and interoperate in order to perform a particular service—sometimes serving multiple components (as in service oriented architectures)—usually exposed to the enterprise via an API or UDDI interface.

Contract. An agreement between two or more parties which includes an agreed upon performance requirement for the contracted service. The performance requirement is expressed in terms of a service level. Service Contract is synonymous with the term 'service level agreement'.

Service Measure. Service measure is the agree upon service level as documented in the contract. A service measure should provide a textual description of the measure; explains how measurement is performed, identify the acceptable minimum service level, identify the maximum required service level, and document the expected service level requirements over an agreed upon timeframe.

Service Operations. This element identifies the organizational unit and business functions to which the contract and service measure apply and the schedule for service measurement.

Service Measurement. Service measurement is the taking of a series of observations of actual performance levels during a given period of service operation or testing scenario.

Governance. In this model, the governance process involves the analysis of service measurement observations. The purpose of the analysis is to determine if action is necessary to improve service performance.

Action. If service performance does meet the standards set out by the service measure, ameliorative action must be taken. This element describes this action.

Capacity Metric. A measure of a component's total capacity to provide service.

Total SLA Load. An enterprise component may be referenced in multiple contracts. The total SLA load is a measure of an enterprise component's commitments to all other enterprise components. When a component's total SLA load is greater than its capacity metric, there is a risk of service slowdown, system disruptions, and total system failure.

SLA Delivered. Components provide service. SLA Delivered is a measure of the total actual performance demands placed on a component in its role as a service provider.

SLA Dependency. Components are service consumers. SLA Dependency is a measure of a component's reliance on services provided by other components.

SLA Profile. Components can be both service providers and service consumers. The SLA profile documents a component's obligation to provide services (SLA Delivered) and a component's dependency on the services of other components (SLA Dependency). Both SLA Delivered and SLA Dependency data are documented in SLA contracts. In this way, the SLA profile documents the total service traffic requirements of, or burden upon, a particular service component.

There are three key things a Service Level Agreement Model can do for the enterprise. First, the model can identify the relationship between an SLA and its related process elements (pattern 1). Second, the model can identify the SLA interactions between multiple technology services (pattern 2). Finally, the model can identify an SLA's relationship to organizational structure (pattern 3).

In pattern 1, the service level is related to: the business service, the contract documenting the SLA, the measure of quality/performance, the system operating under the SLA, the action of measuring quality/performance, the governance mechanism, and the action take in response to SLA issues.

In pattern 2, the SLA interactions between systems are mapped and, for each service, the total SLA load is indicated. If a capacity metric is layered on top of this pattern and that capacity metric is less than the Total SLA Load—you've just identified an important gap in service capacity looks at service level agreements within the context of Organizational Unit, Business Function, and the various Business Services associated with the business function.

Pattern 3 zooms in on a single Organizational Unit/Business Function and creates an SLA Profile model for each business service associated with the business function.

Pattern 1

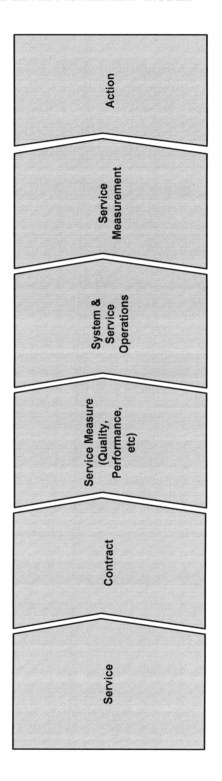

Pattern 2

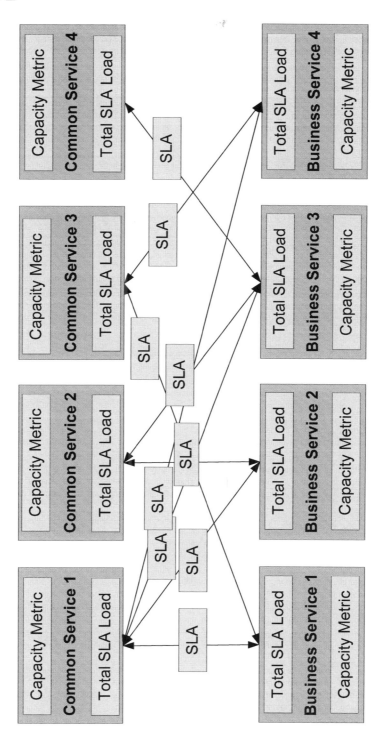

Pattern 3

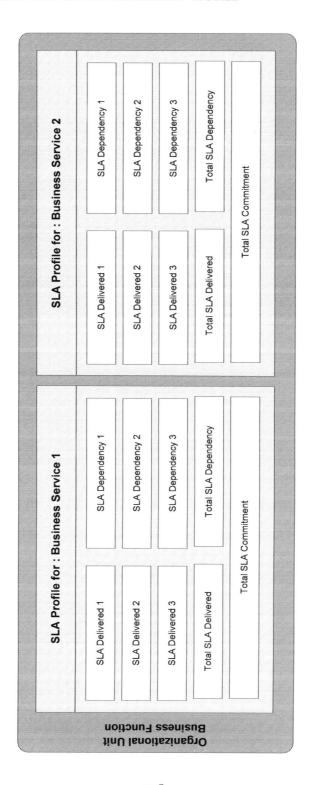

CHAPTER 034

Functional Decomposition Model

The Functional Decomposition Model maps out enterprise capabilities. The model answers a fundamental question: "What does the enterprise do?"

The Functional Decomposition Model contains the following elements:

- Organizational Unit
- Business Function
- Business Service

Organizational Unit. The enterprise is defined by an organizational hierarchy. Below the enterprise top level in the hierarchy is the organizational unit level. Each organizational unit corresponds with a high-level enterprise capability.

Business Function. A business function is a collection of business activities and services, usually organized as a sub-unit of an organizational unit.

Business Service. A business services is a collection of business processes that, together, deliver a particular service.

The Functional Decomposition Model can be parsed to depict just those enterprise capabilities relevant to a particular enterprise business architecture engagement.

The function decomposition model seems closely related to the organizational decomposition model. The Functional Decomposition Model allows the issue of organizational function to be understood and discussed without getting bogged down in distracting debate about 'who' performs what functions.

The Functional Decomposition Model also seems related to the Process Model. The Functional Decomposition Model allows the issue of organizational function to be understood and discussed without getting bogged down with process details or distracting debate on 'how' functions are performed.

Pattern 1 presents a view of organizational units and functions.

Pattern 2 zooms in on an organizational unit and its functions and services.

Pattern 1

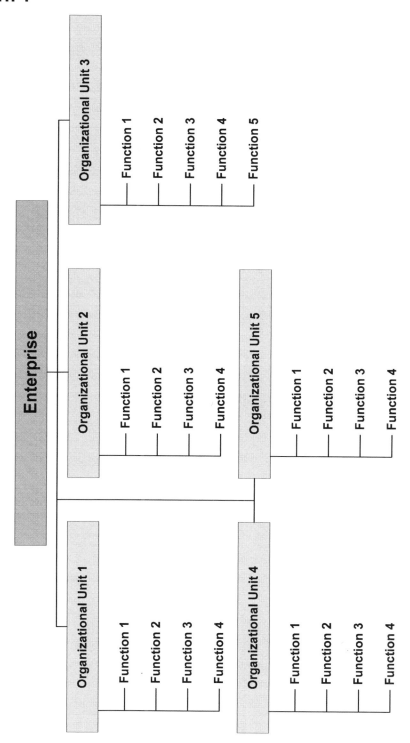

Pattern 2

Organizational Unit

Function 1
- Service 1.1
- Service 1.2
- Service 1.3
- Service 1.4
- Service 1.5
- Service 1.6
- Service 1.7
- Service 1.8
- Service 1.9
- Service 1.10
- Service 1.11

Function 2
- Service 2.1
- Service 2.2
- Service 2.3
- Service 2.4
- Service 2.5

Function 3
- Service 3.1
- Service 3.1

Function 4
- Service 4.1
- Service 4.2
- Service 4.3
- Service 4.4
- Service 4.5
- Service 4.6
- Service 4.7
- Service 4.8

CHAPTER 035

Organization Model

The Organization Model illustrates an organization's decision-making structure—its chain of command—and communicates *who* does *what* in that structure. Each element in the model lists the name of an actor and the role they perform in the organization.

The Organization Model contains the following elements:

- Hierarchy
- Role
- Actor
- Vision
- Goal
- Objective

Hierarchy. The organization and ranking of an enterprise according to authority and capabilities, function, service, and processes. Capabilities are expressed in terms of organizational units. In general, 'organizational unit' can be considered the equivalent of: 'line-of-business', 'high-level business function', and 'enterprise capability'. Functions are expressed as sub-organizational units responsible for delivering services and performing various processes.

Role. A role is a position with the organization that fulfills a particular responsibility or function or plays a part in a particular process.

Actor. An actor is a person, organization or application, system, or service that performs a particular role within the enterprise. An actor may be internal or external to the enterprise

Vision. A vision statement describes a future state which the enterprise desires to work towards.

Goal. Goals are the targets that, when achieved, will transition the enterprise towards its future state vision. Goals guide enterprise decision-making about the type, scope and priority of all enterprise activity.

Objectives. Objectives are the measurable achievements that, when achieved, will move the enterprise towards the realization of its goals.

In the organizational model, organizational hierarchy is depicted in two ways. First, it is graphically laid out as a hierarchy. Second, the taxonomy of the various roles reflect the hierarchical structure.

In pattern 2, a strategic extension is made to the Organization Model by mapping the link between a guiding vision, organizational structure and responsibility for the achievement of certain goals and objectives.

Pattern 1

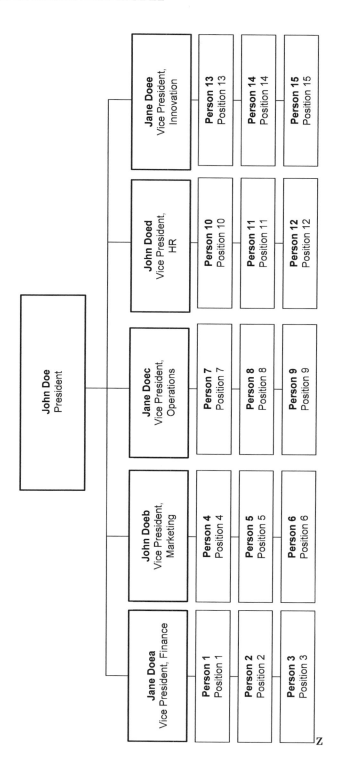

Pattern 2

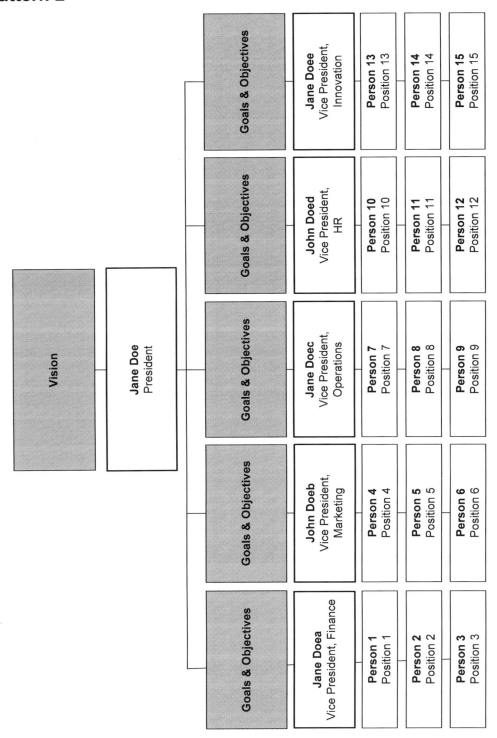

CHAPTER 036

Organizational Unit Model

The Organizational Unit Model identifies the various elements that make up an organizational unit. In general, 'organizational unit' can be considered the equivalent of: 'line-of-business', 'high-level business function', 'business capability', or 'enterprise capability'.

The Organizational Unit Model contains the following elements:

- Organizational Unit
- Motivation
- Service Delivery
- Outputs
- People
- Performance
- Resource
- Location
- Events
- Enabling Technology

Organizational Unit. The enterprise is defined by an organizational hierarchy. Below the enterprise top level in the hierarchy is the organizational unit level. Each organizational unit correspond with a high-level enterprise capability.

Motivation. The motivation component summarizes the goals and objectives which the organizational unit is responsible for fulfilling and the measures of success which indicate whether the organizational unit has or has not been able to fulfill its responsibility.

Service Delivery. The service delivery component identifies the organization's functions, services, processes, and governance processes.

Outputs. The output element identifies the organization's outputs: its products and services. It also identifies the stakeholders that consume those products and services.

People. The people component identifies the roles and actors of the organizational unit. Ironically, the people component also identifies system and group actors.

Performance. A performance measure is a way to assess the effectiveness of business functions, business services, and business processes. The performance component documents the service levels the organizational unit is responsible for meeting and the service quality measures which are used to evaluate the organizational unit's performance.

Resources. The resources element identifies the input supplies used by the organizational unit.

Location. The location element identifies the locations from which the organizational unit conducts business.

Events. The event element identifies the important events in the life of the enterprise.

Enabling Technology. The work of organizational units is supported by technology. The enabling technology element identifies the data, application, and technology components that support the functions and services of the organizational unit.

This organization unit model is based upon a particular organizational ontology and taxonomy. The ontology and taxonomy of this model is only provided as an example, not as a recommendation. Each enterprise should organize itself in a way that makes sense to the enterprise (i.e. decide upon its own ontology) and descriptive vocabulary (i.e. its own taxonomy) to describe it.

In pattern 1 the elements of the organizational unit are grouped into several categories. Motivation: goals, objectives, measures of success. Service Delivery: functions, services, processes, and governance (process controls). People: roles and actors. Output: products & services, and stakeholders (clients or customers). Performance: service level agreements and service quality measures. Standing alone (ungrouped) in the model are: Resources (inputs), locations, events, and enabling technology.

Each element that makes up Organizational Unit Model can be elaborated using the patterns of this model. For example, see: Location Model.

Pattern 1

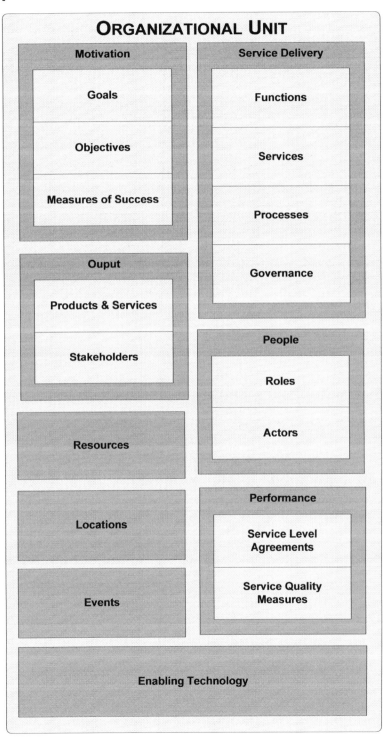

Pattern 2

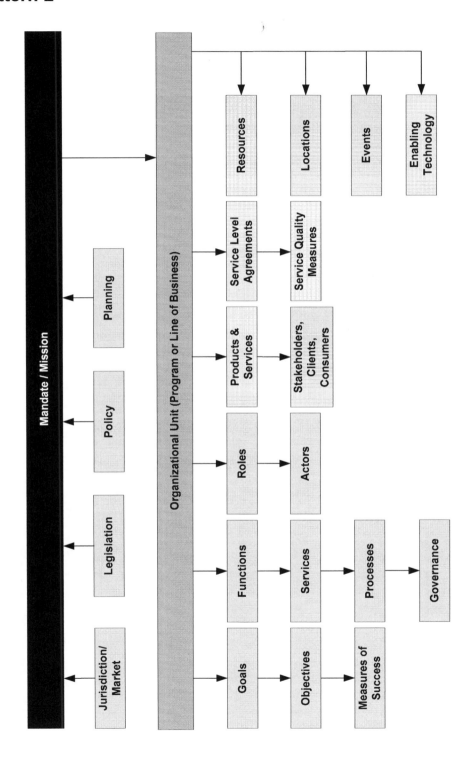

CHAPTER 037

Process Model

The purpose of the Process Model is to show the details of processes that get things get done for the enterprise. The Process Model may take the shape of a simple flowchart, complicated swimlane diagram, or detailed process hierarchy. In short ,this model shows *how* a process is performed.

The Process Model contains the following elements:

- Process Name
- Swimlane Name
- Process Step

Process Name. A process is a series of actions and tasks taken in order to carry out the process. This model element identifies a particular process.

Swimlane Name. A swimlane is an element of the Process Model which shows which actors or roles are responsible for the various tasks, actions, and decision-points at a particular stage of the process.

Process Step. Each process is broken down into steps. The steps involve breaking each process into sub-processes; each sub-process into tasks; and each task into discrete actions.

Pattern 1 shows a complicated swimlane diagram. This pattern shows who owns which parts of the process and their role process decision-making and 'doing'. The pattern also defines sequencing and important events for the process.

The business architect determines the appropriate granularity for the model. Variant patterns based on the Process Model can be produced to show more granular process steps.

Pattern 2 shows a complicated process hierarchy that documents the service-process relationship, sub-process, the tasks associated with each sub-process, and the actions associated with each task.

Pattern 1

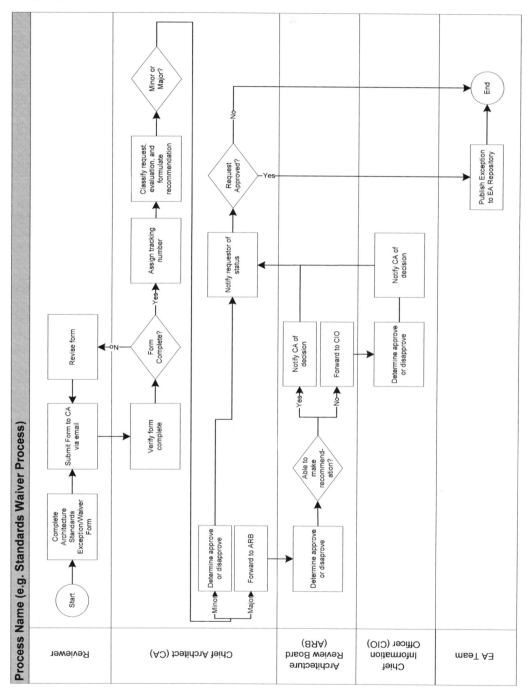

Pattern 2

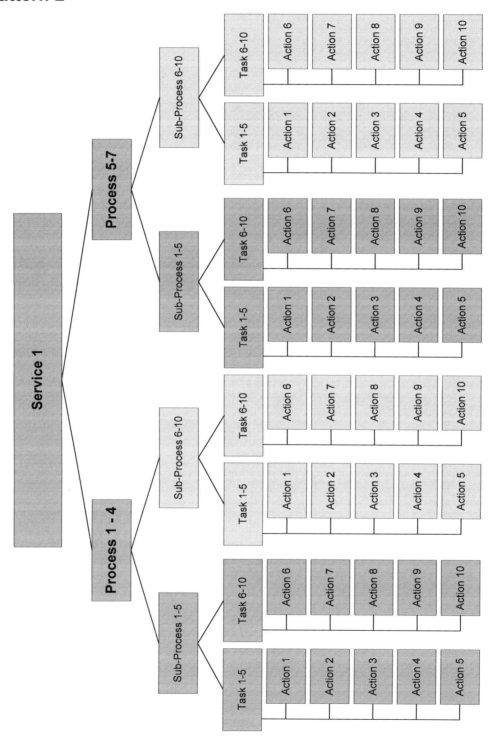

CHAPTER 038

Location Model

The Location Model identifies each physical location at which business is conducted and for each location it identifies the organizational units operating there.

The Location Model contains the following element:

- Location

  Location. The physical location or locations where the organization conducts business.

Locations may be situated anywhere around the globe, the country, state, province, county, city, town, or building.

Pattern 2 depicts a hierarchical relationship between locations.

This model may be elaborated upon by layering over location elements other types of information, such as elements of organizational structure, major functions, major IT systems, major IT services, etc.

Pattern 1

Pattern 2

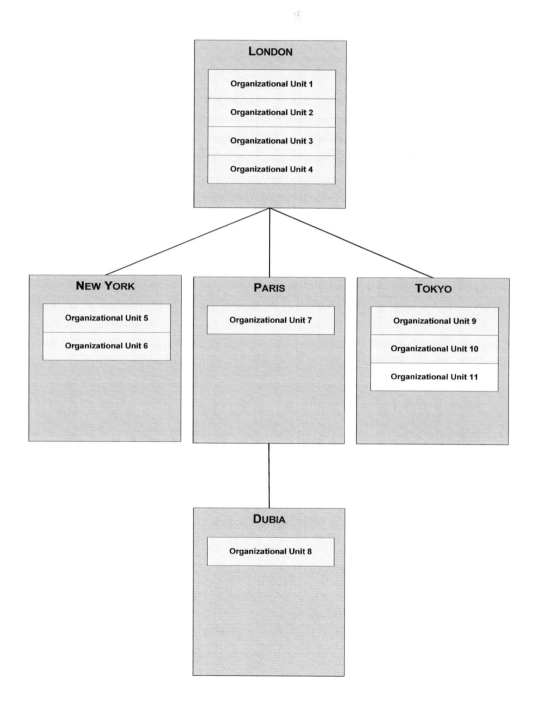

CHAPTER 039

Event Model

The Event Model demonstrates the link between event triggers, a series of subsequent events, and services or service processes.

The Event Model contains the following elements:

- Trigger
- Information Request
- Service
- Event Steps / Flow (Arrow)
- Response

Trigger. A trigger is an inciting incident that 'triggers' the event. The trigger may be a calendar event or process event, like the processing of a sale or an incoming message/ transaction from a system.

Information Request. This is one type of trigger where an external request is made for information, launching a series of event 'steps' to either deny or fulfill the request.

Service. A service may refer to a business service or a technological service. A business service is a collection of business processes that, together, deliver a particular service. A technological service is one or more technologies that integrate and interoperate in order to perform a particular service—sometimes serving multiple components (as in service oriented architectures)—usually exposed to the enterprise via an API or UDDI interface. IT services support business services either directly or indirectly.

Event Steps / Flow (Arrow). Events are a type of process and are made up of sub-processes, tasks, and actions. A flow arrow indicates a step in the event, showing where the step originated and where the step terminates.

Response. The final action of the event is usually a response back to the source system or business process that triggered the event.

The events of an Event Model usually begin with incoming information. In pattern 1, the incoming information is an 'information request'.

In pattern 2, a technology overlay is added to illustrate which systems fulfill which services and process.

And now for something completely different. Event Models often sequence events in technological processes. The enterprise also has the need to sequence business events. Pattern 3 illustrates a calendar of important events in the business cycle of the enterprise. Knowing when important events occur is crucial to any business. Communicating a schedule of those events is, oddly, something that rarely happens. Color coding can be used to highlight important events.

Pattern 1

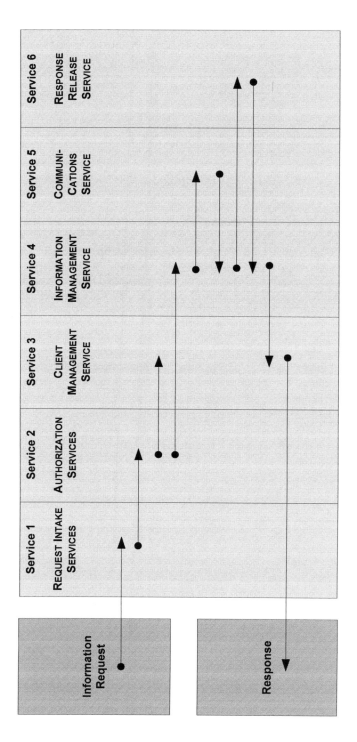

Pattern 2

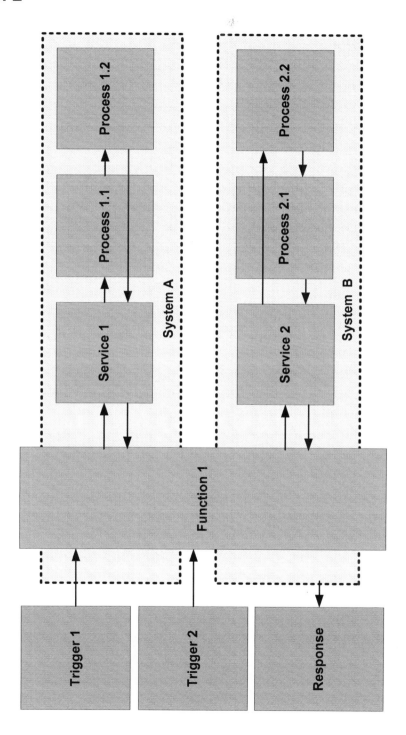

Pattern 3

ENTERPRISE EVENT SCHEDULE

[YEAR]	Organizational Unit 1	Organizational Unit 2	Organizational Unit 3
JANUARY	[Date]: Name of Event 1 [Date]: Name of Event 2		
FEBRUARY	[Date]: Name of Event 1 [Date]: Name of Event 2	[Date]: Name of Event 1 [Date]: Name of Event 2	
MARCH	[Date]: Name of Event 1 [Date]: Name of Event 2	[Date]: Name of Event 1 [Date]: Name of Event 2	[Date]: Name of Event 1 [Date]: Name of Event 2
APRIL	[Date]: Name of Event 1 [Date]: Name of Event 2	[Date]: Name of Event 1 [Date]: Name of Event 2	[Date]: Name of Event 1 [Date]: Name of Event 2
MAY	[Date]: Name of Event 1 [Date]: Name of Event 2		
JUNE	[Date]: Name of Event 1 [Date]: Name of Event 2	[Date]: Name of Event 1 [Date]: Name of Event 2	
JULY	[Date]: Name of Event 1 [Date]: Name of Event 2		[Date]: Name of Event 1 [Date]: Name of Event 2
AUGUST	[Date]: Name of Event 1 [Date]: Name of Event 2	[Date]: Name of Event 1 [Date]: Name of Event 2	[Date]: Name of Event 1 [Date]: Name of Event 2
SEPTEMBER	[Date]: Name of Event 1 [Date]: Name of Event 2	[Date]: Name of Event 1 [Date]: Name of Event 2	
OCTOBER	[Date]: Name of Event 1 [Date]: Name of Event 2		
NOVEMBER	[Date]: Name of Event 1 [Date]: Name of Event 2		[Date]: Name of Event 1 [Date]: Name of Event 2
DECEMBER	[Date]: Name of Event 1 [Date]: Name of Event 2		[Date]: Name of Event 1 [Date]: Name of Event 2

CHAPTER 040

Gap Model

The Gap Model identifies where part or parts of something is missing.

The Gap Model contains the following elements:

- Color Code
- Gap Model Entity

Color Code. A color code is a form of embedded intelligence where the color of an element in the model corresponds with a particular meaning—in this case 'gaps' in the model are assigned a particular color (or shade of grey, as the case may be).

Gap Model Element. In some models the gap is depicted as a model element placed between other entities to indicate that a gap exists between them. For example, a 'performance gap' element may be placed between an 'expected performance' element and an 'actual performance' element.

In patterns 1-3, color coding illustrates which enterprise elements will be implemented during which phases of evolution from current to future states. Any number of interim states may be indicated by color coding.

Pattern 1 uses dark grey shading, a heavy black border, and a key element to identify the gaps—the to-be implemented components—in the Enterprise Model.

Pattern 2 uses dark grey shading, a heavy black dashed border, and a "[GAP]" label to identify the gap. In this pattern, the gap is a strategic misalignment and oversight—there is no strategic IT plan in place. The foundation for this Gap Model is the enterprise business architecture alignment assurance model.

Pattern 3 uses to dark grey bolded and italicized lettering and "(GAP)" label to identify the gaps. This pattern identifies function and service gaps in a Functional Decomposition Model.

Pattern 4 uses a Gap Model element in dark black bolded lettering inside a white box with a heavy black border and "Performance Gap" label to identify the gap. This pattern illustrates a performance gap.

Pattern 5 uses Gap Model elements in dark black bolded lettering inside a white box with a heavy black border and the labels "Gap 1" and "Gap 2", respectively. This pattern illustrates a gap in the communication of a new quality initiative.

For another example of a Gap Model see the Strategic Thinking Heat Map Model.

Ultimately, any model can be used to perform a gap analysis. How so? When you start mapping real enterprise entities to the model, if the entity does not exist but should (now or in the future), then you've just identified a gap.

Pattern 1

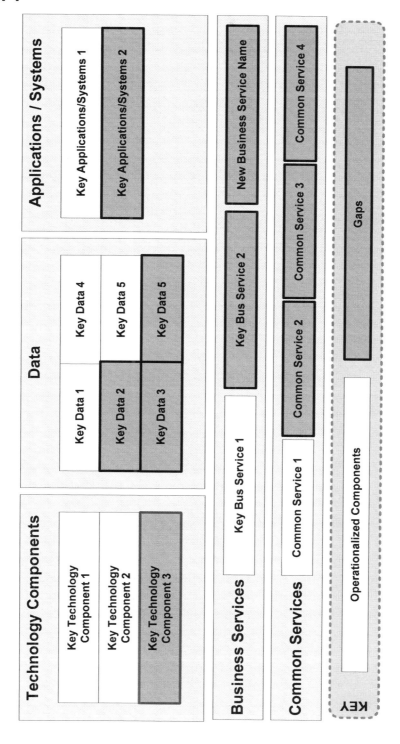

Pattern 2

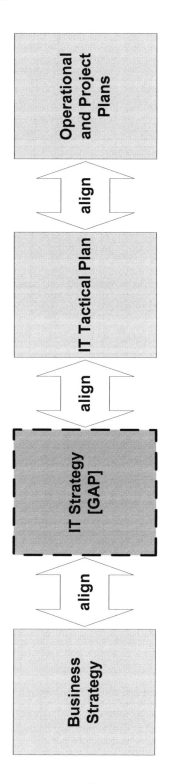

Pattern 3

System Name

Function 1

- Service 1.1
- Service 1.2
- Service 1.3
- Service 1.4
- Service 1.5
- Service 1.6
- *Service 1.7 (GAP)*
- *Service 1.8 (GAP)*
- *Service 1.9 (GAP)*
- Service 1.10
- Service 1.11

Function 2

- Service 2.1
- Service 2.2
- Service 2.3
- Service 2.4
- Service 2.5

Function 3

- Service 3.1
- Service 3.1

Function 4 (GAP)

- *Service 4.1 (GAP)*
- *Service 4.2 (GAP)*
- *Service 4.3 (GAP)*
- *Service 4.4 (GAP)*
- *Service 4.5 (GAP)*
- *Service 4.6 (GAP)*
- *Service 4.7 (GAP)*
- *Service 4.8 (GAP)*

Pattern 4

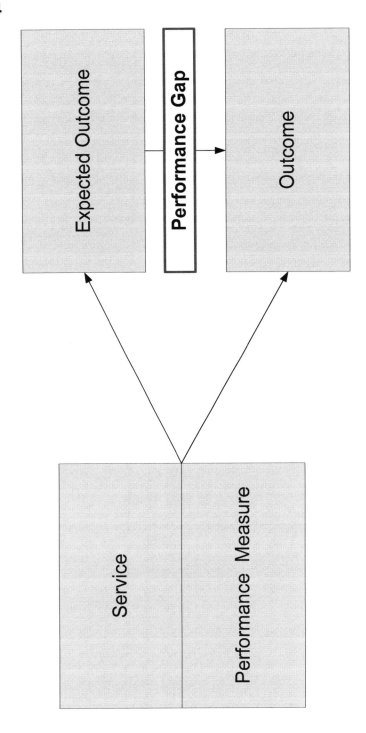

Pattern 5

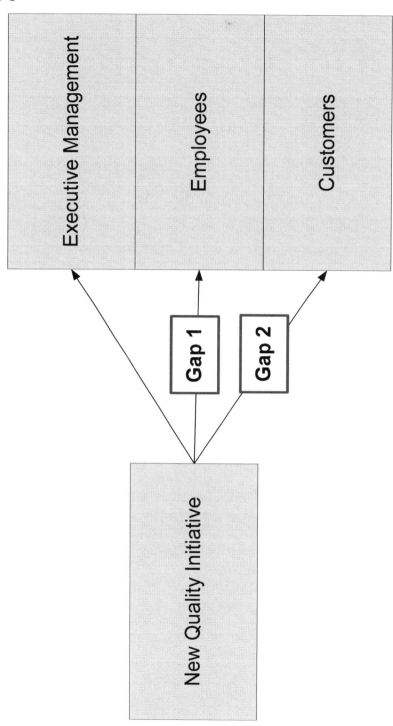

CHAPTER 041

Service Information Model

The Service Information Model identifies the information input, storage, and output requirements for a service.

The Service Information Model contains the following elements:

- Service
- Service Data
- Data Acquired
- Data Shared
- Data Source
- Data Consumer
- Supporting Technology

Service. A service may refer to a business service or a technological service. A business service is a collection of business processes that, together, deliver a particular service. A technological service is one or more technologies that integrate and interoperate in order to perform a particular service—sometimes serving multiple components (as in service oriented architectures)—usually exposed to the enterprise via an API or UDDI interface. IT services support business services either directly or indirectly.

Service Data. Service data is data that is either imported and stored or created and stored by the service's data component.

Data Acquired. Data acquired is data the services acquires from an external data source and is handled in the course of the service's operation.

Data Shared. Data shared is the data output by the service for the consumption of the service's consumers / clients.

Data Source. The external data source or data provider for the service. A service may have any number of data sources.

Data Consumer. The service's external consumers of the data the service provides.

Supporting Technology. To operate, the service depends on three key components: data, application, and technology. To operate, data providers and data consumers depend on these components.

The Service Information Model may be used to depict current, interim, and future states and can help diagnose high-level problems of interoperability, integration, and sustainability of operations.

Pattern 1 sets out the basic relationships between a service and the data is consumes, stores, and shares.

Pattern 2 illustrates the relationship between the service, the information and the supporting technology.

Pattern 3 shows the lifecycle of information consumed and produced by the service.

Pattern 1

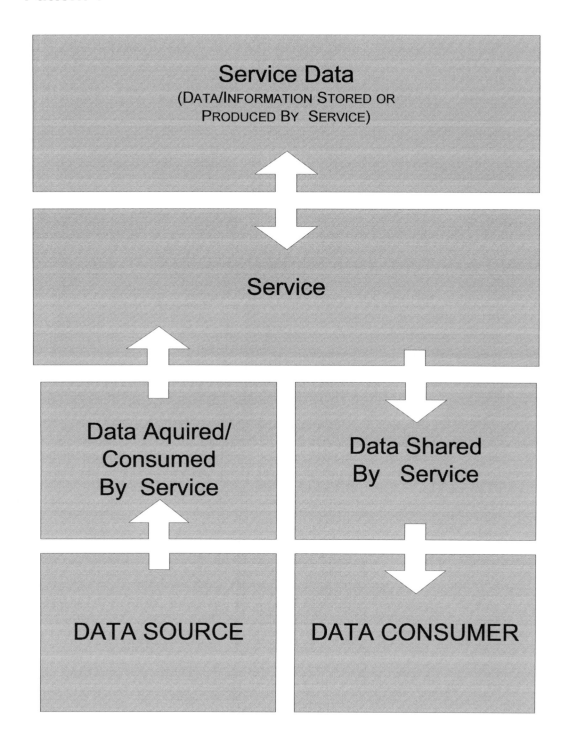

Pattern 2

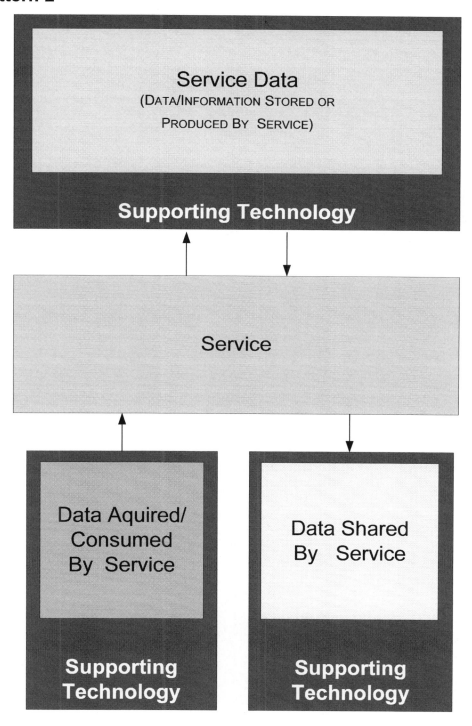

Pattern 3

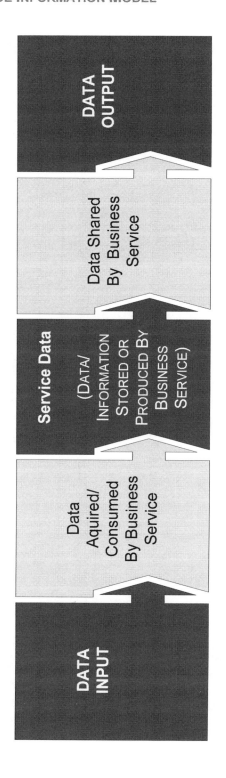

CHAPTER 042

Technology Lifecycle Model

The Technology Lifecycle Model identifies the various stages through which a technology passes during the course of its life within the enterprise.

The Technology Lifecycle Model contains the following elements:

- Technology Review
- Sunrise
- Interim
- Core
- Sunset
- Demoted
- Rejected
- Retired

Technology Review. When new technologies appear, they are reviewed for suitability of use within the enterprise. For mature enterprises, the goal of these reviews is to allow new technology into the enterprise that is not just new for the sake of newness or a useless technology in search of a problem, but a technology that solves existing problems, improves efficiency and effectiveness, or addresses issues before they become problems. The goal is to stay off the bleeding edge to the greatest extent possible, while still affording IT a role in the competitive advantage of the enterprise. As a result of a technology review: a technology can be rejected, but can always be reconsidered at a later date; a technology can be accepted as a 'sunrise' technology; or, immediately assigned 'core' technology status; or, designated an 'interim' technology that is intended as a short term bridge to a permanent, different technological solution. The technology review also has implications for existing technologies because as new technologies are adopted older technologies are demoted and retired.

Sunrise. Sunrise technologies are new technologies that have been accepted for use in the enterprise but which are not yet the preferred or the main technological choice for that type of technology. In general, over time, it is expected that sunrise technologies will replace their equivalent core technologies. By allowing sunrise technologies into the enterprise, there are implications for the operational support team who will require contracted staff with the requisite support skills or require training to develop an internal support capacity for.

Interim. Interim technologies are new technologies that have been accepted for use in the enterprise on a provisional basis: it is not planned that their use will migrate towards 'core' or even 'sunrise' status. An interim technology is strictly used on a short term basis to bridge the enterprise from current state to a future state where a different technology will be deployed in place of the interim technology.

Core. Core technologies are the preferred choice technologies for use in the enterprise. The enterprise has deep experience in the support of core technologies.

Sunset. Sunset technologies are aging technologies, usually former core technologies, that are being phased out. When technologies are considered for the support of new enterprise capabilities, sunset technologies are generally excluded from consideration.

Demoted. When a technology moves from 'core' to 'sunset', it is 'demoted'.

Rejected. When a technology review determines a technology unsuitable for use within the enterprise, the technology is 'rejected'.

Retired. When a technology reaches the end of its useful life within the enterprise, it is 'retired' and no longer used within the enterprise. When an 'interim' technology is replaced, it is no longer used in the enterprise, and is 'retired'.

The lifecycle in pattern 1 follows the technology from first review, to acceptance as a sunrise/emerging technology, promotion to core status, demotion to sunset status, and eventual retirement from use. Some new technologies are immediately rejected. After a short period of use, interim technologies are retired.

Pattern 2 shows the model scoped at the level of an enterprise engagement. In this pattern, technology lists are filtered to itemize only technologies relevant to the engagement.

The Technology Lifecycle Model can serve as a pattern for the lifecycle of various enterprise architecture elements, such as: standards, principles, patterns, building blocks, etc.

Pattern 1

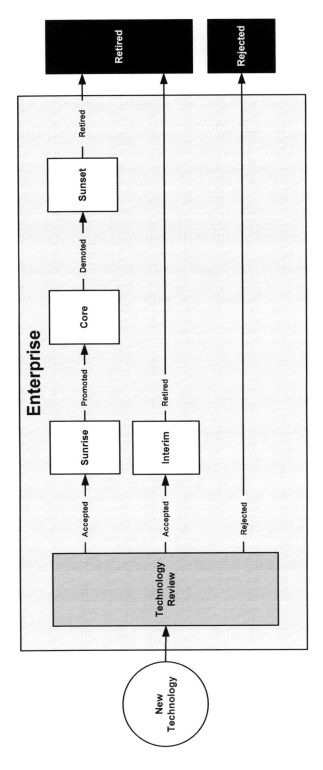

Pattern 2

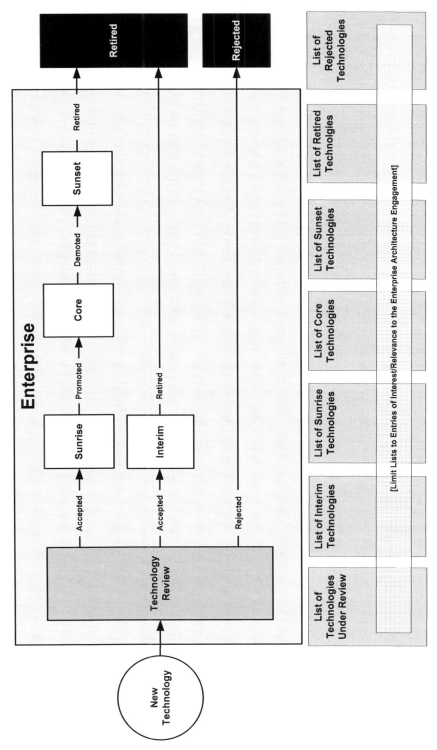

259

CHAPTER 043

Product Lifecycle Model

The Product Lifecycle Model shows the various stages through which a product passes during the course of its life.

The product lifecycle contains the following elements:

- Product Lifecycle
- Product Adoption Pattern
- Risk Perspective Pattern
- Concept to Recycle Pattern

Product Lifecycle. A product lifecycle is a series of stages through which a product passes. The lifecycle is a useful way to understand and analyse a product and the services and processes associated with it. There are many different ways to conceptualize a product lifecycle and each way offers important insight into the product, the enterprise that creates it, and the greater environment in which it is created. Here are three examples. First, there is the product manufacturing and use perspective which looks at the product from its creation to its disposal. Second, there is the product adoption perspective. Third, there is the perspective of the product's changing impact on enterprise risk as it moves through various stages of its lifecycle. Finally, there are many other possible perspectives than the examples presented here.

Product Adoption Pattern. This pattern is based on traditional phases of adoption as originally set out in Everett Roger's diffusion of innovation theory. The Product Adoption Pattern looks at the product in terms of its adoption by groups from the first the last to adopt.

Risk Perspective Pattern. The Risk Perspective pattern looks at the product in terms of the risk it presents to the enterprise over the course of its lifecycle.

Concept to Recycle Pattern. The Concept to Recycle pattern is the most common pattern for product lifecycles, but not always the most useful. This pattern examines the product from its conceptualization, to the resourcing of the products inputs, to its manufacture, to its distribution and sale, to its use and repair, and, finally, to the disposal (preferably recycling) of the product.

Pattern 1 illustrates product adoption over the product's lifecycle.

Pattern 2 illustrates enterprise risk associated with the product over the product lifecycle.

Patterns 1 and 2 can be adapted to present almost any kind of enterprise metric, such as: service support cost, profitability, number of competitors, marketing cost, production costs, etc.

Pattern 3 shows how just about any element internal or external to the enterprise elements can be mapped to the phases of the product lifecycle.

Pattern 1

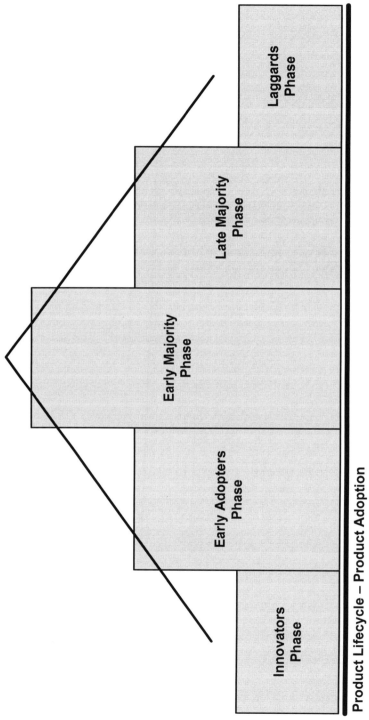

Pattern 2

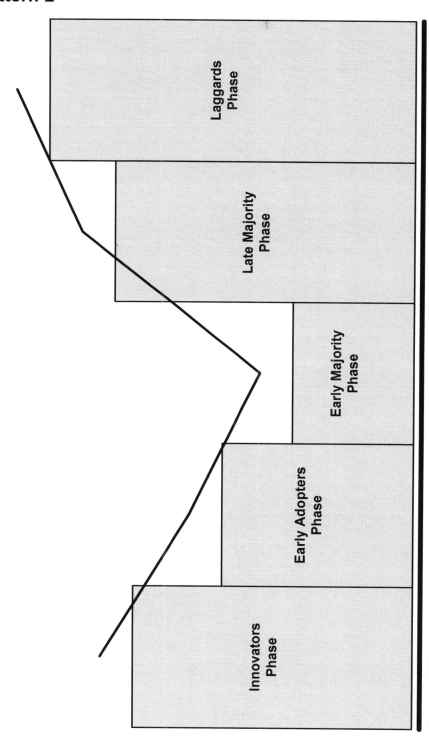

Product Lifecycle – Risk Perspective

Pattern 3

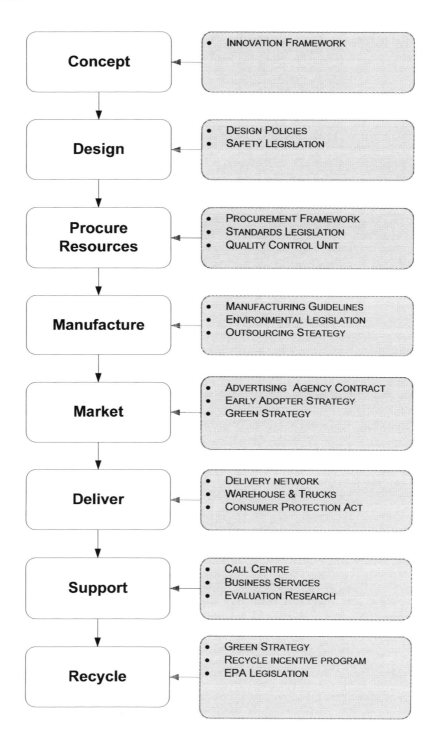

CHAPTER 044

Solution Concept Model

The purpose of the Solution Concept Model is to communicate the high-level shape of the solution to relevant stakeholders.

The Solution Concept Model contains the following elements:

- Solution Statement
- Problem Statement
- Constraint Statement

Solution Statement. The solution statement provides a text description of the envisioned solution to the core problem and key constraints.

Problem Statement. The problem statement explains three things. First, what the core problem is. Second, the seriousness of the problem. Third, the implications for the enterprise if the problem is not addressed.

Constraint Statement. The constraint statement identifies what constraints there are on any potential solution to the problem. For example, budget may be an important constraint on the solution that is envisioned to address the problem.

Pattern 1 presents a simple textual description of the solution. It places the solution in context of business problems and constraints.

Pattern 2 takes the shape of a classic context setting model. It elaborates on the basic solution concept model, by augmenting it with statements on opportunity, data component, application component, technology component, security, staff requirement, location, related strategic goal, related strategic objective, and related tactical initiative.

In pattern 3, classic systems iconography is used to illustrate the shape of a potential solution.

Pattern 4 is particularly useful for discovery consulting—for those engagements where the information necessary to conduct enterprise business architecture effectively is not yet documented and must be 'discovered'.

In all cases, every effort should be taken to ensure the Solution Concept Model remains minimally complex.

Pattern 1

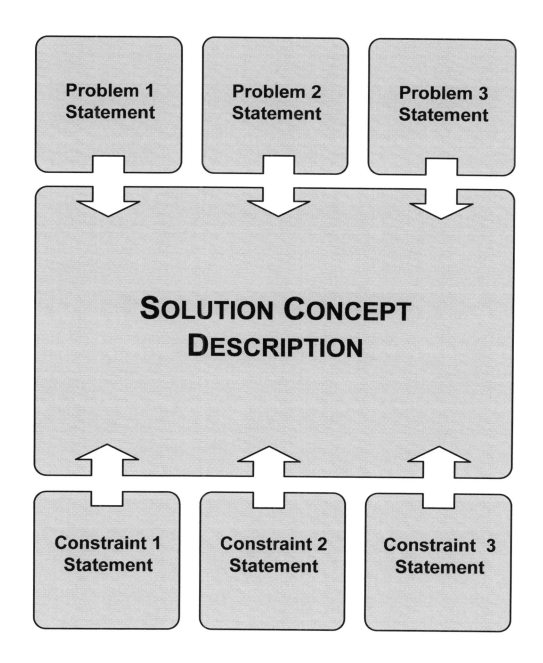

Pattern 2

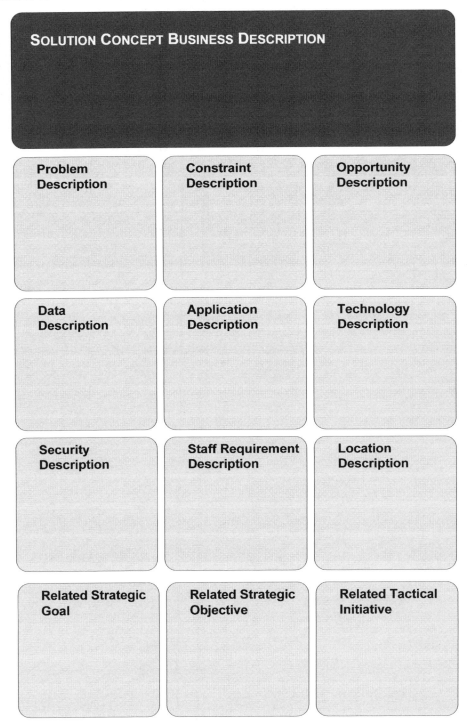

SOLUTION CONCEPT BUSINESS DESCRIPTION

Problem Description	Constraint Description	Opportunity Description
Data Description	Application Description	Technology Description
Security Description	Staff Requirement Description	Location Description
Related Strategic Goal	Related Strategic Objective	Related Tactical Initiative

Pattern 3

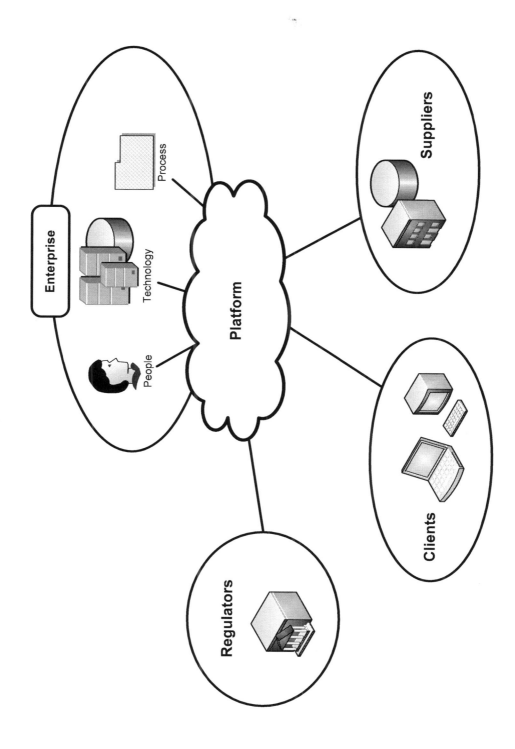

Pattern 4

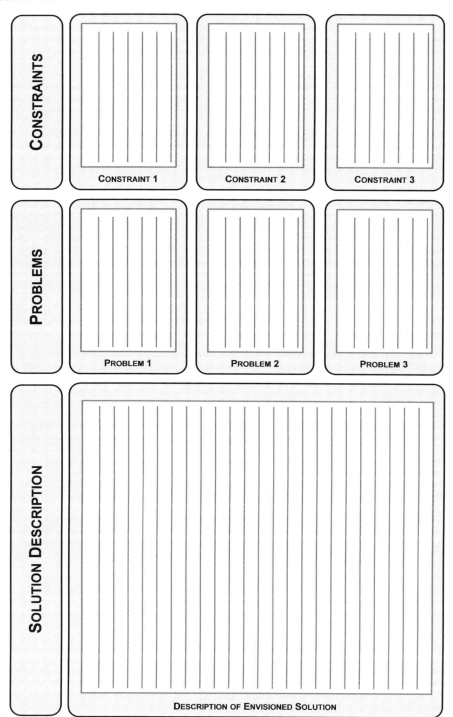

CHAPTER 045

Stakeholder Model

The Stakeholder Model defines who the stakeholders are and identifies each stakeholder's interests (e.g. problems, issues, concerns, key questions, and potential benefits).

The Stakeholder Model contains the following elements:

- Stakeholder Type
- Stakeholder
- Problems
- Issues
- Concerns
- Key Questions
- Anticipated Benefits

Stakeholder Type. Stakeholder type is used to classify the various stakeholders into groups. There are many different ways to classify stakeholders. In this model, the following stakeholder types are identified: client facing staff, administration, IT Unit, Service Providers, Regulators, Suppliers, and Clients. Each enterprise will have its own way to classify its stakeholders.

Stakeholder. A stakeholder is someone with a direct interest in the operations of the enterprise. Stakeholder can be internal or external, including suppliers, customers, and third parties impacted by the operation of the enterprise. This element identifies each stakeholder by a unique name.

Problem. In relation to the architecture engagement, each stakeholder may face a particular set of problems. This element lists the stakeholder's problems.

Issues. In relation to the architecture engagement, each stakeholder faces a particular set of issues. This element identifies the stakeholder's issues.

Concerns. In relation to the architecture engagement, each stakeholder may have a particular set of concerns. This element identifies the stakeholder's concerns.

Key Questions. In relation to the architecture engagement, each stakeholder will have a number of key questions. This element identifies the stakeholder's key questions.

Anticipated Benefits. In relation to the architecture engagement, each stakeholder may experience some benefits as a result of the planned activity and 'solution concept' under consideration. This element lists the anticipated benefit for each stakeholder.

The Stakeholder Model is important. Every facet of enterprise architecture hinges on the enterprise business architect working correctly identifying who the stakeholders are. Accurately identifying each stakeholder and stakeholder type allows the business architect to efficiently address specific stakeholder problems, issues, key questions, and potential benefits.

Few solutions have just one 'type' of stakeholder. Pattern 1 identifies three types of stakeholders: client facing, administrative, and IT. Pattern 2 identifies six types of stakeholders: clients, client facing staff, administration, IT, service providers, regulators, and suppliers.

Pattern 3 is useful when it is necessary to map a large and complex list of stakeholders.

Pattern 4 is useful for discovery consulting—for those engagements where the information necessary to conduct enterprise business architecture effectively is not yet documented and must be 'discovered'.

Pattern 1

Stakeholder Map for [ENGAGEMENT NAME]

Client Facing Stakeholder 1 [Problems, Issues, Concerns, Key Questions, Benefit]	**Administrative Stakeholder 1** [Problems, Issues, Concerns, Key Questions, Benefit]	**IT Stakeholder 1** [Problems, Issues, Concerns, Key Questions, Benefit]
Client Facing Stakeholder 2 [Problems, Issues, Concerns, Key Questions, Benefit]	**Administrative Stakeholder 2** [Problems, Issues, Concerns, Key Questions, Benefit]	**IT Stakeholder 2** [Problems, Issues, Concerns, Key Questions, Benefit]
Client Facing Stakeholder 3 [Problems, Issues, Concerns, Key Questions, Benefit]	**Administrative Stakeholder 3** [Problems, Issues, Concerns, Key Questions, Benefit]	**IT Stakeholder 3** [Problems, Issues, Concerns, Key Questions, Benefit]
Client Facing Stakeholder N [Problems, Issues, Concerns, Key Questions, Benefit]]	**Administrative Stakeholder N** [Problems, Issues, Concerns, Key Questions, Benefit]	**IT Stakeholder N** [Problems, Issues, Concerns, Key Questions, Benefit]]

Pattern 2

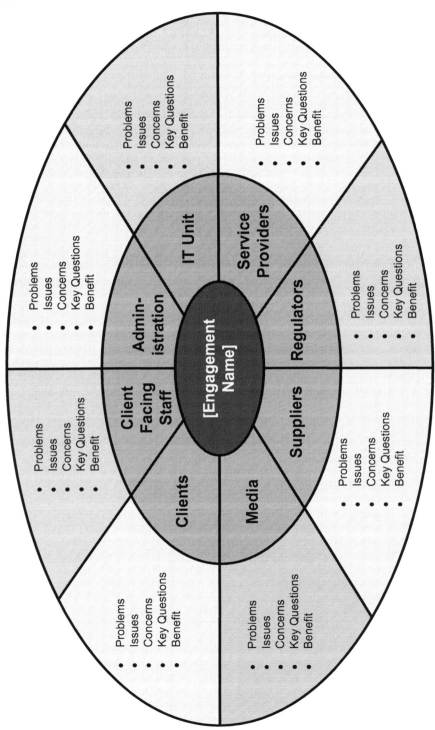

Pattern 3

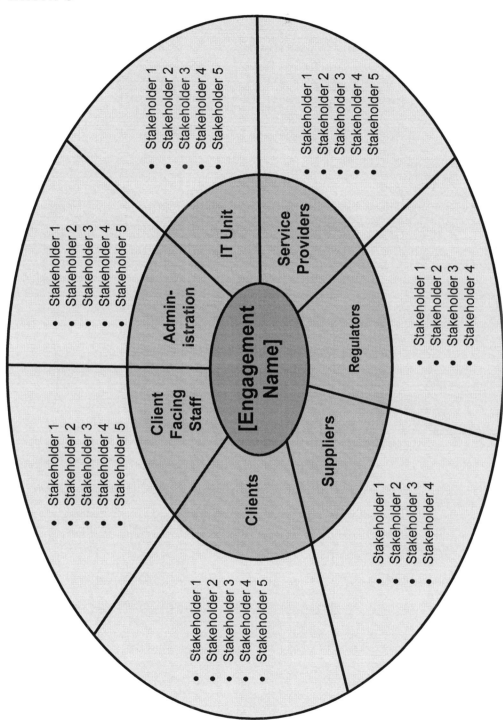

Pattern 4

STAKEHOLDER 1	STAKEHOLDER 2	STAKEHOLDER 3

STAKEHOLDER 1

Problems:
_____
_____
_____
_____

STAKEHOLDER 2

Problems:
_____
_____
_____
_____

STAKEHOLDER 3

Problems:
_____
_____
_____
_____

STAKEHOLDER 1

Issues:
_____
_____
_____
_____

STAKEHOLDER 2

Issues:
_____
_____
_____
_____

STAKEHOLDER 3

Issues:
_____
_____
_____
_____

STAKEHOLDER 1

Concerns:
_____
_____
_____
_____

STAKEHOLDER 2

Concerns:
_____
_____
_____
_____

STAKEHOLDER 3

Concerns:
_____
_____
_____
_____

STAKEHOLDER 1

Key Questions:
_____
_____
_____
_____

STAKEHOLDER 2

Key Questions:
_____
_____
_____
_____

STAKEHOLDER 3

Key Questions:
_____
_____
_____
_____

STAKEHOLDER 1

Anticipated Benefits:
_____
_____
_____
_____

STAKEHOLDER 2

Anticipated Benefits:
_____
_____
_____
_____

STAKEHOLDER 3

Anticipated Benefits:
_____
_____
_____
_____

CHAPTER 046

Socialization-Communication Model

The purpose of the Socialization-Communications Model is to map out a strategy for the dissemination of ideas and innovations among stakeholders.

The Socialization-Communications Model contains the following elements:

- Stakeholder Support Type
- Targeted Message
- Core Message Package
- Sequencing Package
- Method of Delivery Package
- Communicator

Stakeholder Support Type. The content of a message—especially messages of organizational or major technological change—are evaluated by the audience and in response the audience either agrees with the message or does not. Therefore, it is useful to categorize a message's various audiences based on their anticipated response to the message. These categories are: early support, early majority support, late majority support, lagging support, never support. The purpose of classifying stakeholder by their support for the message is so that 'target' messages can be crafted for them, thus increasing the likelihood of the message being accepted.

Targeted Message. A targeted message is a message that is crafted to address the specific concerns, fears, likely misunderstandings, and anticipated objections of a specific stakeholder group or stakeholder support type.

Core Message Package. A core message package is the messages crafted to address all stakeholders rather than individual groups. The delivered message includes the core message package and, as modified by audience, a targeted message.

Sequencing Package. A sequencing package identifies a schedule for communicating the message to the various stakeholders. Sequencing is necessary because in order to grow support for a new idea in the enterprise or new technology in the enterprise some stakeholders need to be addressed before others, and therefore message delivery must be appropriately sequenced.

Method of Delivery Package. A message can be delivered many way: face-to-face in meetings, at conferences, by phone, by email, by letter or memo. Essentially any communication method can be used, however, the nature of the message and the nature of the audience will suggest which methods are preferred—few stakeholders want to learn about major organizational change from an email. This element identifies the preferred method of message delivery for each stakeholder.

Communicator. Stakeholder response to a target message can depend on the person delivering the message as much as on the content of the message itself. For example, it does no good for all stakeholders to learn of a major change initiative from a junior vice president—the CxOs and senior vice presidents must deliver these kinds of messages. This element identifies who the preferred communicators are.

Different messages are targeted at different types of stakeholders. For example, the message to the leadership team of CxOs is different from the message to the IT stakeholders.

The model requires stakeholders be categorized into 'support' categories and socialization messages to be targeted to address the concerns, fears, expectations, or interests of each 'support' category.

Custom messages are adapted within the context of a core message, sequencing is indicated, methods of delivery determined, and a communicator (or group of communicators) is identified to deliver the message to the stakeholders.

A foundational component to any socialization and communication strategy is a common enterprise-wide IT and architecture vocabulary. Shared vocabularies do no happen by accident—they are defined and promoted. A key way to promote a shared vocabulary is through an IT Terms Catalog.

Pattern 1 illustrates the big picture socialization-communication model, showing the various stakeholder support types, the socialization message targeting them, and, then, sets out the components of the socialization-communication action plan.

Pattern 2 is particularly useful for discovery consulting—for those engagements where the information necessary to conduct enterprise business architecture effectively is not yet documented and must be 'discovered'.

Pattern 1

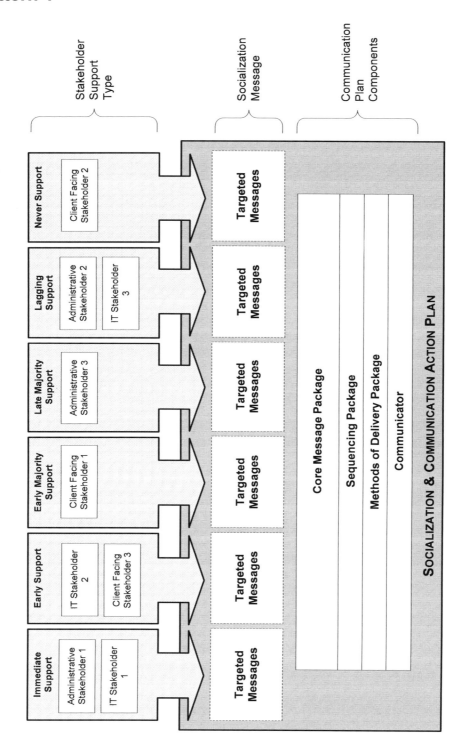

Pattern 2

STAKEHOLDER 4

Stakeholder Type:

SUPPORT TYPE

Targeted Message:

SOCIALIZATION

Preferred Communication Method:

MESSAGE DELIVERY

Communicator:

MESSAGE DELIVERY

STAKEHOLDER 3

Stakeholder Type:

SUPPORT TYPE

Targeted Message:

SOCIALIZATION

Preferred Communication Method:

MESSAGE DELIVERY

Communicator:

MESSAGE DELIVERY

STAKEHOLDER 2

Stakeholder Type:

SUPPORT TYPE

Targeted Message:

SOCIALIZATION

Preferred Communication Method:

MESSAGE DELIVERY

Communicator:

MESSAGE DELIVERY

STAKEHOLDER 1

Stakeholder Type:

SUPPORT TYPE

Targeted Message:

SOCIALIZATION

Preferred Communication Method:

MESSAGE DELIVERY

Communicator:

MESSAGE DELIVERY

CHAPTER 047

Sustainability Model

The Sustainability Model documents the dimensions of sustainability in order to support clear decision-making when evaluating and selecting data, application, or technology components for inclusion in the enterprise.

The enterprise elements of primary concern to the Sustainability Model are:

> *Technology Components.* A technological component of the enterprise is a component which supports the operation of other application, data, and technology components. In this model, a technology component may perform a very specific function or represent a type of technology product. The term technology component includes infrastructure and security components.

> *Data Components.* A data component of the enterprise is an existing enterprise data asset. Data components are usually managed by an application and supported by multiple technology components. Some data components are manage via loosely coupled services like those available via web services or message brokers.

> *Application/System Components.* An application component is an operationalized application or system that supports a specific business service and its various business processes. Applications are used to access and manage specific data components and depend on the support of specific technology components. An application will always have human users directly accessing it via some type of user/client interface—a data or technology component may not.

The Sustainability Model contains the following elements:

- Sustainability Scale

- Sustainability Dimensions
- Name of Component

Sustainability Scale. A sustainability scale is used to determine the level of sustainability of a technological component in relation to a particular dimension of sustainability. Any suitable scale can be used. The scale presented in the model is Lichert Scaling. In this model's example, each square/level is worth 1 point.

Sustainability Dimensions. There are several dimensions to the concept of sustainability. For example, 'fixability' might be considered a dimension of sustainability: if a technological component is hermetically sealed and opening it destroys the component or voids warranty, then the options to 'fix' the component are reduced to sending it away for repair, kicking it, or, worst case, having to swap it out for a new component and trashing the old one. If a component isn't fixable and is expensive, it might score lower on the sustainability scale in comparison to other components.

Name of Component. This element is used to identify a particular application/system, data, or technology component.

In pattern 1, the dimensions of sustainability—supportability, reliability, robustness, agility, integration enabled—are examples only. The leadership of each enterprise must decide for themselves which dimensions to include and how to weight each dimension if a scoring system is to be used. Other dimensions for consideration might include: stability, durability, fixability, and automation capability.

Pattern 2 summarizes the sustainability score of several components. This pattern is useful during procurement processes.

Pattern 3 elaborates on the sustainability model by layering sustainability over top of the Enterprise Model. This pattern presents the results of a sustainability review of the current state enterprise and its key components. This is useful in understanding the true cost of component maintenance and where future investments in sustainability should occur.

Pattern 1

SUSTAINABILITY MODEL FOR [COMPONENT NAME]
SCORE: 14/20

	POOR	FAIR	GOOD	EXCELLENT
Integration Enabled				
Agility				
Robustness				
Reliability				
Suportability				

Pattern 2

COMPONENT 1	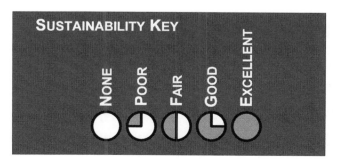
COMPONENT 2	
COMPONENT 3	
COMPONENT 4	
COMPONENT 5	
COMPONENT 6	
COMPONENT 7	
COMPONENT 8	
COMPONENT 9	
COMPONENT 10	

SUSTAINABILITY KEY

NONE   POOR   FAIR   GOOD   EXCELLENT

Pattern 3

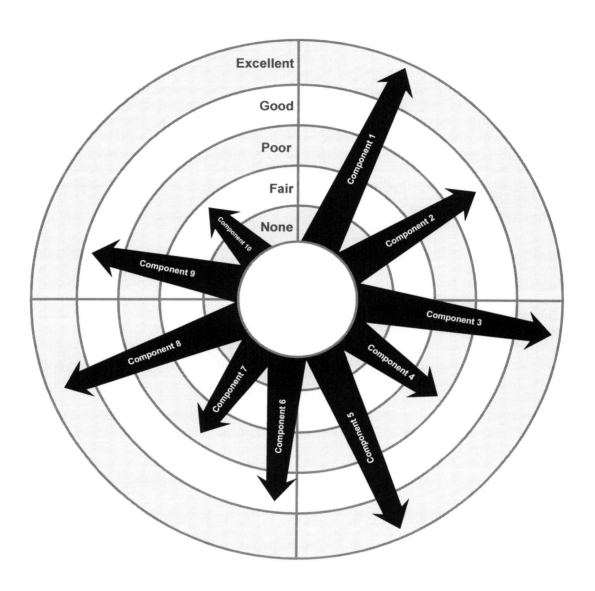

Pattern 3

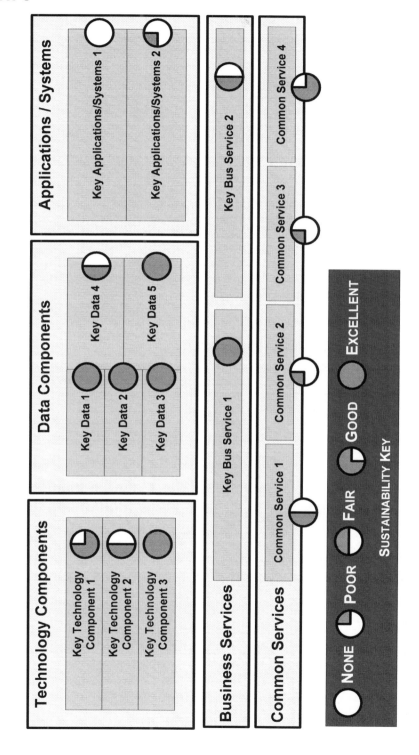

CHAPTER 048

Business Problem Forensics Model

The Business Problem Forensics Model decomposes business problems into three categories: symptom, problem, and source of problem, the model is used to identify the true source of an enterprise problem.

The Business Problem Forensics Model contains the following elements:

- Symptom Statement
- Problem Statement
- Problem Source Statement

Symptom Statement. The symptom statement lists what symptoms are manifesting themselves as the result of some sort of malfunction in the enterprise. Symptoms often appear to be problems, but are merely a by-product/secondary effect of the actual problem.

Problem Statement. The problem statement explains what the core problem is and the acuity of the problem. Problems are the core manifestation of a malfunction within the enterprise.

Problem Source Statement. The problem source statement identifies the primary source of the problem. 'Problem source' is not the problem itself but the reason why the problem is taking place. It asks the question: "What is causing the problem?" Getting to the source of the problem is the goal of the model—for problems are solved by addressing the source of the problem rather than alleviating the problem's symptoms.

The Business Problem Forensics Model is useful in diagnosing problems and facilitating discussion on what the enterprise should be doing to solve the problem.

This model is diagnostic in nature—it does not suggest solutions. When considering solutions, use the Strategic Diagnosis Model.

Pattern 1 sets out the basic shape of this model. Pattern 3 is particularly useful for discovery consulting—for those engagements where the information necessary to conduct enterprise business architecture effectively is not yet documented and must be 'discovered'.

Pattern 1

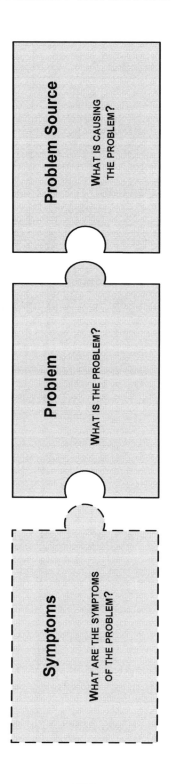

Pattern 2

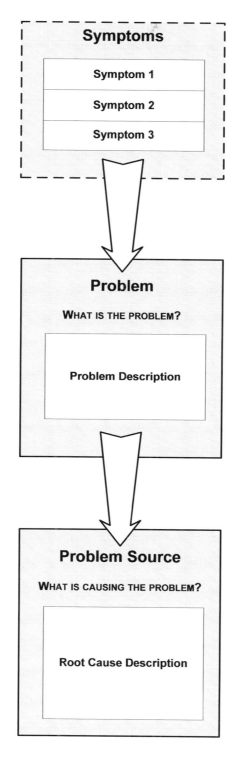

Pattern 3

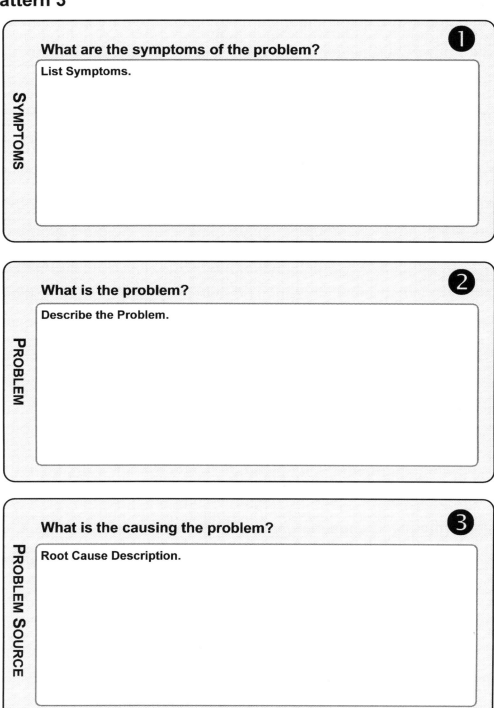

CHAPTER 049

Strategic Diagnosis Model

The Strategic Diagnosis Model identifies both a business problem and a solution via strategic and tactical planning.

The Strategic Diagnosis Model contains the following elements:

- Symptom Statement
- Problem Statement
- Problem Source Statement
- Prescription Statement
- Treatment Plan Statement

Symptom Statement. The symptom statement lists what symptoms are manifesting themselves as the result of some sort of malfunction in the enterprise. Symptoms often appear to be problems, but are merely a by-product/secondary effect of the actual problem.

Problem Statement. The problem statement explains what the core problem is and the acuity of the problem. Problems are the core manifestation of a malfunction within the enterprise.

Problem Source Statement. The problem source statement identifies the primary source of the problem. 'Problem source' is not the problem itself but the reason why the problem is taking place. It asks the question: "What is causing the problem". Getting to the source of the problem is the goal of the model—for problems are solved by addressing the source of the problem rather than alleviating the problem's symptoms.

Prescription Statement. The prescription statement answers the question 'What is to be done?'. In short, this statement tells the enterprise 'what to do'. The prescription statement is a strategic statement about how the source of the problem will be dealt with and, thus, the problem solved. The prescription declares intentions.

Treatment Statement. The treatment statement answers the question "What steps will be taken to follow the prescription?" In short, this statement tells the enterprise 'how' to do what its planning to do. The treatment statement is a tactical list of actions that will be taken in order fulfil the prescription statement. The actions spell out in detail how the source of the problem will be treated and, thus, the problem solved.

Like the business problem forensic model, this model decomposes business problems into three categories: symptom, problem, and source of problem. See the Business Problem Forensics Model for more information. The symptoms, problem, and source of problem elements are part of the problem space.

The Strategic Diagnosis Model presents a solution to the problem in the form of a prescription to cure the problem and a treatment plan to implement the prescription. These elements are part of the solution space.

The Strategic Diagnosis Model is useful when consulting with senior leadership, presenting a simple encapsulation of the problem, a strategic view of the solution, and a high-level tactical view of the solution implementation plan.

Patterns 1 and 2 set out the basic elements of the Strategic Diagnosis Model, showing at a glance the link between a problem and its solution.

Pattern 3 is particularly useful for discovery consulting—for those engagements where the information necessary to conduct enterprise business architecture effectively is not yet documented and must be 'discovered'.

Pattern 1

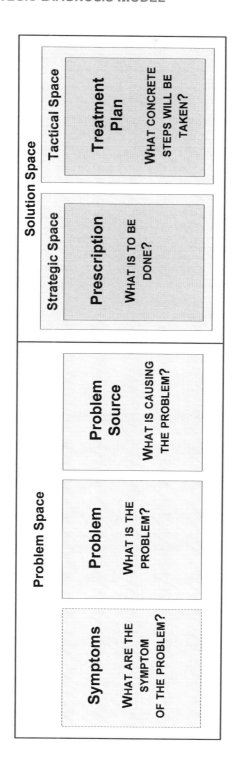

Pattern 2

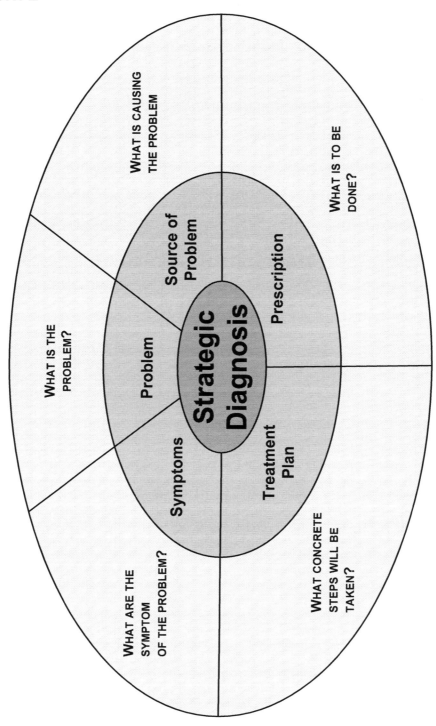

Pattern 3

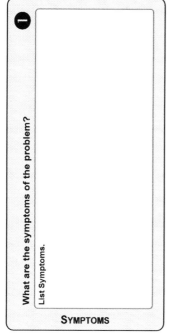

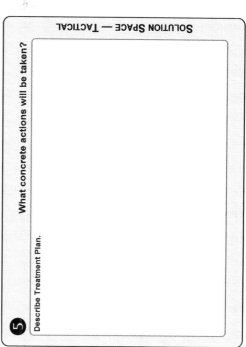

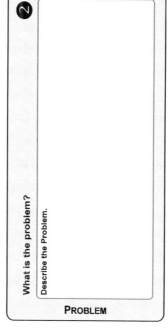

CHAPTER 050

Strategic Thinking Heat Map Model

The Strategic Thinking Heat Map Model identifies areas in the enterprise where strategic thinking has been documented and where gaps in the strategic landscape exist. The Strategic Thinking Heat Map Model helps identify areas where organizational entropy (disorganization) has accelerated in the enterprise. Entropy is (by the way) a bad thing: it destroys efficiency, increase budgets, decreases the efficacy of strategic outcomes, decreases the quality of service and products, de-motivates employees, and robs an organization of credibility—internally and externally.

The Strategic Thinking Heat Map Model contains the following elements:

- Business Activity
- Organization
- Motivation
- Governance
- Information
- Enterprise Context
- Implementation

Business Activity. Business activity is any activity taken in accordance with an enterprise's functions and services. This element identifies which specific part of the business the model is addressing.

Organization. The organization element indicates the level of documentation for: business activity, executive summary description, ownership, stakeholders, business locations, and important events. For business activity, this element asks if functions, services, processes, sub-processes, tasks, and actions have been documented. It asks if executive summary information exists to describe the business activity. It looks to see if business and IT ownership issues are known and delineated in documentation. It looks to see if a definitive list of stakeholders is document. It checks to see if all the locations are known and documented. This element asks if the responsible unit publishes a calendar of important events. The element indicates if staff positions are clearly documented and that a skills inventory exists for each position. Finally, the organization element asks if a business continuity plan is in place.

Motivation. The motivation element of the model indicates the level of explicit strategic planning that has been done around the business activity. It looks for an explicit, definitive, and documented: problem statement, risk statement, strategic direction statement, mission statement, vision statement, inventory of strategic drivers, list of strategic goals, a list of corresponding objectives for each goal, and measures of success for each goal and objective.

Governance. The governance element of the model looks to see if governance mechanisms are known, documented, and actively used. This element looks to see if there are performance measures for services, appropriate contracts (agreements) in place, the applicable policy is documented, and that policy issues and gaps have been identified and are being addressed.

Information. The information element examines the level of information management taking place around the business activity's key information assets. This element looks to see that the key data and application entities are know and there are specific processes and procedures in place to manage (maintain) them in accordance with information management best practices.

Enterprise Context. The enterprise context element is used to gauge the level to which the business activity is aware of its place in the organization. This modules looks to see it an Enterprise Context Model exist for this business activity and whether re-use opportunities and asset creation opportunities have been identified.

Implementation. The implementation element looks at current and future project and program work and whether this work is being handled appropriately. This element looks to see if the following things have been document: a solution statement, a scope statement, a constraint statement, and stakeholder benefit statements.

Enterprise business architects often engage with clients that have not invested sufficient 'thinking' into the areas of organization, motivation, governance, information, and implementation. The Strategic Thinking Heat Map Model helps an enterprise business architect determine where gaps in strategic thinking exist and where the enterprise's intellectual horse-power needs to be focused.

Pattern 1 shows the full model: the white boxes represent the elements which have been documented and the dark boxes represent the elements for which no strategic thinking has been documented.

Pattern 2 shows a summary version of the model. The white boxes represent the elements which have been documented and the dark boxes represent the elements for which no strategic thinking has been documented.

This model is well suited to the use of color. The use of red, yellow, and green can be used to signal strategic thinking: red = no strategic thinking; yellow = inadequate strategic thinking; green = appropriate level of strategic thinking.

Building the Strategic Heat Thinking Map Model

There is a lot of data required to build the strategic heat thinking map model. The model requires data on: organization, motivation, governance, information, enterprise context, and implementation.

The organization data includes:

- o business activity,
- o ownership,
- o stakeholders,
- o business location,
- o important events,
- o staff & skills, and
- o business continuity.

The motivation data includes:

- problem statement,
- risk statement,
- strategic direction statement,
- vision statement,
- mission statement,
- business drivers,
- goals & objectives, and
- success metrics.

The governance data includes:

- performance measures,
- contracts/agreements,
- policy landscape, and
- policy issues/gaps.

The information data includes:

- data,
- application, and
- policy & procedures.

The enterprise context data includes:

- Enterprise Context Model data,
- re-use opportunities, and
- asset creation opportunities.

The implementation data includes:

- solution statement,
- scope statement,
- constraint statement, and
- stakeholder benefit statement.

There needs to be a standardized way to collect all of this data. Of course, there are any number of ways to do this. The suggested way is for the enterprise business architect to use a business profile template, a document which collects all the organization, motivation, governance, information, enterprise context, and implementation information outlined above. The data collected in the business profile document can be used to populate many different models. Bottom-line? This data is extremely useful. Ideally, the business profiles are themselves tracked in a catalog (see: The Business Profile Catalog).

Pattern 1

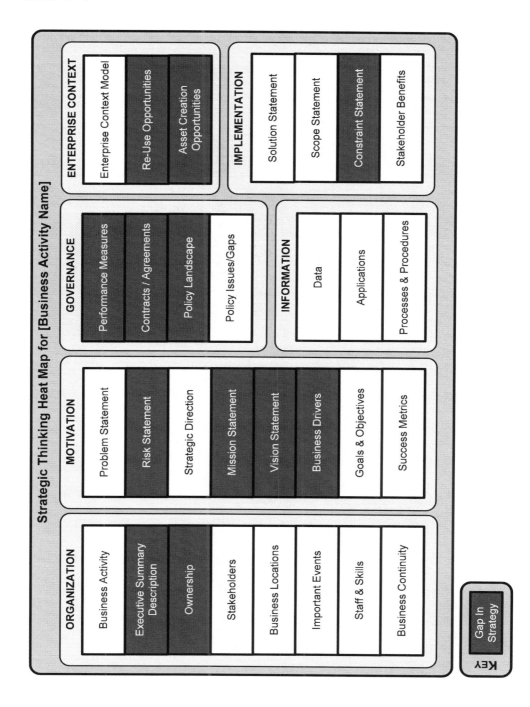

Strategic Thinking Heat Map for [Business Activity Name]

ENTERPRISE CONTEXT
- Enterprise Context Model
- Re-Use Opportunities
- Asset Creation Opportunities

IMPLEMENTATION
- Solution Statement
- Scope Statement
- Constraint Statement
- Stakeholder Benefits

GOVERNANCE
- Performance Measures
- Contracts / Agreements
- Policy Landscape
- Policy Issues/Gaps

INFORMATION
- Data
- Applications
- Processes & Procedures

MOTIVATION
- Problem Statement
- Risk Statement
- Strategic Direction
- Mission Statement
- Vision Statement
- Business Drivers
- Goals & Objectives
- Success Metrics

ORGANIZATION
- Business Activity
- Executive Summary Description
- Ownership
- Stakeholders
- Business Locations
- Important Events
- Staff & Skills
- Business Continuity

KEY
- Gap In Strategy

Pattern 2

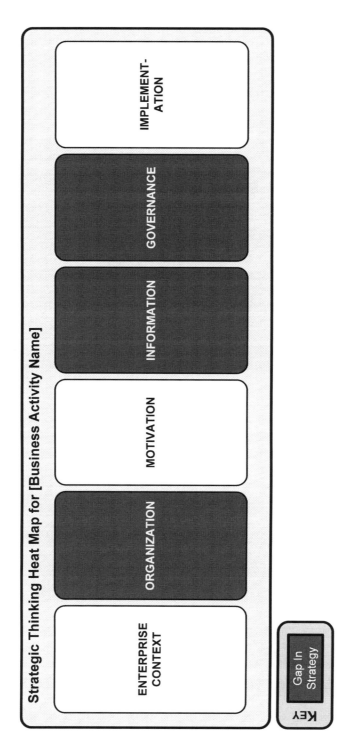

CHAPTER 051

Root Cause Model

The Root Cause Model is used to generate and present ideas about what enterprise elements may be causing a given problem. The Root Cause Model contains the following elements:

- Cause Statements
- Problem Statement

Cause Statements. A list of cause statements is like a list of suspects—the model does not identify the actual perpetrator of the problem. Only the likely suspects are identified via a cause statements.

Problem Statement. The problem statement explains what the core problem is and the acuity of the problem and implication for the enterprise if the problem is not addressed.

In patterns 1 and 2, it is possible to array a vast number of potential enterprise elements around the 'diagnosis' arrow. Use any elements and any number of them when building a Root Cause Model for your problem.

Pattern 1 presents a high-level summary of potential causes for a problem.

Pattern 2 presents a detailed view of potential causes and lists paired primary/secondary causes for each enterprise element of concern.

Pattern 3 is particularly useful for discovery consulting—for those engagements where the information necessary to conduct enterprise business architecture effectively is not yet documented and must be 'discovered'.

The analytical challenge of this model is to understand 1) if the problem actually is the problem; 2) if the listed causes contribute to the problem, or actually are the problem, or are *different* problems in their own right; or 3) if the causes are merely symptoms and not causes at all.

The Root Cause Model often identifies an unwieldy amount of "guesses" about what might be causing a problem. To filter the data collected in a root cause model, try applying logic from the Business Problem Forensics Model or Strategic Diagnosis Model.

Pattern 1

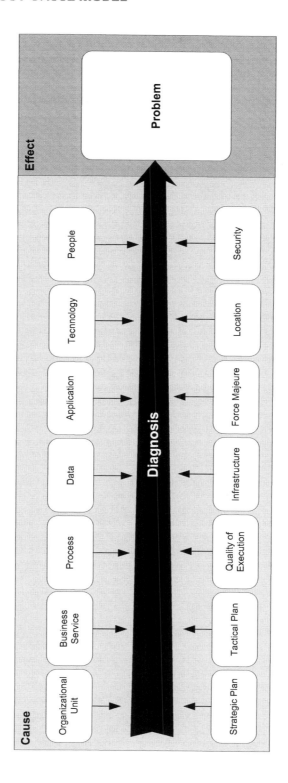

Pattern 2

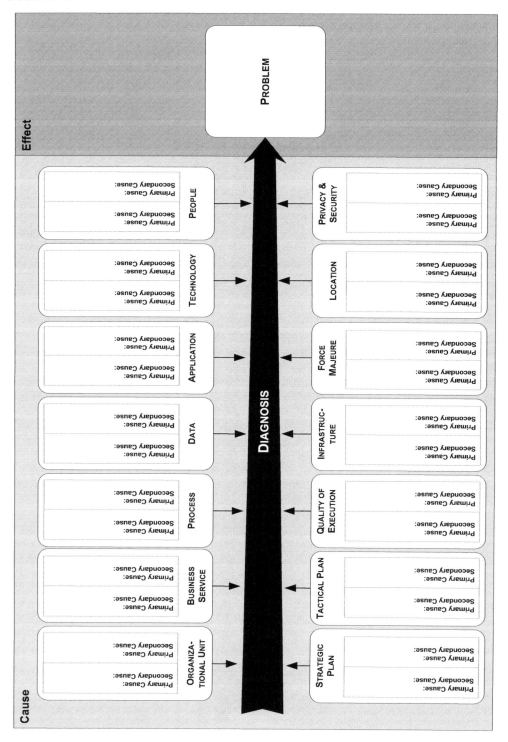

Pattern 3

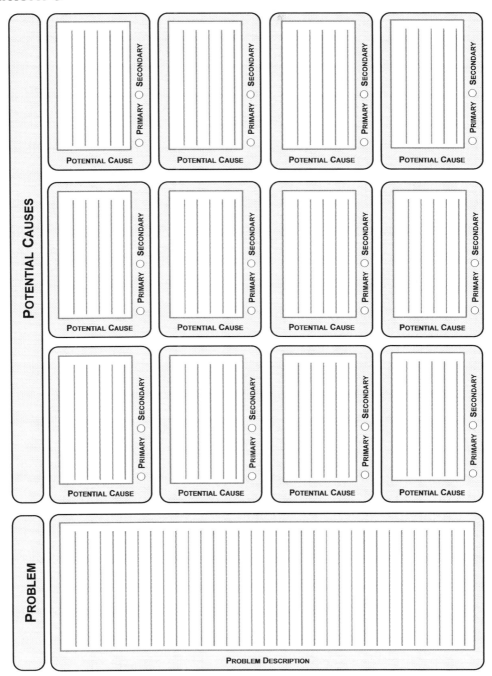

CHAPTER 052

Mission Context Model

The Mission Context Model illustrates the key elements that provide context to the enterprise's mission statement.

The Mission Context Model contains the following elements:

- Mission / Mandate
- Jurisdiction / Market
- Legislation
- Planning
- Policy

Mission / Mandate. A mission or mandate statement describes what the business is in existence to do—its *raison d'être*. (This is different from a vision statement which describes a future state target for the business to work towards.) The terms mission and mandate appear to be synonymous—but there is a difference worth noting. A mission is the enterprise's high-level purpose and completes this statement: *The enterprise exists to _____.* A mandate is a duty the enterprise is authorized and/or required to perform. Mandates are often set out in legislation or legally binding contracts. The mission/mandate statement takes the form of a textual description.

Jurisdiction / Market. The jurisdiction/market describes the playing field on which the enterprise conducts business. Governments work within the context of a specific legal jurisdiction. Private businesses sell their goods and services into particular markets situated in one or more jurisdictions.

Planning. Planning in this model refers to strategic planning, the process of deliberately documenting the vision, mission, goals and objectives of the enterprise—in both the business and IT realms—in order to ensure the enterprise is competitive and possesses or develops the capabilities to fulfil its vision and mission.

Policy. Policies are formal rules used to mandate quality requirements, delineate roles and responsibilities, show where decision-making authority lies, to support consistent and efficient decision-making, to promote or discourage certain organizational behaviours, to articulate performance goals for people and technology, and to set out critical operational rules around each of the enterprise's key functions. The operations of good enterprises are bounded by good, clear policies. This element identifies the key policies that impact on and bound the enterprise.

Patterns 1 and 2 put the key model elements in orbit around the mission / mandate.

Pattern 3 illustrates the elements and their relationship with to the mandate/mission. In this pattern: 1) Jurisdiction/Market limits the mandate/mission; 2) Legislation authorizes the mandate/mission; 3) Policy enables the mandate/mission; and, 4) planning articulates and elaborates the mandate mission.

Pattern 4 is particularly useful for discovery consulting—for those engagements where the information necessary to conduct enterprise business architecture effectively is not yet documented and must be 'discovered'.

Pattern 1

Pattern 2

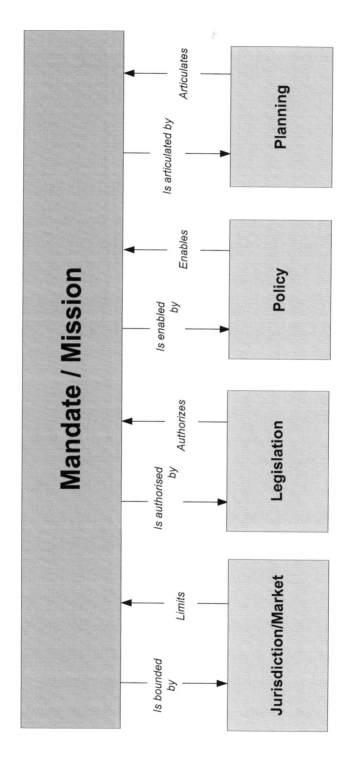

Pattern 3

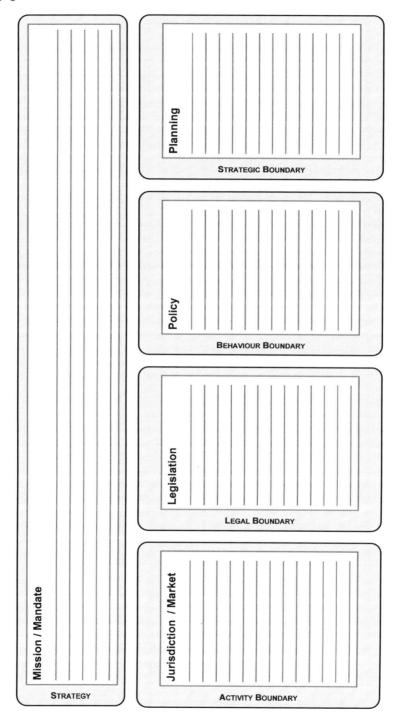

CHAPTER 053

Decision Constraint Model

The Decision Constraint Model maps constraints upon a business architecture decision-item.

The Decision Constraint Model contains the following elements:

- Decision
- Constraint

Decision. A decision is a final judgement resulting from a process of analysis and careful consideration and deliberation. The process for making a decision involves the consideration of constraints on that decision.

Constraint. A constraint is something which limits decision-making. A constraint statement identifies things which limit decision-making options. For example, budget may be an important constraint on a problem-solving decision.

Pattern 1 presents several examples of decision-making constraints: principles, standards, enterprise capabilities, technology, budget, schedule/time, policies, best practices. Examples of other constraints include: legislation, information quality, security concerns, and privacy concerns.

This model is applicable to any type of decision. However, the types of constraint shown in pattern 1 are not—they are merely provided as examples. The decision constraints will be specific to the type of decision to be made.

Pattern 2 illustrates the relationship between an EBA decision and the constraints upon that decision.

Pattern 3 is particularly useful for discovery consulting—for those engagements where the information necessary to conduct enterprise business architecture effectively is not yet documented and must be 'discovered'.

Pattern 1

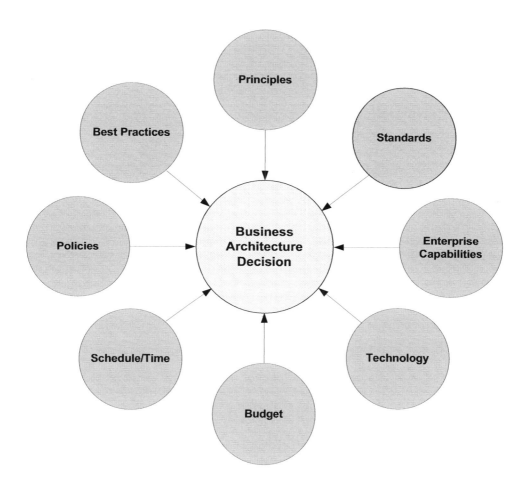

Pattern 2

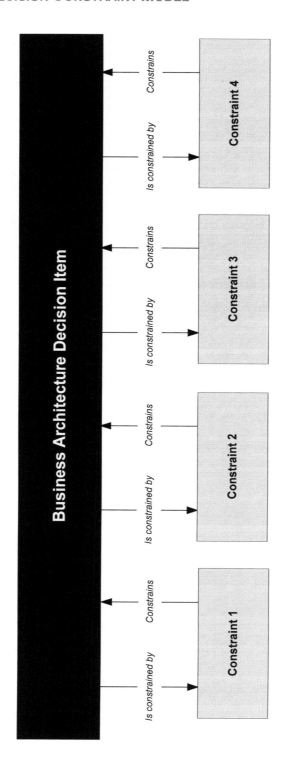

Pattern 3

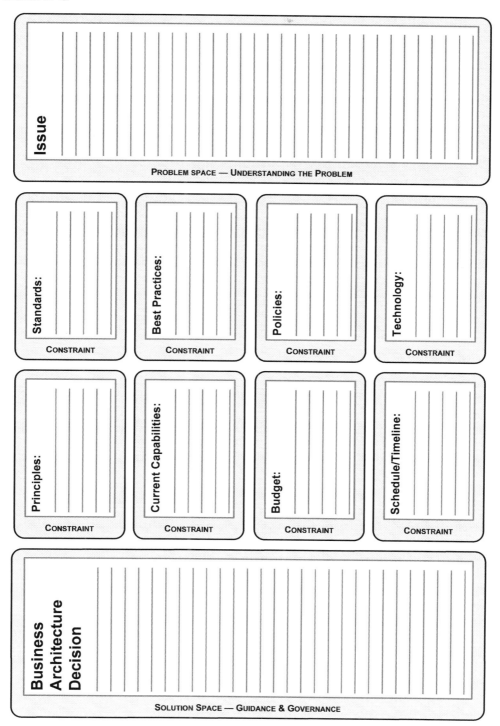

CHAPTER 054

Value Stream Model

The purpose of the Value Stream Model is to provide a high-level overview of the complex relationships and interactions that exist internal to and external to the enterprise and which create value for the enterprise's clients.

The Value Stream Model contains the following elements:

- Value Stream Name
- Value Stream Element Name
- Value Stream Layer

Value Stream Name. The value stream name uniquely identifies the value stream.

Value Stream Element Name. The value stream is made up of a number of 'value' elements—elements that add value. For example, these elements may be phases in a lifecycle, steps in a cross-functional process, of orchestrated services in a function.

Value Stream Layer. The Value Stream Model can be elaborated upon by layering additional data over top of it. For example, in the value stream for a multi-function process, a layer indicating the various responsible units may be included, or a layer indicating service level performance measures.

Pattern 1 shows a classic value stream, following a value creating process from the input of supplies, to manufacturing and management of product, to output to clients.

The value stream in pattern 2 extends the Value Stream Model to include a visual layering of enterprise business functions: enterprise architecture strategic planning service; enterprise architecture guidance and governance service; senior leadership decision-making; the projects unit; and, the operational unit.

Representations of the value stream, as illustrated in pattern 2, can be used to illustrate cross-boundary value creation involving a wide-variety of the enterprise's decision-makers, organizational units, and business services.

A useful technique is to layer the Value Stream Model with LEAN or Six-Sigma annotations (not shown).

Pattern 1

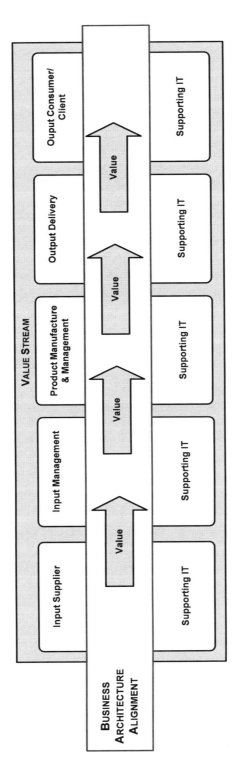

Pattern 2

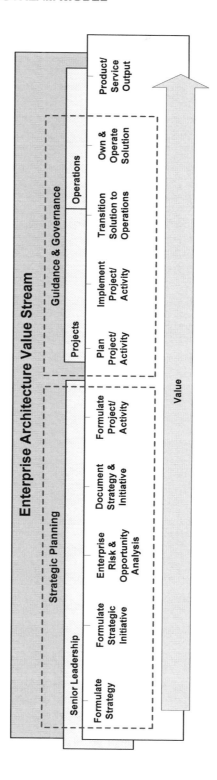

CHAPTER 055

Lean Foundation Process Model

The Lean Foundation Process Model documents six phases of organizational activity necessary to establish and maintain a coherent and smooth running enterprise. The process logic of the Lean Foundation Process Model may be applied to people/business or systems/technology, or both.

The Lean Foundation Process Model contains the following elements:

- Inventory Phase
- Purge Phase
- Store Phase
- Sanitize Phase
- Systematize Phase
- Operate Phase

Inventory Phase. The inventory phase ensures that all assets are known and documented before work on subsequent phases begins.

Purge Phase. The purge phase puts assets into one of three categories: must have, nice to have, and superfluous. The superfluous items are deleted, discarded, or in some way archived.

Store Phase. The store phase focuses on ensuring the 'must have' and 'nice to have' assets are stored effectively so non-experts can find things as easily as experts. The primary focus is on where things are stored. In short, this phase ensures that there is a place for everything and that everything is in its place.

Sanitize Phase. The sanitize phase deals with how things are stored, ensuring that the storage system and its extended environment is neat and tidy. The sanitize phase ensures there are no digital or physical messes lurking in the system.

Systematize Phase. The systematize phase ensures that policy, process, communication channels and training are in place to ensure the work from the first four phases is not a one-time, extravagant, unrepeated exercise. Once these system elements are documented, this phase also sees them launched for the first time.

Operate Phase. The operate phase operationalizes the policy, processes, communication channels, and training from the systematize phase, ensuring that the new system is a living, breathing thing—fully resourced and regularly exercised.

The Lean Foundation Process Model is a useful diagnostic tool for the business architect. Quick scenario: The applications group has set up a system to track all applications in the enterprise. The lean foundational Process Model facilitates some key questions: Does the system focus on key applications and exclude the superfluous? Is the system the right tool to store the information? Does the system track the right application metadata? Does the system have a process attached to it to keep the information up-to-date and useful? And so on.

The Lean Foundation Process Model elaborates on traditional Lean models, atomizing the traditional 'sort' phase into two steps (inventory and purge) and using more familiar IT vocabulary. There are six steps in this new Lean model.

Pattern 1 sets out the traditional elements of the Lean Foundation Process Model.

Pattern 2 shows a Lean foundational Process Model with a table of relevant enterprise elements that relate to each phase. The elements may be organizational units, functions, services, people, policies, systems, technology components, etc.

Pattern 1

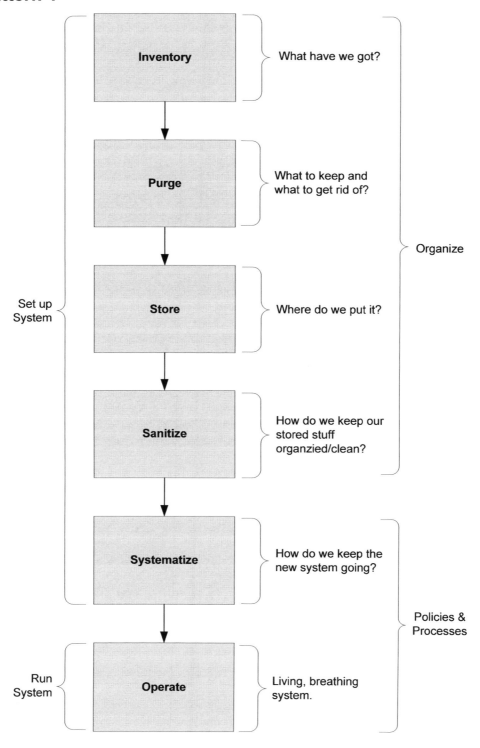

Pattern 2

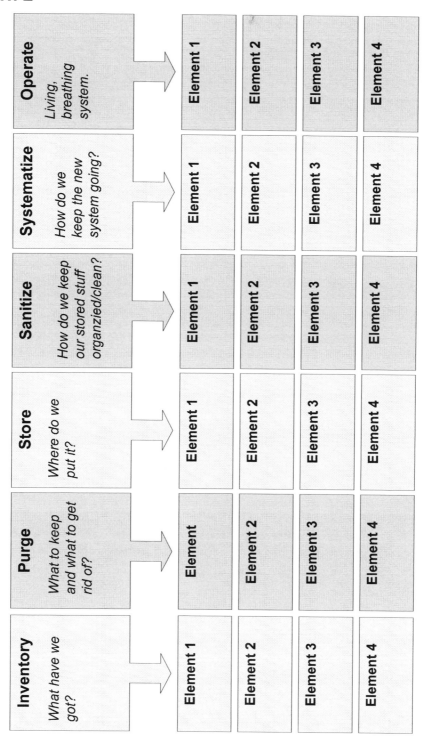

CHAPTER 056

Prioritization Model

The Prioritization Model is used to build a prioritized list of strategic enterprise activities.

What constitutes enterprise activities includes projects, enterprise component development, organizational unit work plan items, etc. An enterprise prioritizes its strategic activities so it can make high quality budget and resourcing decisions.

The Prioritization Model contains the following elements:

- Priority
- Scoring (Scale)
- Weight
- Activity
- Priority Ranking

Priority. When something is given priority it is provided attention and resources before things assigned a lower priority in the priority rankings.

Scoring (Scale). This model uses a scale to set a priority level score for each dimension of priority (cost, time, difficulty, etc). The scale used in this model contains the following quantifications of priority: none (0), low (1), medium (3), high (9).

Weight. Some dimensions of priority are more important than others. The more important dimensions can receive higher weights and, so, contribute more towards the final scoring when scores are calculated.

Activity. An activity is any unit of work contemplated by the enterprise for which resources must be allocated. Resources are not unlimited and therefore each activity must be prioritized so that resources can be allocated accordingly.

Priority Ranking. A priority ranking is list of things with each item on the list assigned a priority score and ranked highest to lowest according to this score. Items at the top of the list receive attention and access to resources before items lower on the list.

The prioritization elements here are: cost, time, quality, difficulty, risk, importance, urgency, and CxO interest. A scoring weight is assigned to each dimension. Each enterprise must decide which dimensions to use in their Prioritization Model and how to weight each dimensions. For example, if a cabal of vice-presidents is keen on supporting IT and have budget influence, then external interest may be highly weighted.

Pattern 1 presents a Prioritization Model as an evaluation table with priority rankings.

Pattern 2 presents the Prioritization Model as a list of prioritized activities.

Pattern 3 uses strategic goals to help make prioritization decisions. This pattern begins with a functional decomposition of the enterprise that has been filtered to show just those organizational units that contribute the realization of the strategic goal that has been made the focus for this prioritization exercise. Each organizational unit and function has been assigned two scores, a performance score (excellent, acceptable, poor) and a goal importance score (high, medium, low). Organizational units and functions with poor performance and high importance have been prioritized for investment to improve performance. Pattern 3 highlights prioritized organizational units/function in two ways, first by color (they are marked by a dark grey background) and in the priority summary they are identified by name.

Pattern 2

PRIORITY	COST	TIME	QUALITY	DIFFICULTY	RISK	IMPORTANCE	URGENCY	CxO INTEREST	PRIORITY RANKING
Scoring	1 – High 3 – Medium 9 - Low	1 – Low 3 – Medium 9 - High	1 – Hight 3 – Medium 9 - Low	1 – High 3 – Medium 9 - Low	1 – High 3 – Medium 9 - Low	1 – Low 3 – Medium 9 - High	1 – Low 3 – Medium 9 - High	1 – High 3 – Medium 9 - Low	
Weight	1	1.5	1	2	1.5	2	1.5	3	
Activity 1									
Activity 2									
Activity 3									
Activity 4									
Activity 5									

Pattern 2

HIGH PRIORITY	MEDIUM PRIORITY	LOW PRIORITY	NO PRIORITY	
				Activity 5
				Activity 4
				Activity 3
				Activity 2
				Activity 1
HIGH PRIORITY	MEDIUM PRIORITY	LOW PRIORITY	NO PRIORITY	

Pattern 3

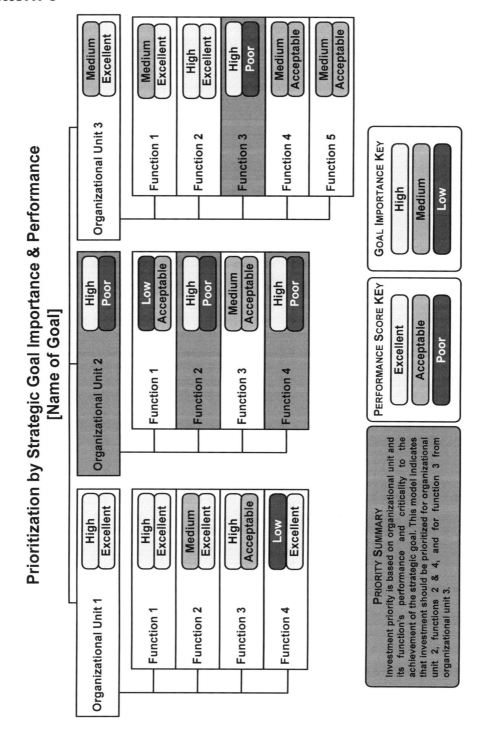

Prioritization by Strategic Goal Importance & Performance
[Name of Goal]

Organizational Unit 1

Function	Importance	Performance
Function 1	High	Excellent
Function 2	Medium	Excellent
Function 3	High	Acceptable
Function 4	Low	Excellent

Organizational Unit 2

Function	Importance	Performance
Function 1	Low	Acceptable
Function 2	High	Poor
Function 3	Medium	Acceptable
Function 4	High	Poor

(Organizational Unit 2: High / Poor)

Organizational Unit 3

(Organizational Unit 3: Medium / Excellent)

Function	Importance	Performance
Function 1	Medium	Excellent
Function 2	High	Excellent
Function 3	High	Poor
Function 4	Medium	Acceptable
Function 5	Medium	Acceptable

GOAL IMPORTANCE KEY
- High
- Medium
- Low

PERFORMANCE SCORE KEY
- Excellent
- Acceptable
- Poor

PRIORITY SUMMARY

Investment priority is based on organizational unit and its function's performance and criticality to the achievement of the strategic goal. This model indicates that investment should be prioritized for organizational unit 2, functions 2 & 4, and for function 3 from organizational unit 3.

CHAPTER 057

Information Lifecycle Model

The Information Lifecycle Model illustrates the services, information processes and states as they relate to the information value stream.

The Information Lifecycle Model contains the following elements:

- Planning
- Collection
- Storage
- Analysis
- Reports
- Distribution
- Use
- Evaluation

Planning. Planning in this model refers to strategic planning, the process of deliberately documenting the vision, mission, goals and objectives of the enterprise—in both the business and IT realms—in order to ensure the enterprise is competitive and possesses or develops the capabilities to fulfil its vision and mission. In this stage of the lifecycle, planning sets out the information requirements to measure success. To enable the measurement of success, data will have to be collected, stored, analysed, turned into digestible report forms, distributed, used to support high-quality decision-making within the enterprise, and, finally, used to evaluate strategic outcomes.

Collection. In this stage of the lifecycle, information is collected. Sometimes collecting data to measure success is done as a special project. However, this is not the most efficient or most effective way to go about things. The best way is to collect data to measure success as a by-product of regular operations. In this stage, the information is used for primary purposes. Applications allow users to use information in support of their delivery of services and products—and while this may be the primary reason for the existence of this information, the useful life of this information has only just begun.

Storage. In this stage of the lifecycle, collected information is stored in two important ways. First, data is stored in an operational context and structured to support the primary uses of data. Second, data is stored in an enterprise warehouse context where information is structured for the secondary use of data. A key component of the enterprise is the enterprise data warehouse, which gives the enterprise the capability to store and manage fixed/persistent data and correctable meta-data over time. The enterprise data warehouse becomes the *source-of-truth* for all questions about the enterprise which require analysis to be performed over one or more years of data and/or across one or more enterprise datasets.

Analysis. In this stage of the lifecycle, information is analysed. While every stage of the lifecycle is important, this stage is the first important step towards aggregating and filtering vast amounts of data in order to support decision-makers with clear and relevant information. This is the stage that begins the transition of raw data into actionable business intelligence.

Reports. In this stage of the lifecycle, information is packaged into reports—information products carefully crafted to support decision-making in a wide variety of ways. The term 'report' is used here in its widest sense. A report may be a document, a collection of statistic, a custom dataset, a balanced scorecard, a chart, an online user-manipulated business intelligence tool, a dashboard data widget, etc.

Distribution. In this stage of the lifecycle, information is once again on the move. Distribution may involve pushing reports out to users or publishing reports to a system that allows users to seek out information using business intelligence tools. The goal of this stage is to get the right information into the hands of the right decision-makers at the right time and in the right security context.

Use. In this stage, information is consumed by end users. These 'data consumer' use the information in their reports to make decisions. It is the quality of these decisions that determine the success of the enterprise.

Evaluation. Those involved in enterprise planning are deeply interested in the success of their plans, which is to say they are interested in the success of the enterprise. The plan to measure success in a number of ways. Once the work of the enterprise has been done—usually with the context of a time period or lifecycle of an asset or project—evaluations are performed. The evaluation of informational effectiveness looks at the usefulness of available information to measure success, which is the same notion as the usefulness of information to support high-quality decision-making throughout the organization. The results of evaluating informational effectiveness feed into new rounds of enterprise planning and to formulate corrective action for in-flight projects and programs.

Any enterprise element can be associated with one or more phases of the information lifecycle.

Pattern 1

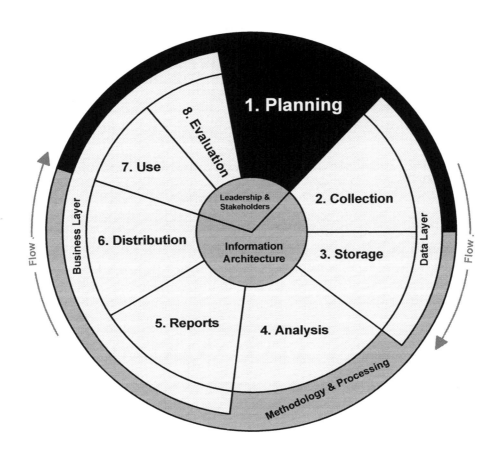

Pattern 2

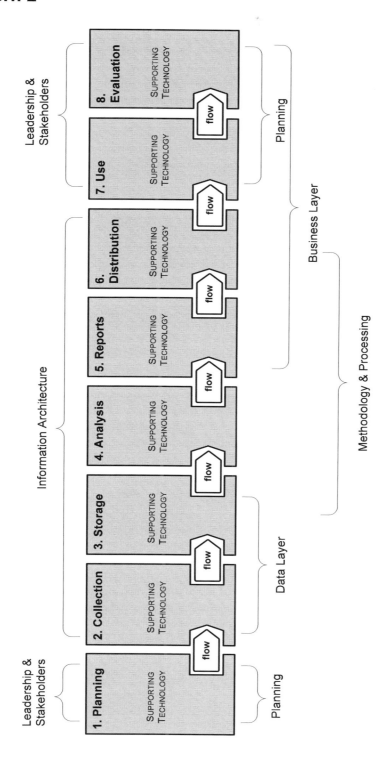

Pattern 3

INFORMATION LIFECYCLE ANALYSIS

1. PLANNING

2. COLLECTION

3. STORAGE

4. ANALYSIS

5. REPORTS

6. DISTRIBUTION

7. USE

8. EVALUATION

CHAPTER 058

Information Risk Model

The Information Risk Model maps the dimensions of information risk for collections of data, information, and for systems. The model can be used as an input to both strategic and tactical planning processes.

The Information Risk Model contains the following elements:

- Name (of Data, Information, Application, or System)
- Relevance
- Quality
- Authorization
- Security
- Availability
- Architecture
- Scale

Name (of Data, Information, Application, or System). This element identifies the enterprise data, information, application or system component by name.

Relevance. Relevance of information measures the usability of the information. In short, is the information relevant to decision-making?

Quality. Quality of information measures the completeness, accuracy, and timeliness of information.

Authorization. Authorization measures compliance with external legislation and internal policy and procedure.

Security. Security determines whether information is restricted on a need-to-know basis.

Availability. Availability measures the extent to which

appropriate information is available to the right decision-makers, at the right time, and in an appropriate context.

Architecture. The architecture element measures whether the right IT infrastructure and systems are in place, that they meet today's needs and will meet enterprise needs into the future, and that they meet those needs in an effective and efficient way.

Scale. This model uses a scale to determine the level of risk to the enterprise in relation to a particular dimension of risk (relevance, quality, authorization, etc). The scale used in this model contains the following quantifications of risk: no risk, low risk, medium risk, and high risk.

At a glance, the Information Risk Model illustrates challenges to the making of evidence-based decisions by highlighting data flow/lifecycle dysfunction, issues with business use/management of information, and issues with IT's technical management of the data.

The scale here is only an example and has four levels: no risk, low risk, medium risk, and high risk. 'No Risk' are areas where risk is acceptable and no impacts are expected, and nothing needs to be done. 'Low Risk' are areas where a business process usually addresses issues impacting confidence in a business service. 'Medium Risk' situations where a business process and/or a technical process addresses risk issues impacting on the enterprise. 'High Risk' situations are unacceptable situation requiring immediate action before the risk impacts the enterprise's ability to carry out its mission/mandate and strategic plans.

For a look at an another way to score a model similar to this one, see the Sustainability Model.

Pattern 1

INFORMATION RISK MODEL FOR [NAME OF DATA OR INFORMATION OR SYSTEM]

SCORE: _____

	HIGH RISK	MEDIUM RISK	LOW RISK	NO RISK
Architecture				
Availability				
Security				
Authorizattion				
Quality				
Relevance				

	HIGH RISK	MEDIUM RISK	LOW RISK	NO RISK

Pattern 2

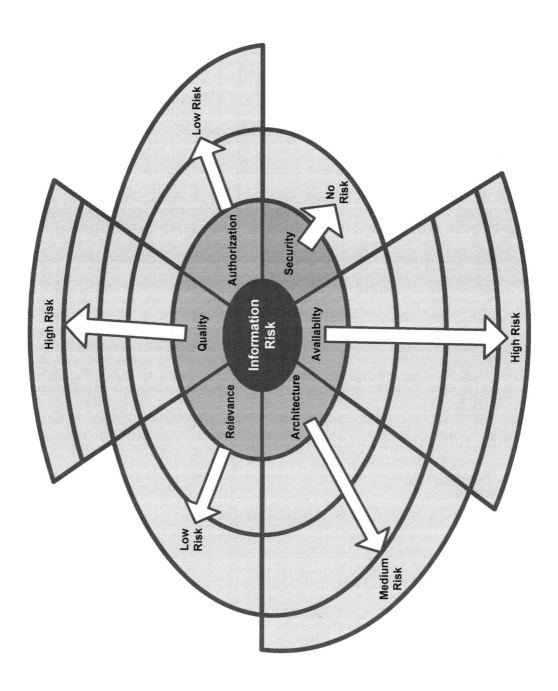

CHAPTER 059

Essential Complexity Model

The Essential Complexity Model demonstrates the link between any given topic and any other enterprise element or issue. The model is useful for demonstrating essential complexity to senior leaders before that complexity has been conquered by an architectural plan of attack. In short, the model presents all the parts of a problem before you know how to solve the problem.

The Essential Complexity Model contains the following elements:

- Topic
- Enterprise Elements

Topic. A topic is an area of interest to the enterprise, usually the topic is a problem that requires solving.

Enterprise Element. Enterprises are made up of elements. Depending on context, many things can be described as an enterprise element.

Pattern 1 shows the bubbles version of the model. The topic statement can be placed anywhere and the bubbles (each labelled with the name of an enterprise) can be arranged around the issue statement in any way.

Pattern 2 drops the topic statement and places related enterprise elements on the page and connects the elements. This pattern is useful to illustrate the essential complexity of the relationships that make up the enterprise.

Pattern 1

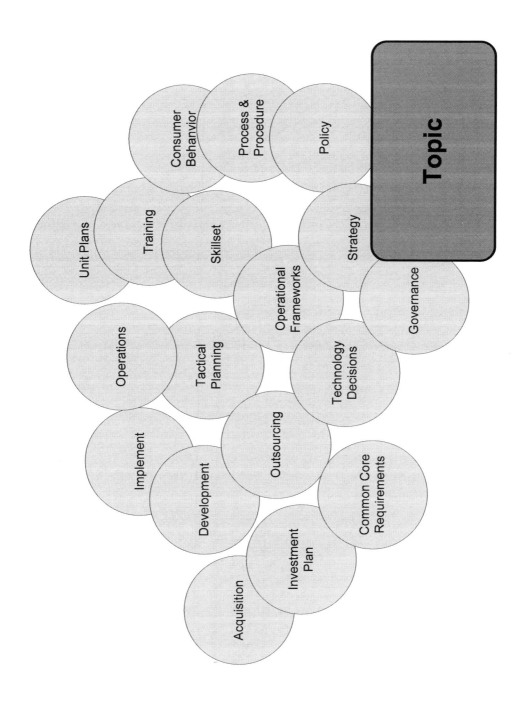

Pattern 2

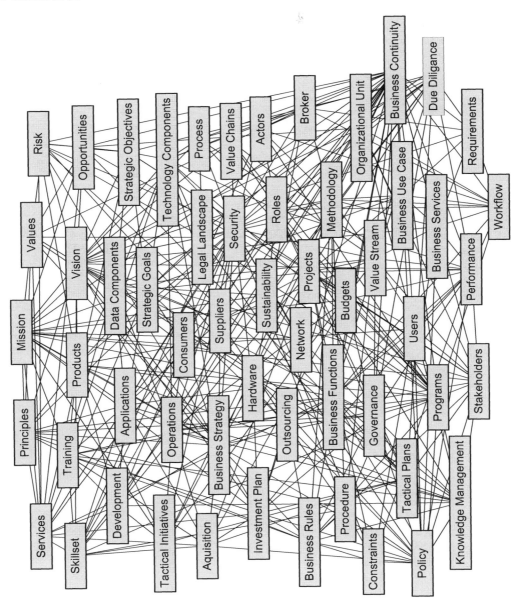

CHAPTER 060

Business Reference Model

The Business Reference Model defines a functional view of an organization's lines of business from a client perspective. This model has been adapted from the Business Reference Model first developed and popularized by the US Federal Enterprise Architecture (FEA) program. Both this and the FEA model reflect the business perspectives prominent in such schools of thought as LEAN and Six Sigma.

The Business Reference Model contains the following elements:

- Services for Clients
- Mode of Delivery
- Support Delivery of Services
- Management of Resources

Services for Clients. This element deals with an enterprise's core services and conceptualizes them in a client-centric manner. As core services, these services answer the question: "What is the purpose of the business?" The answer usually describes a line of business or a high-level organizational unit.

Mode of Delivery. The second element of the model answers the question: "How are *services for clients* delivered?" The answer usually describes the business functions and services that make up the line of business or high-level organizational units.

Support Delivery of Services. The third element of the model answers the question: "What support functions deliver direct value to the clients?" The answer is usually an inventory of enterprise services that directly support the delivery of *services for clients*.

Management of Resources. The fourth and final element asks: "What functions deliver secondary (enabling) value to clients?" The FEA model can be confusing. The intent is to identify enterprise management functions that support all the other functions—in this sense they are the equivalent of technology components, which are not interacted with directly by the client, but which must be in place in order for primary components—application and data components—to function.

In patterns 1 and 2, the syntax has adapted for public or private application.

Pattern 2 is particularly useful for discovery consulting—for those engagements where the information necessary to conduct enterprise business architecture effectively is not yet documented and must be 'discovered'.

For the enterprise, the primary implications of the Business Reference Model is this: "If a business function cannot be shown to directly provide value to clients or provide critical support to those client-linked functions, then those functions are of very low or no value to the enterprise." In general, functions of very low or no value to the enterprise should be terminated.

Pattern 1

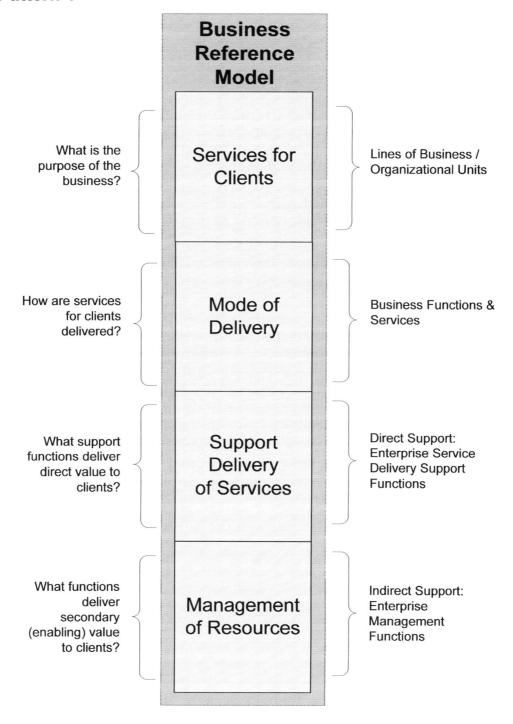

Pattern 2

ORGANIZATION

What is the purpose of the business?

Describe Services for Clients.

FUNCTIONS & SERVICES

How are services for clients delivered?

Describe the Mode of Delivery.

DIRECT SUPPORT FUNCTIONS

What support functions deliver direct value to the clients?

Describe Support Delivery of Services.

INDIRECT SUPPORT FUNCTIONS

What functions deliver secondary (enabling) value to clients?

Describe Management of Resources.

CHAPTER 061

Business Use Case Model

The Business Use Case Model illustrates the link between clients, business functions, business services, and supporting IT.

The Business Use Case Model contains the following elements:

- Client Objective
- Activity/Functions
- Business Services
- Technology

Client Objective. A client objective is something a client wishes to achieve. For example, 'a client wishes to buy a car', 'a client wishes to buy insurance', 'a client needs to procure a new fleet of vehicles'.

Activity/Functions. Business activity is any activity taken in support of an enterprise's capabilities or an organizational unit's functions and services. A business function is a collection of business activities and services, usually organized as a sub-unit of an organizational unit. Services are owned and operated by a responsible organizational unit.

Business Services. A business service is a collection of business processes that, together, deliver a particular service. Business services are owned and operated by a responsible organizational unit. Business services are supported by technological services, which are composed of data, application, and technology components that are integrated and interoperate in order to support the business activity.

Technology. In this model, 'technology' refers to the components that enable the business services. The types of components that support the business are: technology components, data components, and application/system components.

Technology Components. A technological component of the enterprise is a component which supports the operation of other application, data, and technology components. In this model, a technology component may perform a very specific function or represent a type of technology product. The term technology component includes infrastructure and security components.

Data Components. A data component of the enterprise is an existing enterprise data asset. Data components are usually managed by an application and supported by multiple technology components. Some data components are manage via loosely coupled services like those available via web services or message brokers.

Application/System Components. An application component is an operationalized application or system that supports a specific business service and its various business processes. Applications are used to access and manage specific data components and depend on the support of specific technology components. An application will always have human users directly accessing it via some type of user/client interface—a data or technology component may not.

The business use case model demonstrates how enterprise functions and services are organized in support of client objectives and emphasizes the importance of the client perspective

Pattern 1

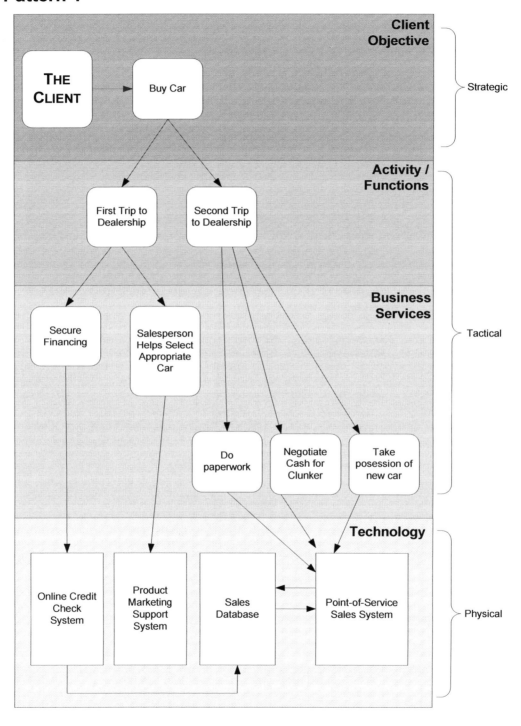

CHAPTER 062

Enterprise Business Rules Discovery Model

The Enterprise Business Rules Discovery Model is used to generate enterprise business rules from enterprise business scenarios/use cases.

The Enterprise Business Rules Discovery Model contains the following elements:

- Enterprise Business Scenario
- Scenario Variations
- Unique Workflows
- Enterprise Business Rules

Enterprise Business Scenario. An enterprise business scenario is a description of a series of sequenced actions that perform a task and/or a series of tasks that perform a process.

Scenario Variations. For every process there are exceptions and few processes can run smoothly without planning for a few contingencies. The core enterprise business scenario may be extended with scenario variations in order to account for process exceptions and varying input and environmental conditions.

Unique Workflows. Theoretical scenarios are mapped to actual workflows—process activity steps. Each scenario and its variation can be mapped to a 'unique workflow'.

Enterprise Business Rules. For a workflow to be efficient and effective, it must abide by certain rules. A rule is a statement that defines important aspects of performing the business. Enterprise business rules are discovered by working through unique workflows and determining and documenting rules necessary to promote an effective and efficient process.

The Enterprise Business Rules Discovery Model generates business scenario variations based on a core business scenario. The variations may explore special case business scenarios.

Each business scenario variation requires a unique workflow to be documented. It is through the process of documenting these workflows that enterprise business rules are discovered.

This model can be applied to both business use cases and system use cases.

Pattern 1

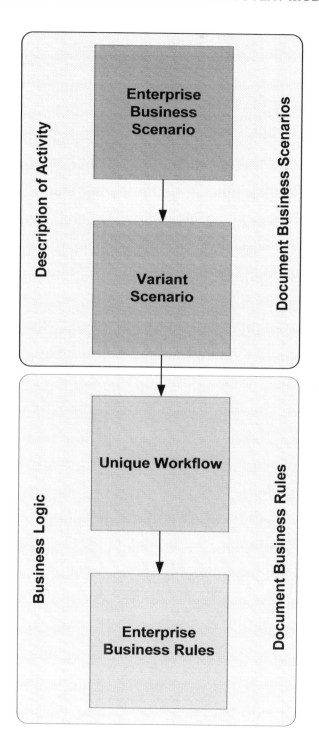

Pattern 2

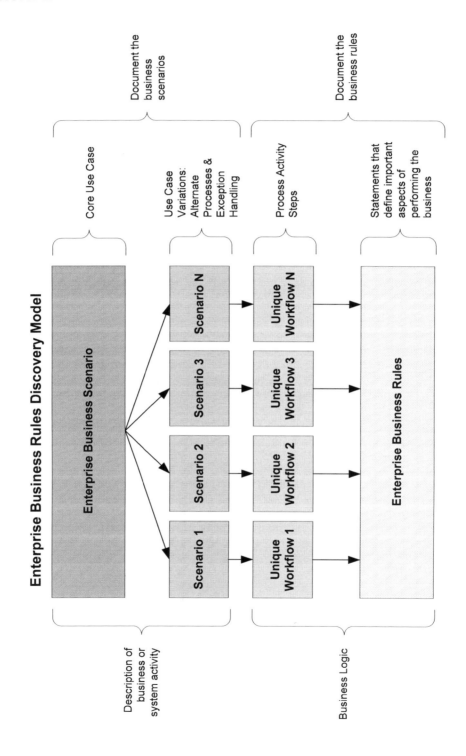

CHAPTER 063

Enterprise Architecture Governance Model

The purpose of the Enterprise Architecture Governance Model is to illustrate enterprise decision-making relationships.

The Enterprise Architecture Governance Model contains the following elements:

- Senior Leadership
- Oversight Layer
- Enterprise Architecture Group
- EA Clients

Senior Leadership. The senior leadership of an enterprise are its high-level executives and most responsible decision-makers: CEOs, CIOs, presidents, vice-presidents, and directors. The role of senior leadership is to resolves disputes regarding architecture.

Oversight Layer. A body or board may be constituted to 'approve' the work of the enterprise architecture team. Only implement an architecture review board if the organization has enough expert members to provide credible oversight.

Enterprise Architecture Group. The business function of enterprise architecture is often embodied in organizational structure by creating a permanent group of enterprise architects. Membership in this group might include: chief architect, business architect, data architect, application architect, and technology architect.

Enterprise Architecture Clients. When enterprise architects undertake enterprise architecture engagements, their clients are often the staff members and consultants undertaking new programs and projects. When these programs and projects come across architecture issues that require decision-making, they bring these issues to an enterprise architect for an architecture decision.

The enterprise business architect uses this model to explain to stakeholders how enterprise architecture decisions are made.

In pattern 1, enterprise architects make decisions, chief architects support them, and the CIO and CEO arbitrate them.

Formal enterprise business architecture governance activity is also mapped as 'checkpoints / approval gates' in the Enterprise Business Architecture and IT Project Touchpoints Model. Governance is a formal activity described in the Enterprise Business Architecture Lifecycle Model.

Pattern 1

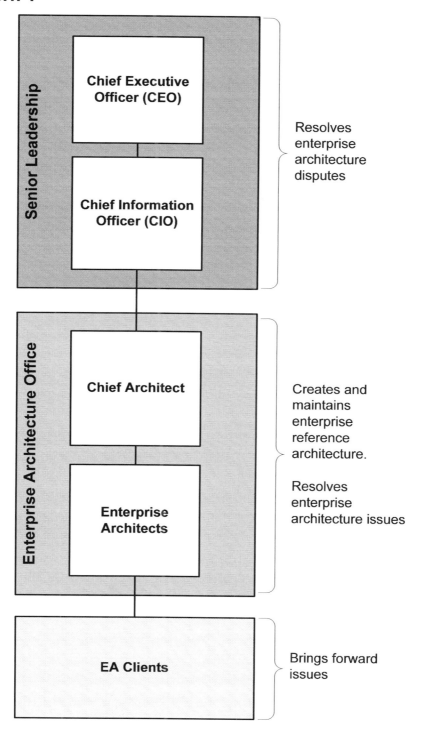

Pattern 2

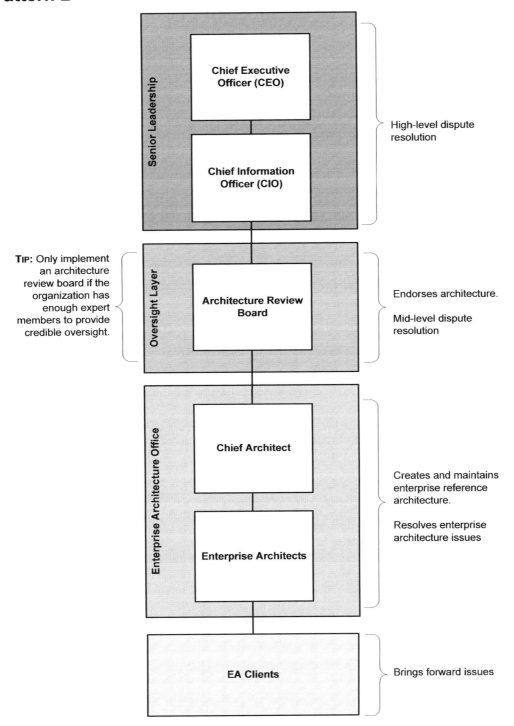

CHAPTER 064

IT Asset Lifecycle and Project Lifecycle Relationship Model

The IT Asset Lifecycle and Project Lifecycle Relationship Model does exactly what its name suggests: the model depicts the relationship between the asset lifecycle and the project lifecycle.

The IT Asset Lifecycle and Project Lifecycle Relationship Model contains the following elements:

- IT Asset Lifecycle
- IT Project Lifecycle

IT Asset Lifecycle. The IT Asset lifecycle describes the stages through which an IT asset passes over the course of its life within the enterprise, from its first selection and deployment to its final retirement from use.

IT Project Lifecycle. The IT Project Lifecycle describes the stages through which an IT project passes from its first inception to it final closing.

Business architects will find the utility of this model lies in its ability to surface the role of projects within the IT asset lifecycle. Often projects are seen as an end unto themselves—rather than the 'means of asset creation' that they are. This models clarifies the role of project and by doing this, allows weight to be given to big picture questions of asset sustainability and utility—from both the planning perspective and the operational perspective.

Pattern 1

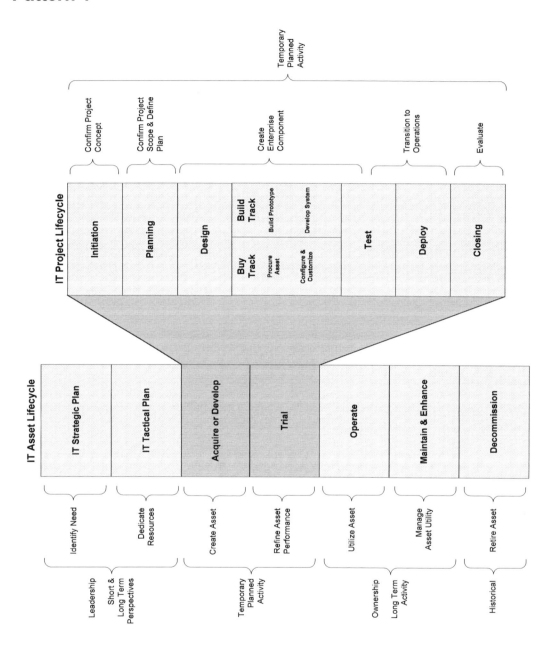

CHAPTER 065

Standards Lifecycle Model

The Standards Lifecycle Model shows the business architect's perspective on the lifecycle of standards.

The Standards Lifecycle Model contains the following elements:

- Standards Review
- Sunrise
- Interim
- Core
- Sunset
- Demoted
- Rejected
- Retired

Standards Review. When new standards appear, they are reviewed for suitability of use within the enterprise. As a result of a standards review: a standards can be rejected, but can always be reconsidered at a later date; a standard can be accepted as a 'sunrise' standard or immediately assigned 'core' standard status or designated an 'interim' standard as a short term bridge to a permanent, different standard. The standards review has implications for existing standards for as new standards are adopted older standards may be demoted and retired.

A key guideline for conducting standards reviews is to only allow standards into the organization that directly enable business value. Avoid crippling the organization's ability to change with standards for standard's sake. In short, standards must solve problems, not create them.

Sunrise. Sunrise standards are new standards that have been accepted for use in the enterprise but which are not yet the preferred or 'go to' standard. In general, over time, it is expected that sunrise standards will replace their equivalent core standards.

Interim. Interim standards are new standards that have been accepted for use in the enterprise on a provisional basis: they will not migrate towards 'core' or even 'sunrise' status. An interim standard is strictly used on a short term basis to bridge the enterprise from a current state to a future state where a different standards will be deployed in place of the interim standard.

Core. Core standards are the preferred standards for use in the enterprise. The enterprise has deep experience in the use of core standards and core standards have usually influenced the implementation of many important enterprise components.

Sunset. Sunset standards are aging standards that are being phased out of regular use. When new IT work is being undertaken, sunset standards are not considered for use.

Demoted. When a standard moves from 'core' to 'sunset', it has been 'demoted'.

Rejected. When a standard review determines a standard unsuitable for use within the enterprise, the standard has been 'rejected'.

Retired. When a standard reaches the end of its useful life within the enterprise, it is 'retired' and no longer used within the enterprise. When an 'interim' standard is replaced, it is no longer used in the enterprise and is 'retired'.

The lifecycle in pattern 1 follows standards from first review, to acceptance as a sunrise/emerging standard, promotion to core status, demotion to sunset status, and eventual retirement from use. Some potential standards are immediately rejected.

The Standards Lifecycle Model and Technology Lifecycle Model share the same elements and conceptual purpose. The underlying lifecycle pattern to both of these models is useful when modeling other enterprise architecture elements, such as: principles, patterns, building blocks, etc.

Pattern 1

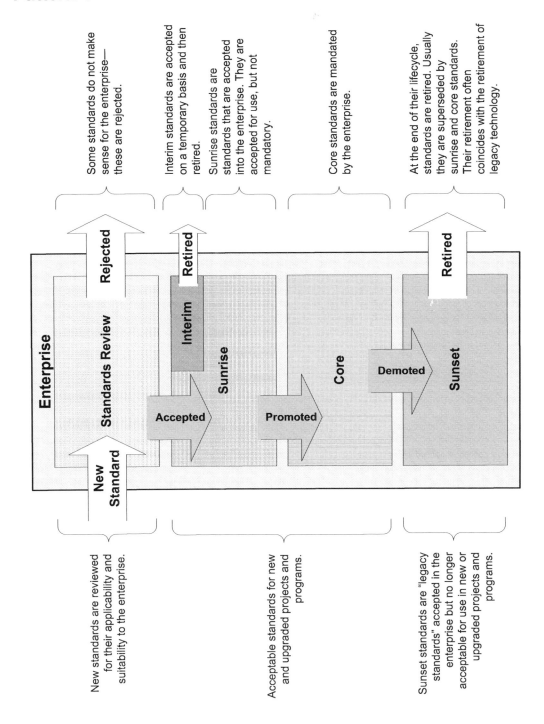

Some standards do not make sense for the enterprise—these are rejected.

Interim standards are accepted on a temporary basis and then retired.

Sunrise standards are standards that are accepted into the enterprise. They are accepted for use, but not mandatory.

Core standards are mandated by the enterprise.

At the end of their lifecycle, standards are retired. Usually they are superseded by sunrise and core standards. Their retirement often coincides with the retirement of legacy technology.

New standards are reviewed for their applicability and suitability to the enterprise.

Acceptable standards for new and upgraded projects and programs.

Sunset standards are "legacy standards" accepted in the enterprise but no longer acceptable for use in new or upgraded projects and programs.

CHAPTER 066

Business Continuity Model

The Business Continuity Model documents the enterprise approach to maintaining critical enterprise functions in the event of disaster and how the enterprise will recover in the wake of the disaster.

The Business Continuity Model contains the following elements:

- Analysis & Assessment
- Strategize & Plan
- Execute Plan

Analysis & Assessment. In this element of the model—the first phase of the business continuity process—the primary task is to understand the business and threats to the business. There are three key activities in the analysis and assessment phase. The first key activity is to undertake a business impact analysis (to understand the business). The second activity is to undertake a threat/risk assessment (to understand the threats). The final activity is to correlate the business impact assessment with the threat/risk assessment and examines the impact of each unique threat upon the business.

Strategize & Plan. In this element—the second phase of the business continuity process—the primary task is to consider the analysis and assessment and make important judge-ments and decisions. A business continuity strategy and tactical plan is developed, tested, and refined.

Execute Plan. This is the third phase of the business continuity process and the final element of the model. The primary purpose of this element is to map out the actions necessary to operationalized and exercise (maintain, test and review) the plan.

Pattern 1 shows the three key dimensions of this model. First, analysis and assessment of threats to the enterprise. Second, strategy and plans to mitigate threats. Finally, the approach to keeping the plans effective and up-to-date.

Pattern 2 elaborates on the basic structure in pattern 1. In this pattern, the model answers key questions about business continuity: What is the business? What are the threats? How serious are the threats and what are their impacts? What is the strategy to mitigate the threats? What is the tactical plan to implement the strategy? How will the plan be embedded in the everyday life of the enterprise?

Pattern 1

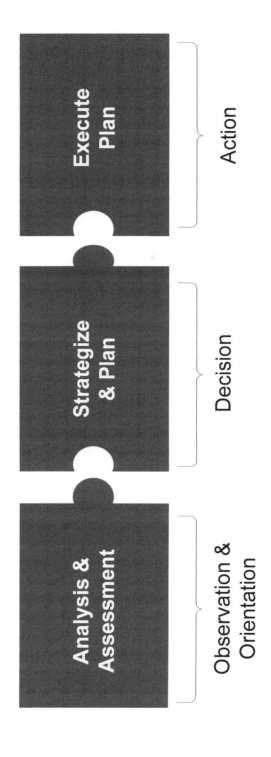

Pattern 2

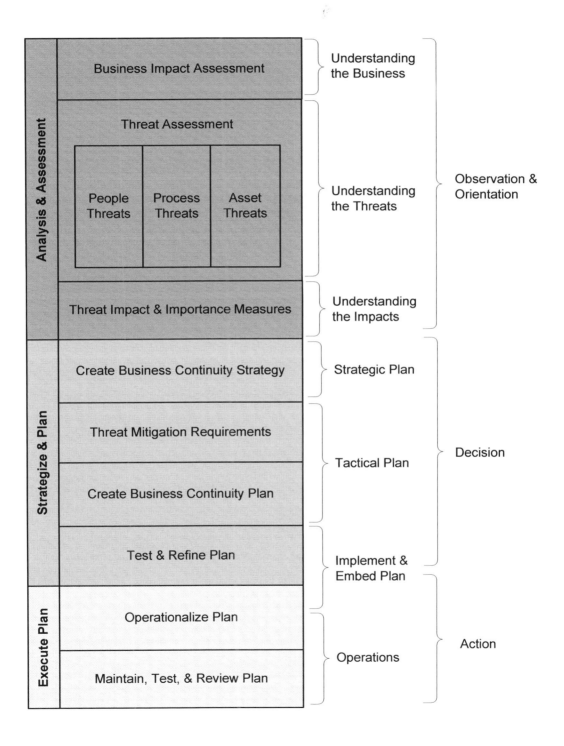

CHAPTER 067

Business Continuity Impact Assessment Model

The Business Continuity Impact Assessment Model illustrates the business continuity impact assessment process. The model looks at the impact a disruption might have on the enterprise's ability to function. Disruptions are caused by natural disaster, strike, epidemic, utility failure, etc. However, exactly *what the disruption is* not relevant to the business impact assessment.

The Business Continuity Impact Assessment Model contains the following elements:

- Disruption
- Key Services
- Disruption Duration
- Impact On...
- Acceptable Disruption Interval (ADI)
- Disruption Recovery Targets (DRT)
- Critical Process Resources
- Impact Scoring

Disruption. A disruption is a break in the continuity of enterprise operations.

Key Services. Key services are enterprise services that, if disrupted, would result in harm to health & safety, destruction of physical enterprise assets and IT components, unacceptable financial recovery costs, damage to the reputation of the enterprise, or loss of confidence in the enterprise by either its staff or stakeholders.

Disruption Duration. Any given impact may have different effects based on the duration of the disruption. Therefore, impact is measured at standards intervals of relevance to the particular enterprise. For example, impact may be measured at 1 day, 2-3 days, 7 days, 14 days, greater than 14 days.

Impact On.... An enterprise can measure the impact of a disruption on many different things. The determination of what impacts to consider will vary from enterprise to enterprise. In this example, the effects of 'impact on' is considered for: clients, stakeholders, and the ability of enterprise meet its goals and objectives.

Acceptable Disruption Interval (ADI). Each key service will have an acceptable duration interval—the maximum time a disruption may carry on before it is necessary to resume operation of the service.

Disruption Recovery Targets (DRT). Each key service will be assigned a disruption recovery target—the point in time after the commencement of a disruption that the enterprise plans to resume the service.

Critical Process Resources. When a disruption hits a key service, it is important to understand the impact in terms of the resource that are critical to the functioning of the service. This component of the model asks the question: What resources are required to keep the critical processing running and meet Disruption Recovery Targets?" The critical resources to consider are: people (staffing), data components, application components, technology components, location, and inputs/supplies.

Impact Scoring. The impact of a disruption is quantified by impact scoring. The determination of a score for the disruption of each key service is made through the evaluation of the service, the disruption duration, the ADI and DRT, and the service's critical process resources.

The Business Continuity Impact Assessment Model suggests a six step business impact assessment process.

The first step in the assessment is to create an inventory of the enterprise's key services—the key services are often called 'critical services'.

The second step considers the impact of a disruption on clients and stakeholders and on the enterprise's ability to fulfil its goals and objectives. As impact varies over time, impact effects are examined at various time intervals (one day, two days, one week, etc).

The third step looks at disruption impacts from a pragmatic perspective. First, it determines what the maximum time a key service can be 'down' before unacceptable consequences occur. Second: Once down what is the specific disruption recovery target for each service? By setting disruption recovery targets for each service, a de-facto service recovery sequence is created.

The fourth step determines which processes in the service are critical to the delivery of the service.

The fifth step elaborates on the identified critical processes. This step decomposes each critical process into its constituent parts: people, data, applications, technology, location, and inputs. Each enterprise will determine which process resources are of relevance to their impact analysis.

The sixth and final step assigns each service and service resource an 'impact score' of high or low. (This is, perhaps, an oversimplified approach to the 'impact score' step. Some enterprises will require a more complex approach to assigning impact scores.) By assigning 'impact scores', disruption impacts can be ranked. The 'impact score' is an input to the business continuity risk analysis model.

Pattern 1

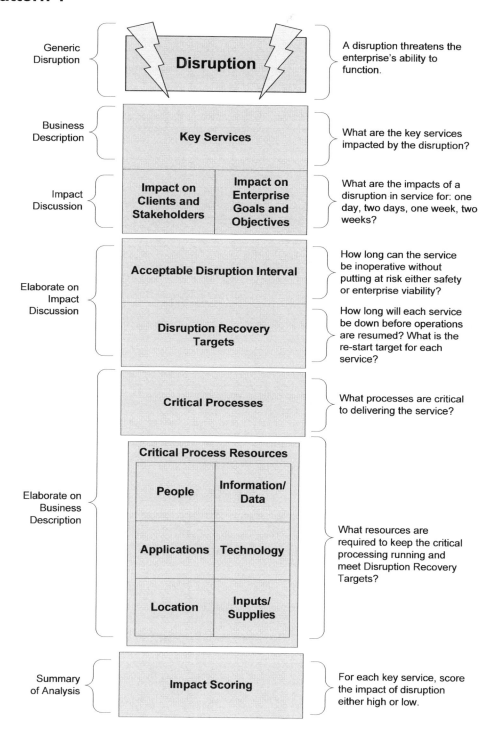

Generic Disruption
Disruption
A disruption threatens the enterprise's ability to function.

Business Description
Key Services
What are the key services impacted by the disruption?

Impact Discussion
Impact on Clients and Stakeholders | **Impact on Enterprise Goals and Objectives**
What are the impacts of a disruption in service for: one day, two days, one week, two weeks?

Elaborate on Impact Discussion
Acceptable Disruption Interval
How long can the service be inoperative without putting at risk either safety or enterprise viability?

Disruption Recovery Targets
How long will each service be down before operations are resumed? What is the re-start target for each service?

Critical Processes
What processes are critical to delivering the service?

Elaborate on Business Description
Critical Process Resources
People | **Information/ Data**
Applications | **Technology**
Location | **Inputs/ Supplies**
What resources are required to keep the critical processing running and meet Disruption Recovery Targets?

Summary of Analysis
Impact Scoring
For each key service, score the impact of disruption either high or low.

CHAPTER 068

Business Continuity Risk Assessment Model

The Business Continuity Risk Assessment Model is used to measure and rank potential threats to the enterprise's ability to function. (Risk assessment is, in general, a synonym for threat assessment.)

The Business Continuity Risk Assessment Model contains the following elements:

- Risk Inventory
- Risk Likelihood Analysis
- Current State Risk Mitigation
- Future State Risk Mitigation
- Risk Likelihood Scoring
- Risk Score Plot
- Risk Ranking

Risk Inventory. A risk inventory is a comprehensive catalog of risks faced by the enterprise. In terms of this model, the terms 'risk' and 'threat' mean essentially the same thing— both threaten to disrupt the normal operations of the enterprise.

Risk Likelihood Analysis. A risk likelihood analysis is the process of examining each risk faced by the enterprise, judging its likelihood and impact, assigning it a risk ranking, and, finally, ranking the risks accordingly.

Current State Risk Mitigation. The current state risk mitigation component is an inventory of all current risk mitigation strategies and plans.

Future State Risk Mitigation. In consideration of the current state risk mitigation efforts and the Risk Inventory, the future state risk mitigation component lists all appropriate risk mitigation strategies and plans that should be put in place.

Risk Likelihood Scoring. Some risks are more likely to happen than others. For example, a tropical monsoon is less likely in Arizona than in Hawaii; an earthquake is more likely in California than North Dakota. Risk likelihood scoring is an element of the risk likelihood analysis and explicitly considers the likelihood and impact of a risk and generates a risk likelihood score for each risk in the risk inventory.

Risk Score Plot. Some risks are more damaging than others. For example: a flu pandemic has the potential to be more damaging than a brief disruption in electrical service; a temporary evacuation from a building due to a small fire is less damaging than a terrorist bomb that destroys an entire building. The Risk Score Plot takes into consideration each risk's likelihood, assigns an impact value to that risk and then plots likelihood and impact. The plot point for each risk constitutes a risk scoring. In this simple model a risk may be deemed: high likelihood – high impact, high likelihood – low impact, low likelihood – low impact, or low likelihood – high impact.

Risk Ranking. The 'risk score plot' is used to generate a 'risk score' and it is this 'risk score' that allows the risk inventory items to be ranked by likelihood and severity.

The Business Continuity Risk Assessment Model suggest a six step risk assessment process.

The first step of the risk assessment process is to create an inventory of potential risks. This inventory might include the threat of disruption from: natural disasters, disease, political upheaval, labour relations, failed utilities, system hackers, etc.

The second step is to assign each risk a likelihood of occurring. The risk assessment team usually meets, discusses, assesses, and assigns each risk to a likelihood category: often, seldom, almost never, etc.

The third step considers two things. First: What is the enterprise currently doing to mitigate each risk in the inventory? Second: What should the enterprise be doing to mitigate each risk in the inventory?

The fourth step involves assigning each risk in the inventory a 'risk score' based on its likelihood of happening. Each risk is assigned a score of either high or low. (This score is, perhaps, oversimplified. Each enterprise will have to determine the appropriate granularity of its own risk likelihood scoring system.)

In step five, the impact and likelihood of each risk in the inventory is plotted. Once on the graph, the quadrant into which the risk falls determines its final risk score.

In the final step, risks are ranked by their risk score. Within each quadrant there may be several risks: Intra-quadrant rankings are qualitative decisions made by the risk assessment team.

Pattern 1

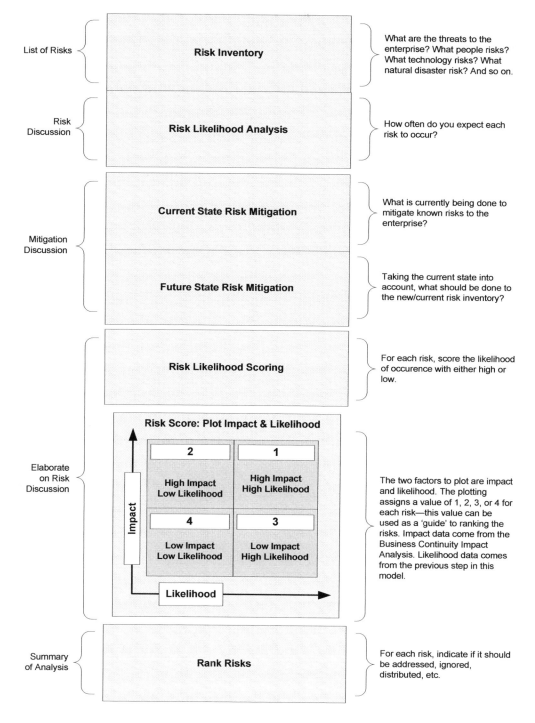

PART 3

CATALOGS

CHAPTER 069

Strategic Context Catalog

The Strategic Context Catalog is the enterprise's authoritative and complete listing of strategic vision, business drivers, goals, objectives, and measures. This includes the strategic vision, drivers, goals, objectives, and measures of the enterprise itself and for each of the enterprise's major organizational units (lines of business).

The catalog provides 'strategic context' to the past, present, and future actions of the enterprise. The catalog provides a way to search, filter, query, investigate relationships, analyze, and report on the enterprise's strategic context information.

The following elements are included in the Strategic Context Catalog:

- Organizational Unit
- Vision
- Drivers
- Goals
- Objectives
- Measures
- Source
- Year

Organizational Unit. The enterprise is defined by an organizational hierarchy. Below the enterprise top level in the hierarchy is the organizational unit level. Each organizational units usually correspond with a high-level enterprise capability. What is the name of the organizational unit?

Vision. A vision statement describes a future state which the enterprise desires to work towards. What is the organizational unit's vision statement?

Drivers. Business drivers are the events and situations which motivate the business to take particular actions. What are the organizational unit's business drivers?

Goals. Goals are the targets that, when achieved, will transition the enterprise towards its future state vision. Goals guide enterprise decision-making about the type, scope and priority of all enterprise activity. What are the organizational unit's goals?

Objectives. Objectives are the measurable achievements that, when achieved, will move the enterprise towards the realization of its goals. What are the organizational unit's objectives?

Measures. Measures are the qualitative or quantitative metrics used to determine if a goal or objective has been successfully achieved. What are the identified measures?

Source. Where did this catalog entry come from? Reference the document from which the vision, drivers, goals, objectives, and measures came.

Year. In what year did this information become official strategy?

CHAPTER 070

Business Alignment Catalog

The Business Alignment Catalog is the enterprise's authoritative collection of business and IT resource alignment data.

The catalog documents information captured in Enterprise Business Architecture Alignment Assurance Models, which show the relationship between strategy (strategic goals and objectives), the owners responsible for achieving the strategy (organizational unit, function and services), and the IT application, data, and technology components of the enterprise that enable the owners to fulfil their strategic responsibilities. The catalog provides a way to search, filter, query, investigate relationships, analyze, and report on business alignment data.

The following elements are included in the Business Alignment Catalog:

- Enterprise Goal
- Enterprise Objective
- Responsible Organizational Unit
- Aligned Capabilities
- Aligned Business Functions
- Aligned Business Services
- Aligned Strategic Plans
- Aligned Tactical Plans
- Aligned Applications
- Aligned Data Component
- Aligned Technology Component

Enterprise Goal. Goals are the targets that, when achieved, will transition the enterprise towards its future state vision. Goals guide enterprise decision-making about the type,

383

scope and priority of all enterprise activity. In this catalog, everything is traceable to the enterprise level goals. What is the goal?

Enterprise Objectives. Objectives are the measurable achievements that, when achieved, will move the enterprise towards the realization of its goals. What is the objective?

Aligned Capabilities. Capabilities represent organizational capacity to provide a particular service or group of services to its clients or stakeholders. What capabilities are necessary for the enterprise to deliver on the enterprise goal?

Responsible Organizational Unit. What is the name of the organizational unit responsible for achieving the goal and objectives and which posses the appropriate capability to achieve the enterprise goal and related objectives?

Aligned Business Functions. A business function is a collection of business activities and services, usually organized as a sub-unit of an organizational unit. In this catalog, these services are owned and operated by the responsible organizational unit. What are the names of the business functions that will help fulfil the enterprise goal and objectives?

Aligned Business Service. A business services is a collection of business processes that, together, deliver a particular service. In this catalog, the aligned business services are owned and operated by the responsible organizational unit. What are the names of the aligned business services that support the achievement of the enterprise goals and objectives?

Aligned Strategic Plans. What business and IT strategic plans support the fulfillment of the enterprise goals and objectives?

Aligned Tactical Plans. What business and IT tactical plans support the fulfilment of the strategic plans?

Aligned Applications. Identify which applications support the business service and its various processes.

Aligned Date Components. Identify which date components

support the business service and its various processes.

Aligned Technology Components. Identify which technology components support the business service and its various processes. The term technology component includes infrastructure and security components.

Chapter 071

Performance Catalog

The Performance Catalog is the enterprise's authoritative and complete listing of all service contracts and performance measures associated with enterprise services.

This catalog is essentially a master list of service levels agreed to across the enterprise and it provides a way to search, filter, query, discover relationships, and report on the contracts and performance measures that set out those SLAs. The catalog documents the SLAs depicted in the Service Level Agreement Model.

The following elements are included in the Performance Catalog:

- Service
- Service Contract
- Performance Measure Name
- Performance Measure Type
- Performance Measure Description

Service. A service may refer to a business service or a technological service. A business services is a collection of business processes that, together, deliver a particular service. A technological service is one or more technologies that integrate and interoperate in order to perform a particular service—sometimes serving multiple components (as in service oriented architectures)—usually exposed to the enterprise via an API or UDDI interface. What is the name of the service?

Service Contract. An agreement between two parties which includes an agreed upon performance requirement for the service in question. The performance requirement is expressed in terms of a service level. Service Contract is a synonym for 'service level agreement'.

Performance Measure Name. A performance measure is a way to assess the effectiveness of functions, services, and processes. What is the name of the performance measure (service level)?

Performance Measure Type. Is the measure qualitative or quantitative?

Performance Measure Description. The description of a performance measure provides a textual description of the measure; it explains how measurement is performed, the acceptable minimum service level, maximum required service level, and service level requirements by time.

Chapter 072

Stakeholder Catalog

The Enterprise Stakeholder Catalog is the enterprise's definitive, authoritative, and complete listing of stakeholders that directly consume services provided by the enterprise's information technology unit or are stakeholders indirectly impacted by IT services.

The catalog includes all stakeholders along the IT value stream: data providers, application providers, technology providers, IT system users, IT system owners, staff, contractors, other business units, senior leaders and decision-makers, data consumers/customers/clients, and shareholders.

The catalog provides a way to search, filter, query, investigate relationships, analyze, and report on enterprise stakeholder information.

The following elements are included in the Stakeholder Catalog:

- Stakeholder Name
- Stakeholder Type
- Stakeholder Abbreviation

Stakeholder Name. A stakeholder is someone with a direct interest in the operations of the enterprise. Stakeholder can be internal or external, and include suppliers, customers, and third parties impacted by the operation of the enterprise. The first question: What stakeholder classification is right for the enterprise? The second, element specific question: What is the stakeholder's name?

Stakeholder Type. There are many different ways to classify stakeholders. In the Stakeholder Model the following stakeholder types are identified: client facing staff, administration, IT Unit, Service Providers, Regulators, Suppliers, and Clients. What is the stakeholder type?

Stakeholder Abbreviation. Is there an abbreviation for the stakeholder name?

Chapter 073

Business Issues Catalog

The Business Issues Catalog is the enterprise's authoritative and complete listing of active issues or problems within the domain of enterprise business architecture. The catalog provides a way to search, filter, query, investigate relationships, analyze, prioritize, and report on these business issues and problems.

The following elements are included in the Business Issues Catalog:

- Issue Name
- Issue Description
- Organizational Unit
- Issue Acuity
- Issue Status

Issue Name. What name as been given to this issue or problem?

Issue Description. Describe important characteristics of the issue or problem.

Organizational Unit. The enterprise is defined by an organizational hierarchy. Below the enterprise top level in the hierarchy is the organizational unit level. Each organizational units usually correspond with a high-level enterprise capability. What is the name of the organizational unit that owns this issue?

Issue Acuity. Is the issue/problem of high, moderate, or low importance?

Issue Status. Is the issue/problem open or closed?

Chapter 074

Business Services Catalog

The Business Services Catalog is the enterprise's authoritative and complete listing of business services, organized by organizational unit and business function.

This catalog provides a detailed decomposition of the enterprise's business structure and provides a way to search, filter, query, investigate relationships, analyze, and report on business services.

The following elements are included in the Business Service Catalog:

- Organizational Unit
- Business Function
- Business Service
- Business Service Description

Organizational Unit. The enterprise is defined by an organizational hierarchy. Below the enterprise top level in the hierarchy is the organizational unit level. Each organizational units usually correspond with a high-level enterprise capability. What is the name of the organizational unit?

Business Function. A business function is a collection of business activities and services, usually organized as a sub-unit of an organizational unit. What is the name of the business function?

Business Service. A business services is a collection of business processes that, together, deliver a particular service. What is the name of the business service?

Business Service Description. A statement describing the essential nature and characteristics of the business service.

Chapter 075

Value Stream Catalog

The Value Stream Catalog is the enterprise's authoritative and complete listing of the enterprise's documented value streams.

The catalog provides a way to search, filter, query, investigate relationships, analyze, and report on value stream data.

The following elements are included in the Value Stream Catalog:

- Organizational Unit
- Value Stream Name
- Value Statement
- Core Services
- Upstream Organizational Units and Services
- Downstream Organizational Units and Services
- Suppliers and Inputs
- Clients and Outputs

Organizational Unit. The enterprise is defined by an organizational hierarchy. Below the enterprise top level in the hierarchy is the organizational unit level. Each organizational units usually correspond with a high-level enterprise capability. What is the name of the organizational unit?

Value Stream Name. For any given organizational unit, there are services and processes (from inputs to output and points in between) that provide value to the unit's clients—this is the value stream.

Value Statement. The value statement describes the value stream and each of its services and processes.

Core Services. In relation to the value steam, there are

services of primary importance delivering direct value to the client—these are the core services. List these core services.

Upstream Organizational Unit and Services. Value streams almost always run between organizational boundaries. In terms of inputs, list upstream organizational units and services.

Downstream Organizational Unit and Services. Value streams almost never begin and end inside an organizational unit's boundaries. In terms of outputs, list downstream organizational units and services dependent on the value stream.

Suppliers and Inputs. List the suppliers and inputs of the value stream.

Clients and Outputs. List the clients and outputs of the value stream.

Chapter 076

Critical Services Catalog

The Critical Services Catalog is the enterprise's authoritative and complete listing of critical services—critical services as defined by enterprise business architecture and the enterprise's business continuity plan.

The catalog provides a way to search, filter, query, investigate relationships, analyze, and report on critical services.

The following elements are included in the Critical Services Catalog:

- Service
- Critical Service Ranking

Service. A service may refer to a business service or a technological service. A business services is a collection of business processes that, together, deliver a particular service. A technological service is one or more technologies that integrate and interoperate in order to perform a particular service—sometimes serving multiple components (as in service oriented architectures)—usually exposed to the enterprise via an API or UDDI interface. What is the name of the service?

Critical Service Ranking. Critical services are ranked according to their criticality, with the most critical services being ranked higher than other critical services. What is this service's critical service ranking?

Chapter 077

Organization Structure Catalog

The Organization Structure Catalog is the enterprise's authoritative and complete listing of the organizational units that make up the enterprise. This catalog decomposes the enterprise's internal organization structure, which is depicted in the 'Organizational Model'. The catalog provides a way to search, filter, query, investigate relationships, analyze, and report on enterprise structure data.

The following elements are included in the Organization Structure Catalog:

- Organizational Unit
- Organization Description
- Organization Abbreviation

Organizational Unit. The enterprise is defined by an organizational hierarchy. Below the enterprise top level in the hierarchy is the organizational unit level. Each organizational units usually correspond with a high-level enterprise capability. What is the name of the organizational unit?

Organization Description. A statement describing the essential nature and characteristics of the organizational unit.

Organization Abbreviation. What is the standard abbreviation for the organizational unit?

Chapter 078

Principles Catalog

The Principles Catalog is the enterprise's authoritative and complete listing of enterprise architecture principles. Principles are included from all domains of enterprise architecture, including: business, data, applications, technology, and security. The catalog provides a way to search, filter, query, investigate relationships, analyze, and report on enterprise architecture principles.

The following elements are included in the Principles Catalog:

- Principle Category
- Principle
- Statement (Description of Principle)
- Rationale
- Implications

Principle Category. Principles can be categorized. Enterprise architecture groups often use the following categories to organize their principles: business principles, data principles, application principles, technology principles, and security principles. What is the category?

Principle. A principle is a basic underlying assumption used to guide and govern decision-making. What is the name of this principle?

Statement (Description of Principle). The statement describes the essential nature and characteristics of the principle. Describe the principle.

Rationale. A rationale is an underlying reason for something. What is the rationale—the underlying reason—for this principle? What is the justification for the principle?

Implications. What are the wider implications of this

principle? What are the consequences of applying this principle to the various areas of enterprise endeavour?

Chapter 079

Event Catalog

The Event Catalog is the enterprise's authoritative and complete listing of important events in the life of the enterprise. The event catalog serves as the event repository from which enterprise calendars/event schedules are constructed. The catalog provides a way to search, filter, query, investigate relationships, prioritize, analyze, and report on enterprise events.

The following elements are included in the Event Catalog:

- Organizational Unit
- Event name
- Event Description
- Event Date
- Event Frequency

Organizational Unit. The enterprise is defined by an organizational hierarchy. Below the enterprise top level in the hierarchy is the organizational unit level. Each organizational units usually correspond with a high-level enterprise capability. What is the name of the organizational unit?

Event Name. An event is any important incident in the life of the enterprise. The event may occur just once or on a reoccurring basis. What is the name of this event?

Event Description. The event description is a statement describing the essential nature and characteristics of the event.

Event Date. What date or series of dates are associated with this event?

Event Frequency. Is this event a one-off or does it re-occur? If it is a reoccurring event, what is its frequency?

CHAPTER 080

Governance Catalog

The Governance Catalog is the enterprise's authoritative and complete listing of the governance elements—the legislation, regulation, policies, contracts, and authoritative groups/bodies—that impact each of the enterprise's organizational units and business services. The catalog provides a way to search, filter, query, investigate relationships, analyze, and report on the elements of the governance landscape.

The following elements are included in the Governance Catalog:

- Organizational Unit
- Business Function
- Business Service
- Business Service Description
- Legislation
- Regulation
- Policy
- Contract
- Authoritative Groups/Bodies

Organizational Unit. The enterprise is defined by an organizational hierarchy. Below the enterprise top level in the hierarchy is the organizational unit level. Each organizational units usually correspond with a high-level enterprise capability. What is the name of the organizational unit?

Business Function. A business function is a collection of business activities and services, usually organized as a sub-unit of an organizational unit. What is the name of the business function?

Business Service. A business services is a collection of

business processes that, together, deliver a particular service. What is the name of the business service?

Business Service Description. This element is a statement that describes the essential nature of the business service.

Legislation. Legislation refers to the laws that govern the operations of the organizational unit's business services. List all relevant legislation.

Regulation. A regulation is a governmental interpretation of legislation—it usually clarifies the meaning of legislation. List the regulations that apply to the operations of the organizational unit's business service.

Policy. Policies are formal organizational rules used to: mandate quality requirements, delineate roles and responsibilities, show where decision-making authority lies, support consistent and efficient decision-making, promote or discourage certain organizational behaviours, articulate performance goals for people and technology, and set out critical operational rules around each of the enterprise's key functions. What polices guide and govern the organizational unit's business service?

Contract. Business services are designed to meet performance targets. Contracts are an agreement between two or more parties which set out agreed upon performance requirements for the service. What contracts govern the organizational unit's business service?

Authoritative Group/Bodies. An organizational unit or business service and their operation are often governed by an authoritative group or body which provides approvals or general oversight. What authoritative group or body provides approvals or general oversight to the organizational unit's business service?

Chapter 081

Location Catalog

The Location Catalog is the enterprise's authoritative and complete listing of the locations from which the enterprise conducts business. The catalog provides a way to search, filter, query, investigate relationships, analyze, and report on the enterprise's various locations.

The following elements are included in the Location Catalog:

- Organizational Unit
- Location

Organizational Unit. The enterprise is defined by an organizational hierarchy. Below the enterprise top level in the hierarchy is the organizational unit level. Each organizational units usually correspond with a high-level enterprise capability. What is the name of the organizational unit?

Location. What is the name of the physical location where the organization does business?

The Location Catalog may be elaborated upon by adding specific information associated with each location, information such as, but not limited to: business functions, business services, technology, people or positions at location, location contact information, location address, related geographic locations, location GPS coordinates, and location emergency information.

Chapter 082

Process Catalog

The Process Catalog is the enterprise's authoritative and complete listing of the processes that make up the enterprise's various business services. The catalog also decomposes each process into its constituent resources: people, technology, information, location, and inputs/supplies. The catalog provides a way to search, filter, query, investigate relationships, analyze, and report on the enterprise's various processes.

The following elements are included in the Process Catalog:

- Business service
- Process Name
- Process Description
- Resources — People
- Resources — Technology
- Resources — Location
- Resources — Information
- Resources — Supplies/Inputs

Business Service. A business services is a collection of business processes that, together, deliver a particular service. What is the name of the business service?

Process Name. A process is a series of actions and tasks. What's he name of this process?

Process Description. Describe the essential nature of the process.

Resources — People. What roles and what people are key resources for the process?

Resources — Technology. What are the key applications/systems, technological components, and infrastructure components for the process? What are the key dependencies for these IT resources?

Resources — Location. What are the key locations for the process?

Resources — Information. What is the key information for the process?

Resources — Supplies/Inputs. What are the key supplies/inputs for the process?

Chapter 083

Role Catalog

The Role Catalog is the enterprise's authoritative and complete listing of the roles performed in accordance with the enterprise's business functions and services and the actors (people and systems) that perform those roles. The catalog provides a way to search, filter, query, investigate relationships, analyze, and report on the enterprise's various roles and actors and associated organizational units and business functions and services.

The following elements are included in the Role Catalog:

- Organizational Unit
- Business Function
- Business Service
- Role
- Actor
- Actor Type

Organizational Unit. The enterprise is defined by an organizational hierarchy. Below the enterprise top level in the hierarchy is the organizational unit level. Each organizational units usually correspond with a high-level enterprise capability. What is the name of the organizational unit?

Business Function. A business function is a collection of business activities and services, usually organized as a sub-unit of an organizational unit. What is the name of the business function?

Business Service. A business services is a collection of business processes that, together, deliver a particular service. What is the name of the business service?

Role. A role is a position with the organization that fulfills a particular responsibility or function. What is the role?

Actor. An actor is a person, organization or application, system, or service that performs a particular role within the enterprise. An actor may be internal or external to the enterprise. Who is the actor?

Actor Type. What type of actor performs this role? A person, application/system, service, other?

Chapter 084

Prioritization Catalog

The Prioritization Catalog is the enterprise's authoritative and complete prioritized listing of scheduled enterprise activity, including project and program activity. When enterprise resource requirements need to be understood, interrelated, and aligned with priorities, the prioritization catalog is the enterprise's first stop.

The catalog provides a way to search, filter, query, investigate relationships, analyze, and report on prioritization data.

The following elements are included in the Prioritization Catalog:

- Activity Name
- Activity Description
- Priority Level
- Priority Ranking

Activity Name. An activity is any course of action taken by the enterprise. An activity may be a project or a program. An activity may be a course of action taken in relation to IT projects and programs. What is the name of this activity?

Activity Description. Describe the essential nature of the activity.

Priority Level. How has the enterprise prioritized the activity? Is it a high, medium, or low level activity?

Priority Ranking. Activities are assigned resource priority based on their importance. What is the priority ranking

Chapter 085

Lessons Learned Catalog

The Lessons Learned Catalog is the enterprise's authoritative and complete listing of lessons learned. Its purpose is to promote learning and sharing among enterprise staff and, by doing this, help the enterprise increase the efficiency of its decision-making and solution development. The catalog provides a way to search, filter, query, investigate relationships, analyze, and report on lessons learned across the entire enterprise.

When post-project evaluations are conducted, the process should result in a formal list of 'lessons learned' which is posted to the lessons learned catalog. Note, it is important to conduct post-mortems on all closing projects, for not all successful projects are all successful and not all failed projects are all bad. There are positive and negatives to all projects and learning about them can only help future enterprise endeavour.

The following elements are included in the Lessons Learned Catalog:

- Lesson Date
- Submitting Organization
- Lesson Title
- Lesson Summary
- Description of Driving Event
- Lessons Learned (list)
- Recommendations (list)
- Related Documents

Lesson Date. When was this lesson learned entered into the catalog?

Submitting Organization. Which organizational unit submitted these lessons learned?

Lesson Title. What is the title of this lesson learned?

Lesson Summary. Briefly describe the lessons learned.

Description of Driving Event. Describe the activity or situation that led to the identification of these lessons learned.

Lessons Learned. Lessons learned are units of enterprise knowledge identified by a formal evaluation process applied to completed units of work. List the lessons learned.

Recommendations. When lessons learned identify things the enterprise could improve, what action is recommended?

Related Documents. What documents are related to the lessons learned? These may be documents that provide more information on the submitting organization, the driving event, or the lessons learned and recommendations.

Chapter 086

IT Terms Catalog

The IT Terms Catalog is the enterprise's authoritative and complete listing of information technology terms—especially the terms of enterprise architecture. The purpose of the catalog is to facilitate clear communication and understanding across the enterprise's disparate business units and among old staff and newcomers to the enterprise. The catalog provides a way to search, filter, query, investigate relationships, analyze, and report on the technical language used by the enterprise.

The following elements are included in the IT Terms Catalog:

- IT Term
- Definition
- Acronym
- Reference
- Synonym

IT Term. An IT term is a word or phrase that identifies something pertaining to information technology or information management. What is the IT term in question?

Definition. What is the definition of the IT term?

Acronym. What is the acronym for the IT term?

Reference. Where did the IT term and definition come from?

Synonym. What other terms mean the same as this IT term?

Chapter 087

Application/System Catalog

The Application/System Catalog is the enterprise's authoritative and complete listing of the enterprise's conceptual, logical, and physical applications/systems. This catalog draws on data from the current, future, roadmap, and interim state blueprints and plans, and from operational lists.

The catalog provides a way to search, filter, query, investigate relationships, analyze, and report on the enterprise's various applications/systems.

The following elements are included in the Application/System Catalog:

- State
- Application Category
- Application Name
- Description

State. For enterprise architects there are three main states for applications: conceptual, logical, and physical. What is the state?

Application Category. Applications serve may purposes in the enterprise and, therefore, can be categorized in many different ways. The big picture question: What is the categorization system of most use to the enterprise? The question specific to this catalog element: What is the application category?

Application Name. What is the name of the application?

Description. Describe the purpose of the application.

Chapter 088

Data Component Catalog

The Data Component Catalog is the enterprise's authoritative and complete listing of the enterprise's conceptual, logical, and physical date components. The catalog provides a way to search, filter, query, investigate relationships, analyze, and report on the enterprise's various date components.

The following elements are included in the Data Component Catalog:

- State
- Data Category
- Data Component Name
- Description

State. For enterprise architects there are three main states for date components: conceptual, logical, and physical. What is the state?

Data Category. Date components are containers for computerized information. Date components serve may purposes in the enterprise and, therefore, can be categorized in many different ways and for many different purposes. The big picture question: What is the categorization system of most use to the enterprise? The question specific to this catalog element: What is the data category?

Data Component Name. What is the name of the data component?

Description. Describe the purpose of the data component?

Chapter 089

Technology Catalog

The Technology Catalog is the enterprise's authoritative and complete listing of the conceptual, logical and physical technology components that make up the enterprise. This catalogs includes infrastructure and security components. The catalog provides a way to search, filter, query, investigate relationships, analyze, and report on the enterprise's various technology components.

The following elements are included in the Technology Catalog:

- State
- Technology Category
- Technology Component Name
- Description

State. For enterprise architects there are three main states for technological components: conceptual, logical, and physical. What is the state?

Technology Category. Technological components serve may purposes in the enterprise and, therefore, can be categorized in many different ways and for many different purposes. The big picture question: What is the categorization system of most use to the enterprise? The question specific to this catalog element: What is the technology category?

Technology Component Name. What is the name of the technology component?

Description. Describe the purpose of the technology component?

Chapter 090

Business Profile Catalog

The Business Profile Catalog is comprised of data from business profile documents. Business profile documents collect data specific to organizational units. Data from business profile documents—or the business profile catalog—can be used to build the strategic heat thinking map model. Information from the business profile catalog can be used to populate other catalogs. The catalog provides a way to quickly locate business profile information collected on various organizational units.

The following elements are included in the Business Profile Catalog:

- Organizational Unit
- Document Name
- Document Title
- Document Date

Organizational Unit. The enterprise is defined by an organizational hierarchy. Below the enterprise top level in the hierarchy is the organizational unit level. Each organizational units usually correspond with a high-level enterprise capability. What is the name of the organizational unit?

Document Name. Where on the on the enterprise's file system is the file with the strategic heat thinking map model (e.g.: c:\busprofiles\example1.doc)? Where is the document stored and what is the file name?

Document Title. What is the title of the strategic heat thinking map model? This title will usually include the name of the organizational unit.

Document Date. What is the date the strategic heat thinking map model was completed?

Chapter 091

Business Standards Catalog

The Business Standards Catalog is the enterprise's authoritative and complete listing of business standards. The catalog provides a way to search, filter, query, investigate relationships, analyze, and report on business standards.

The following elements are included in the Business Standards Catalog:

- Standard Name
- Standard Description
- Status
- Effective Date

Standard. A standard is a rule, guideline, specification or identified level of quality or performance to which the enterprise is expected to conform. What is the name of this business standard?

Description. Clearly describe the essential nature of the standard.

Status. What is the status of the standards: sunrise, core, sunset, rejected, or retired?

Effective Date. On what date was this standards accepted for use in the enterprise?

Chapter 092

Architecture Decisions Catalog

The Architecture Decisions Catalog is the enterprise's authoritative and complete listing of architecture decision items, including architecture waivers. The catalog provides a way to search, filter, query, investigate relationships, analyze, and report on architecture decision items.

The following elements are included in the Architecture Decisions Catalog:

- Issue
- Issue Description
- Related Organizational Unit
- Project Name
- Date
- Architecture Decision

Issue. What name as been given to this issue or problem?

Issue Description. Describe important characteristics of the issue or problem.

Related Organizational Unit. What is the name of the organizational unit related to this issue?

Project Name. What is the name of the related project?

Date. On what date was this issue added to the catalog?

Architecture Decision. What decision did the enterprise architectures make in regards to this issue?

Chapter 093

Policy Catalog

The Policy Catalog is the enterprise's authoritative and complete listing of enterprise architecture policy, not just business architecture policy. The catalog provides a way to search, filter, query, investigate relationships, analyze, and report on the enterprise architecture team's collection of policies.

The following elements are included in the Policy Catalog:

- Policy Name
- Policy Description
- Policy Document

Policy Name. Policies are formal organizational rules used to mandate quality requirements, delineate roles and responsibilities, show where decision-making authority lies, to support consistent and efficient decision-making, to promote or discourage certain organizational behaviours, to articulate performance goals for people and technology, and to set out critical operational rules around each of the enterprise's key functions. What is the policy's name?

Policy Description. Clearly describe the essential nature of the policy.

Policy Document. Policies are documents stored on the enterprise's file system (e.g.: c:\policies\example1.doc). Where is the policy document stored and what is its name?

Chapter 094

Threat Catalog

The Threat Catalog is the enterprise's authoritative and complete listing of the threats faced by the enterprise. The catalog provides a way to search, filter, query, investigate relationships, prioritize, rank, analyze, and report on these threats.

The following elements are included in the Threat Catalog:

- Threat Category
- Threat Name
- Likelihood/Probability
- Impact — Health & Safety
- Impact — Assets
- Impact — Critical Service Delivery
- Threat Ranking

Threat Category. Threats can be categorized in many ways. What is the best way for the enterprise to categorize the threats it faces. The specific question this element asks: What is this threat's category?

Threat Name. A threat is something that disrupts the operations of the enterprise. Tornados, pandemics, earthquakes, strikes, and riots are all potential threats. What is the name of the threat?

Likelihood/Probability. What is the likelihood/probability of the threat disrupting enterprise operations?

Impact — Health & Safety. Should this threat occur, what will its impact be on the health and safety of staff, clients, and stakeholders? In one day? In two days? In one week? In two weeks? In greater than two weeks?

Impact — Assets. Should this threat occur, what will the impact of the disruption be on enterprise assets (IT assets, buildings, etc)? In one day? In two days? In one week? In two weeks? In greater than two weeks?

Impact — Critical Service Delivery. Should this threat occur, what will the impact of the disruption be on the enterprise's ability to provide critical services? In one day? In two days? In one week? In two weeks? In greater than two weeks?

Threat Ranking. Each threat is ranked according to the severity of its impact on health and safety, assets, and critical services of the enterprise. What is the threat ranking?

Chapter 095

Consultation Log

The Consultation Log is the enterprise's authoritative and complete listing of the consultations and interactions of the business architect and all other groups in the enterprise.

The business architect spends a lot of time socializing new IT ideas, new business ideas, and change initiatives. This activity requires structured and sustained communication and interaction with senior leaders, strategic planners, program-project-change managers, operational managers, and other architects and IT professionals. To prevent unnecessary overlap or duplication of effort, it is important for the enterprise business architect to record who was consulted, on what, and when.

The Consultation Log is a catalog that provides a way to search, filter, investigate relationships, analyze, and report on consultation data.

The following elements are included in the Consultation Log:

- Meeting Date
- Subject Name
- Subject Description
- Audience Organization
- Audience (Who was there?)
- Number of Persons
- Notes

Meeting Date. On what date did the consultation take place?

Subject Name. What was the subject of the consultation?

Subject Description. Describe the meeting subject in detail.

Audience Organization. What organization does the

audience belong to, if any?

Audience. List who attended this consultation.

Number of Persons. How many people were at the consultation?

Notes. Is there anything pertinent to the consultation that needs to be recorded?

Chapter 096

Enterprise Business Architecture Asset Catalog

The Enterprise Business Architecture Asset Catalog is where the enterprise business architect stores and manages enterprise business architecture assets—including, but not limited to models, catalogs, interactions, program and project artifacts, strategic planning artifacts, engagement artifacts, governance artifacts, evaluation artifacts, and related EA program documentation.

The assets in this catalog define and clarify business strategy, IT strategy, tactical plans, guidance activity and tools, governance activity and tools, evaluation activity and tools, and help bring definition and clarity to the enterprise's key business functions, services, and processes.

These assets form part of the enterprise reference architecture, which allows the enterprise to pro-actively manage business change, technological change, and increasing complexity, and, ultimately, control costs and increase organizational agility.

These assets are important components of baseline architectures, target architectures, and the roadmaps that guide enterprise change from the baseline to the target architecture.

This catalog provides a way to search, filter, query, investigate relationships, analyze, and report on enterprise business architecture assets.

The following elements are included in the Consultation Log:

- Asset Name
- Asset Type

- Asset Description
- Asset Status
- Asset Date

Asset Name. What is the name of the asset?

Asset Type. A system may be used to classify the artifacts. What type of asset is the asset?

Asset Description. Clearly describe the essential nature of this asset.

Asset Status. What is the status of the asset: sunrise, core, sunset, rejected, or retired?

Asset Date. When was this asset created?

PART 4

INTERACTIONS

Chapter 097

Strategic Context Interaction

Strategic context interactions describe the relationship between one or more of the elements from the strategic context catalog—organizational unit, vision, drivers, goals, objectives, measures—and other catalogs and the elements that they contain.

The key Strategic Context Interactions are:

- Strategic Context - Application/System Interaction
- Strategic Context - Architecture Decisions Interaction
- Strategic Context - Business Alignment Interaction
- Strategic Context - Business Profile Interaction
- Strategic Context - Business Services Interaction
- Strategic Context - Business Standards Interaction
- Strategic Context - Consultation Interaction
- Strategic Context - Data Component Interaction
- Strategic Context - Governance Interaction
- Strategic Context - Lessons Learned Interaction
- Strategic Context - Location Interaction
- Strategic Context - Organization Structure Interaction
- Strategic Context - Policy Interaction
- Strategic Context - Prioritization Interaction
- Strategic Context - Process Interaction
- Strategic Context - Stakeholder Interaction
- Strategic Context - Technology Interaction
- Strategic Context - Value Stream Interaction

Example Interaction: Strategic Context - Business Services Interaction.

There are several elements to each of these source catalogs and, so, many possible ways to map this interaction. In this example, the interaction identifies which goals are supported by which business services.

The process for creating this interaction table involved selecting the element 'goal' from the Strategic Context Catalog and the element 'business service' from the Business Services Catalog. This selection process is depicted in the following diagram.

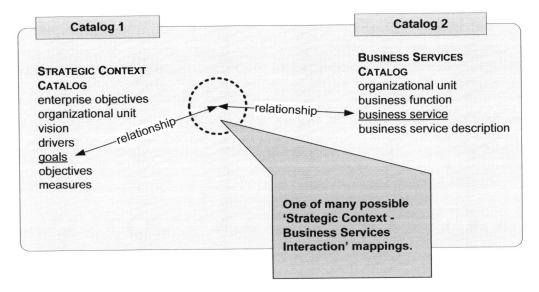

The resulting interaction table looks like this:

Interaction	Business Service			
Strategic Context	Service 1	Service 2	Service 3	Service N
Goal 1	X	X	X	X
Goal 2			X	
Goal 3	X	X	X	X
Goal N				X

Chapter 098

Business Alignment Interaction

Business alignment interactions describe the relationship between one or more of the elements from the business alignment catalog—enterprise goal, enterprise objectives, aligned capabilities, responsible organizational unit, aligned business functions, aligned business services, aligned tactical plans, aligned strategic plans, aligned tactical plans, aligned applications, aligned data component, aligned technology component, aligned infrastructure component—and other catalogs and the elements that they contain.

The key Business Alignment Interactions are:

- Business Alignment - Application/System Interaction
- Business Alignment - Architecture Decisions Interaction
- Business Alignment - Business Profile Interaction
- Business Alignment - Business Services Interaction
- Business Alignment - Business Standards Interaction
- Business Alignment - Consultation Interaction
- Business Alignment - Data Component Interaction
- Business Alignment - Event Interaction
- Business Alignment - Governance Interaction
- Business Alignment - Lessons Learned Interaction
- Business Alignment - Location Interaction
- Business Alignment - Organization Structure Interaction
- Business Alignment - Performance Interaction
- Business Alignment - Policy Interaction
- Business Alignment - Prioritization Interaction
- Business Alignment - Process Interaction

- Business Alignment - Stakeholder Interaction
- Business Alignment - Strategic Context Interaction
- Business Alignment - Technology Interaction
- Business Alignment - Value Stream Interaction

Example Interaction: Strategic Context – Stakeholder Interaction.

There are several elements to each source catalog and, so, many possible ways to map this interaction. In this example, the interaction reveals the relationship between enterprise goals and the technology component supporting that goal and the relationship between the goals/technology and the stakeholder groups impacted by them.

The process for creating the example interaction table involved selecting the elements 'goal' and 'aligned technology component' from the Business Alignment Catalog and the element 'stakeholder type' (a synonym for 'stakeholder group') from the Stakeholder Catalog. This selection process is depicted in the following diagram.

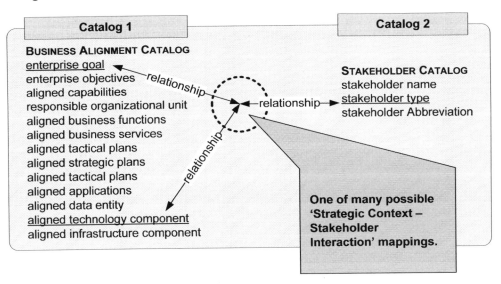

The resulting interaction table looks like this:

Interaction	Stakeholder			
Business Alignment	Stakeholder Group 1	Stakeholder Group 2	Stakeholder Group 3	Stakeholder Group N
Goal 1 and Technology Component 1	X	X	X	X
Goal 2 and Technology Component 2			X	
Goal 3 and Technology Component 3	X	X	X	X
Goal N and Technology Component N				X

CHAPTER 099

Performance Interaction

Performance interactions describe the relationship between one or more of the elements from the performance catalog—service, service contract, performance measure name, performance measure type, performance measure description—and other catalogs and the elements that they contain.

The key Performance Interactions are:

- Performance - Application/System Interaction
- Performance - Architecture Decisions Interaction
- Performance - Business Alignment Interaction
- Performance - Business Profile Interaction
- Performance - Business Services Interaction
- Performance - Business Standards Interaction
- Performance - Consultation Interaction
- Performance - Critical Services Interaction
- Performance - Data Component Interaction
- Performance - Event Interaction
- Performance - Governance Interaction
- Performance - Lessons Learned Interaction
- Performance - Location Interaction
- Performance - Organization Structure Interaction
- Performance - Policy Interaction
- Performance - Prioritization Interaction
- Performance - Process Interaction
- Performance - Technology Interaction
- Performance - Value Stream Interaction

Example Interaction: Performance - Application/System

Interaction.

There are several elements to each of these source catalogs and, therefore, many possible ways to map this interaction. In this example, the interaction maps the relationship between applications and the measures used to evaluate application performance.

The process for creating the interaction table involved selecting the element 'performance measure name' from the Performance Catalog and the element 'application name' from the Application/System Catalog. This selection process is depicted in the following diagram.

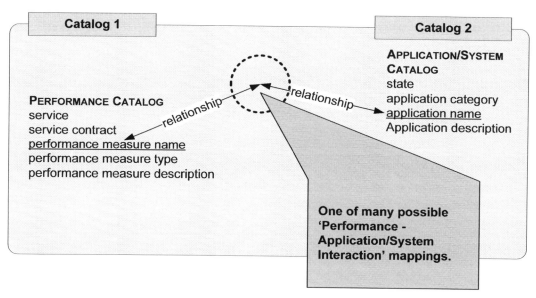

The resulting interaction table looks like this:

Interaction	Applications			
Performance	App 1	App 2	App 3	App N
Measure 1	X	X	X	X
Measure 2			X	
Measure 3	X	X	X	X
Measure N				X

Chapter 100

Stakeholder Interaction

Stakeholder interactions describe the relationship between one or more of the elements from the stakeholder catalog—stakeholder name, stakeholder type, stakeholder abbreviation—and other catalogs and the elements that they contain.

The key Stakeholder Interactions are:

- Stakeholder - Application/System Interaction
- Stakeholder - Architecture Decisions Interaction
- Stakeholder - Business Alignment Interaction
- Stakeholder - Business Issues Interaction
- Stakeholder - Business Profile Interaction
- Stakeholder - Business Services Interaction
- Stakeholder - Business Standards Interaction
- Stakeholder - Consultation Interaction
- Stakeholder - Critical Services Interaction
- Stakeholder - Data Component Interaction
- Stakeholder - Governance Interaction
- Stakeholder - Lessons Learned Interaction
- Stakeholder - Location Interaction
- Stakeholder - Organization Structure Interaction
- Stakeholder - Policy Interaction
- Stakeholder - Prioritization Interaction
- Stakeholder - Process Interaction
- Stakeholder - Strategic Context Interaction
- Stakeholder - Technology Interaction
- Stakeholder - Value Stream Interaction

Example Interaction: Stakeholder - Technology Interaction.

There are several elements to each of the source catalogs and, so, many possible ways to map this interaction. In this example, the interaction maps the relationship between stakeholders and technology components.

The process for creating this interaction table involved selecting the element 'stakeholder name' from the Stakeholder Catalog and the element 'technology name' from the Technology Catalog. This selection process is depicted in the following diagram.

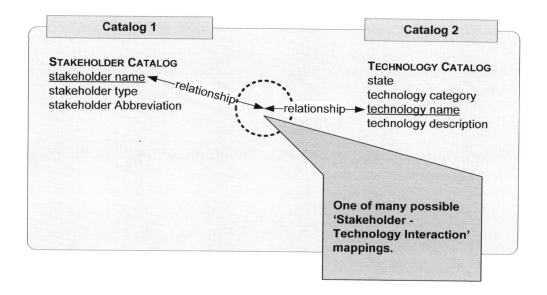

The resulting interaction table looks like this:

Interaction	Technology			
Stakeholder	Component 1	Component 2	Component 3	Component N
Stakeholder 1	X	X	X	X
Stakeholder 2			X	
Stakeholder 3	X	X	X	X
Stakeholder N				X

Chapter 101

Business Issues Interaction

Business issues interactions describe the relationship between one or more of the elements from the business issues catalog—issue name, issue description, organizational unit, acuity, status—and other catalogs and the elements that they contain.

The key Business Issue Interactions are:

- Business Issues - Architecture Decisions Interaction
- Business Issues - Consultation Interaction
- Business Issues - Stakeholder Interaction
- Business Issues - Lessons Learned Interaction
- Business Issues - Value Stream Interaction

Example Interaction: Business Issues – Value Stream Interaction.

There are several elements to each of these source catalogs and, therefore, many possible ways to map this interaction.

In this example, the interaction maps the relationship between business issues and value streams.

This particular example interaction reveals where there are issues or problems in each value stream.

In reading the example interaction, the frequency with which the problem repeats in multiple value streams points towards the scope of the problem and is one factor in judging the acuity of the problem.

The interaction can also be considered one possible way to measure the relative health of the enterprise's various value streams. Creating the

Business Issues – Value Stream Interaction is a good way to take the figurative temperature of the enterprise.

The process for creating this interaction table involved selecting the element 'issue name' from the Business Issues Catalog and the element 'value stream name' from the Value Stream Catalog. This selection process is depicted in the following diagram.

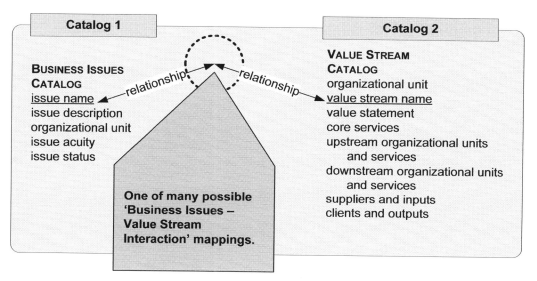

The resulting interaction table looks like this:

Interaction	Value Streams			
Business Issues	VS 1	VS 2	VS 3	VS N
Issue 1	X	X	X	X
Issue 2			X	
Issue 3	X	X	X	X
Issue N				X

Chapter 102

Business Services Interaction

Business service interactions describe the relationship between one or more of the elements from the business services catalog—organizational unit, business function, business service business service description—and other catalogs and the elements that they contain.

The key Business Services Interactions are:

- Business Services - Application/System Interaction
- Business Services - Business Alignment Interaction
- Business Services - Business Services Interaction
- Business Services - Consultation Interaction
- Business Services - Critical Services Interaction
- Business Services - Data Component Interaction
- Business Services - Event Interaction
- Business Services - Governance Interaction
- Business Services - Lessons Learned Interaction
- Business Services - Location Interaction
- Business Services - Organization Structure Interaction
- Business Services - Performance Interaction
- Business Services - Process Interaction
- Business Services - Role Interaction
- Business Services - Stakeholder Interaction
- Business Services - Strategic Context Interaction
- Business Services - Technology Interaction
- Business Services - Value Stream Interaction

Example Interaction: Business Services - Business Services Interaction.

There are several elements to each of these source catalogs and, so, many possible ways to map this interaction. In this example, the interaction maps the relationship between different business services.

The process for creating this interaction table involved selecting the element 'business' from the Business Service Catalog and using this element for both the catalog one element and the catalog two element.

This selection process is illustrated in the following diagram.

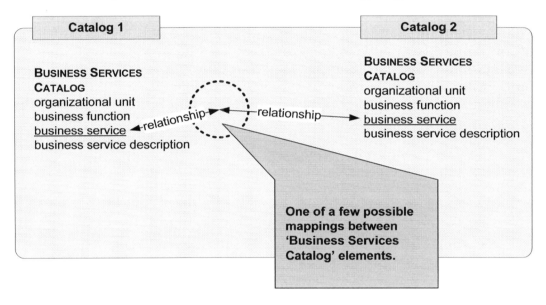

The resulting interaction table looks like this:

Interaction	Business Services			
Business Services	Service 1	Service 2	Service 3	Service N
Service 1	X	X	X	X
Service 2			X	
Service 3	X	X	X	X
Service N				X

Chapter 103

Value Stream Interaction

Value stream interactions describe the relationship between one or more of the elements from the value stream catalog—organizational unit, value stream name, value statement, core services, upstream organizational units and services, downstream organizational units and services, suppliers and inputs, clients and outputs—and other catalogs and the elements that they contain.

The key Value Stream Interactions are:

- Value Stream - Application/System Interaction
- Value Stream - Business Alignment Interaction
- Value Stream - Business Issues Interaction
- Value Stream - Business Profile Interaction
- Value Stream - Business Services Interaction
- Value Stream - Consultation Interaction
- Value Stream - Critical Services Interaction
- Value Stream - Data Component Interaction
- Value Stream - Event Interaction
- Value Stream - Lessons Learned Interaction
- Value Stream - Location Interaction
- Value Stream - Organization Structure Interaction
- Value Stream - Performance Interaction
- Value Stream - Prioritization Interaction
- Value Stream - Process Interaction
- Value Stream - Role Interaction
- Value Stream - Stakeholder Interaction
- Value Stream - Strategic Context Interaction
- Value Stream - Technology Interaction
- Value Stream - Value Stream Interaction

Example Interaction: Value Stream - Organization Structure Interaction.

There are several elements to each of these source catalogs and, so, many possible ways to map this interaction. In this example, the interaction maps the relationship between value streams and related organizational units.

The process for creating this interaction table involved selecting the element 'value stream name' from the Value Stream Catalog and the element 'organizational unit name' from the Organizational Structure Catalog.

This selection process is illustrated in the following diagram.

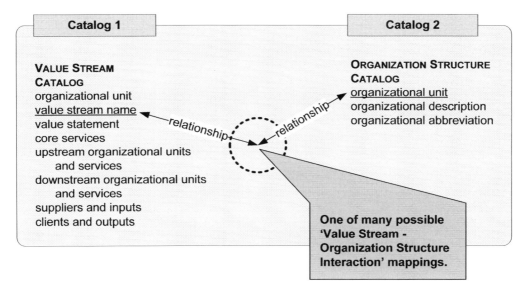

The resulting interaction table looks like this:

Interaction	Organizational Structure			
Value Stream	Unit 1	Unit 2	Unit 3	Unit N
VS 1	X	X	X	X
VS 2			X	
VS 3	X	X	X	X
VS N				X

Chapter 104

Critical Services Interaction

Critical services interactions describe the relationship between one or more of the elements from the critical services catalog—service, critical service ranking—and other catalogs and the elements that they contain.

The Critical Services Interactions are:

- Critical Services - Application/System Interaction
- Critical Services - Architecture Decisions Interaction
- Critical Services - Business Profile Interaction
- Critical Services - Business Services Interaction
- Critical Services - Business Standards Interaction
- Critical Services - Consultation Interaction
- Critical Services - Data Component Interaction
- Critical Services - Governance Interaction
- Critical Services - Lessons Learned Interaction
- Critical Services - Location Interaction
- Critical Services - Organization Structure Interaction
- Critical Services - Performance Interaction
- Critical Services - Policy Interaction
- Critical Services - Prioritization Interaction
- Critical Services - Process Interaction
- Critical Services - Role Interaction
- Critical Services - Stakeholder Interaction
- Critical Services - Technology Interaction
- Critical Services - Threat Interaction
- Critical Services - Value Stream Interaction

Example Interaction: Critical Services - Location Interaction.

There are several elements to each of these source catalogs and, so, many possible ways to map this interaction. In this example, the interaction maps the relationship between critical services and the locations from which the critical services are delivered.

The process for creating this interaction table involved selecting the element 'critical service name' from the Critical Services Catalog and the element 'location' from the Location Catalog.

This selection process is illustrated in the following diagram.

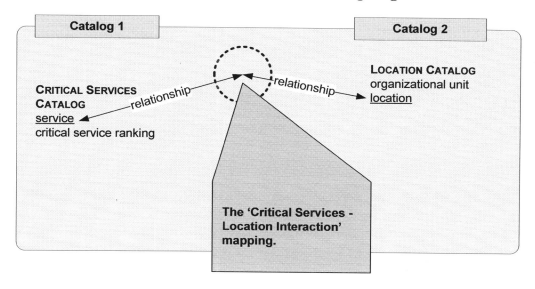

The resulting interaction table looks like this:

Interaction	Location			
Critical Services	Location 1	Location 2	Location 3	Location N
Critical Service 1	X	X	X	X
Critical Service 2			X	
Critical Service 3	X	X	X	X
Critical Service N				X

Chapter 105

Organization Structure Interaction

Organization structure interactions describe the relationship between one or more of the elements from the organization structure catalog—organizational unit, organizational description, organizational abbreviation—and other catalogs and the elements that they contain.

The key Organization Structure Interactions are:

- Organization Structure - Application/System Interaction
- Organization Structure - Business Alignment Interaction
- Organization Structure - Business Profile Interaction
- Organization Structure - Business Services Interaction
- Organization Structure - Consultation Interaction
- Organization Structure - Critical Services Interaction
- Organization Structure - Data Component Interaction
- Organization Structure - Event Interaction
- Organization Structure - Governance Interaction
- Organization Structure - Lessons Learned Interaction
- Organization Structure - Location Interaction
- Organization Structure - Performance Interaction
- Organization Structure - Prioritization Interaction
- Organization Structure - Process Interaction
- Organization Structure - Role Interaction
- Organization Structure - Stakeholder Interaction
- Organization Structure - Strategic Context Interaction
- Organization Structure - Technology Interaction
- Organization Structure - Value Stream Interaction

Example Interaction: Organization Structure - Data Component Interaction.

There are several elements to each of these source catalogs and, therefore, many possible ways to map this interaction. In this example, the interaction maps the relationship between organizational units and the physical databases that hold the organizational information.

The process for creating this interaction table involved selecting the element 'organizational unit' from the Organizational Structure Catalog and the composite element 'physical date components' (DB – databases) based the 'state' (physical) and 'data component name' elements from the Data Component Catalog.

This selection process is illustrated in the following diagram.

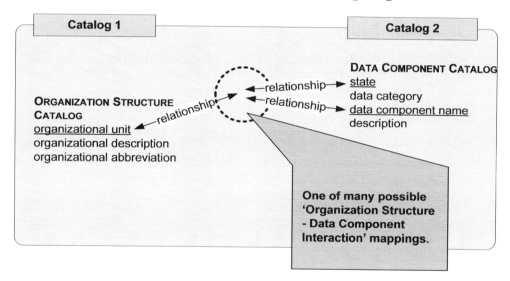

The resulting interaction table looks like this:

Interaction	Physical Date Components			
Organizational Structure	DB 1	DB 2	DB 3	DB N
Unit 1	X	X	X	X
Unit 2			X	
Unit 3	X	X	X	X
Unit N				X

Chapter 106

Principles Interaction

Principles interactions describe the relationship between one or more of the elements from the principles catalog—principle category, principle, statement (description of principle), rationale, implications—and other catalogs and the elements that they contain.

The key Principles Interactions are:

- Principles - Application/System Interaction
- Principles - Business Profile Interaction
- Principles - Consultation Interaction
- Principles - Data Component Interaction
- Principles - Lessons Learned Interaction
- Principles - Process Interaction
- Principles - Technology Interaction

Example Interaction: Principles - Consultation Interaction.

There are several elements the Principles Catalog and the Consultation Log and, so, many possible ways to map this interaction.

In this example, the interaction maps the relationship between principles and the consultations sessions during which the principles were presented to clients.

This sample interaction can serve as one measure of the velocity of education in the enterprise. When the principles are enterprise architecture principles, it can serve as one possible way to measure the effectiveness of the enterprise's enterprise architecture program.

The interaction can also serve as a map of the diffusion of principles and best practices in the enterprise.

The process for creating this interaction table involved selecting the element 'principle' from the Principles Catalog and the element 'meeting date' elements from the Consultation Log.

This selection process is illustrated in the following diagram.

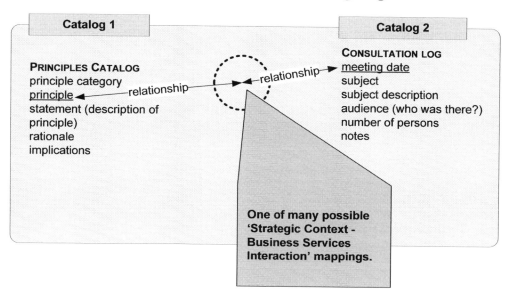

The resulting interaction table looks like this:

Interaction	Consultations			
Principles	Date 1	Date 2	Date 3	Date N
Business Architecture Principles	X	X	X	X
Data Management Principles			X	
Application Architecture Principles	X	X	X	X
Technology Architecture Principles				X

Chapter 107

Event Interaction

Event interactions describe the relationship between one or more of the elements from the event catalog—organizational unit, event name, event description, event date, event frequency—and other catalogs and the elements that they contain.

The key Event Interactions are:

- Event - Application/System Interaction
- Event - Business Alignment Interaction
- Event - Business Profile Interaction
- Event - Business Services Interaction
- Event - Consultation Interaction
- Event - Lessons Learned Interaction
- Event - Location Interaction
- Event - Organization Structure Interaction
- Event - Performance Interaction
- Event - Process Interaction
- Event - Role Interaction
- Event - Technology Interaction
- Event - Value Stream Interaction

Example Interaction: Event - Process Interaction.

There are several elements the Principles Catalog and the Consultation Log and, so, many possible ways to map this interaction. In this example, the interaction maps the relationship between an organization's events and processes.

The process for creating this interaction table involved selecting the elements 'organizational unit name' and 'event name' from the Event Catalog and the elements 'process name' and 'resources-information' from the Event Catalog.

This selection process is illustrated in the following diagram.

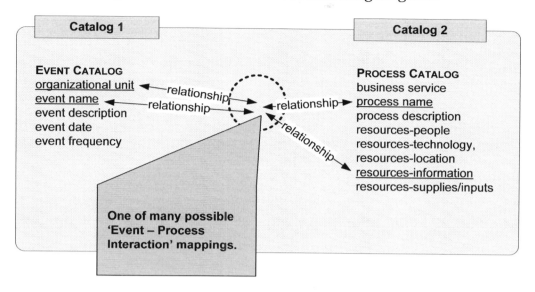

The resulting interaction table looks like this:

Interaction	Processes 1			
Organization Event	Resource Info 1	Resource Info 2	Resource Info 3	Resource Info N
Event 1	X	X	X	X
Event 2			X	
Event 3	X	X	X	X
Event N				X

Chapter 108

Governance Interaction

Governance interactions describe the relationship between one or more of the elements from the governance catalog—organizational unit, business function, business service, business service description, legislation, regulation, policy, contract, authoritative groups/bodies—and other catalogs and the elements that they contain.

The key Governance Interactions are:

- Governance - Application/System Interaction
- Governance - Architecture Decisions Interaction
- Governance - Business Alignment Interaction
- Governance - Business Profile Interaction
- Governance - Business Services Interaction
- Governance - Business Standards Interaction
- Governance - Consultation Interaction
- Governance - Critical Services Interaction
- Governance - Data Component Interaction
- Governance - Governance Interaction
- Governance - Lessons Learned Interaction
- Governance - Organization Structure Interaction
- Governance - Performance Interaction
- Governance - Policy Interaction
- Governance - Prioritization Interaction
- Governance - Process Interaction
- Governance - Stakeholder Interaction
- Governance - Strategic Context Interaction
- Governance - Technology Interaction

Example Interaction: Governance - Governance Interaction.

There are several elements to this source catalogs and, therefore, many possible ways to map interactions. In this example, the interaction maps the relationship between the two governance catalog elements (legislation and policy) and a third element (organizational unit name) from the catalog.

The process for creating this interaction table involved selecting the elements 'legislation' and 'policy' from the Governance Catalog and listing them down the first column of the table and the element 'organizational unit name' from the Governance Catalog, and listing it across a top row.

This selection process is illustrated in the following diagram.

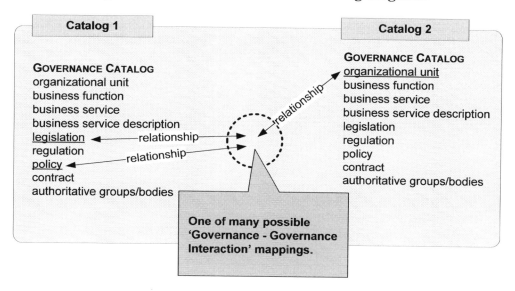

The resulting interaction table looks like this:

Interaction	Organizational Unit			
Governance	Unit 1	Unit 2	Unit 3	Unit N
Legislation 1	X	X	X	X
Legislation 2			X	
Policy 1	X	X	X	X
Policy 2				X

Chapter 109

Location Interaction

Location interactions describe the relationship between one of the two elements from the location catalog—organizational unit, location—and other catalogs and the elements that they contain.

The key Location Interactions are:

- Location - Application/System Interaction
- Location - Business Alignment Interaction
- Location - Business Profile Interaction
- Location - Business Services Interaction
- Location - Consultation Interaction
- Location - Critical Services Interaction
- Location - Data Component Interaction
- Location - Event Interaction
- Location - Lessons Learned Interaction
- Location - Organization Structure Interaction
- Location - Performance Interaction
- Location - Process Interaction
- Location - Role Interaction
- Location - Stakeholder Interaction
- Location - Strategic Context Interaction
- Location - Technology Interaction
- Location - Value Stream Interaction

Example Interaction: Location - Technology Interaction.

There are several elements the Location Catalog and the Technology Catalog and, so, many possible ways to map this interaction. In this example, the interaction maps the relationship between locations and technology components.

The process for creating this interaction table involved selecting the element 'location' from the Location Catalog and the element 'technology name' from the Technology Catalog.

This selection process is illustrated in the following diagram.

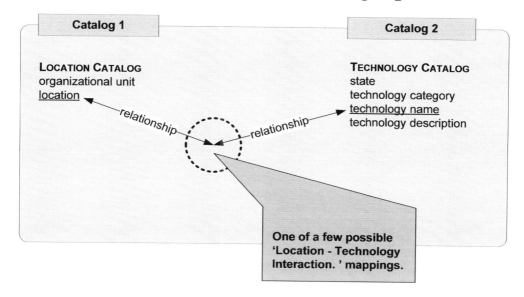

The resulting interaction table looks like this:

Interaction	Technology Component			
Location	Component 1	Component 2	Component 3	Component N
Location 1	X	X	X	X
Location 2			X	
Location 3	X	X	X	X
Location N				X

Chapter 110

Process Interaction

Process interactions describe the relationship between one or more of the elements from the process catalog—business service, process name, process description, resources-people, resources-technology, resources-location, resources-information, resources-supplies/inputs—and other catalogs and the elements that they contain.

The key Process Interactions are:

- Process - Application/System Interaction
- Process - Business Alignment Interaction
- Process - Business Profile Interaction
- Process - Business Services Interaction
- Process - Business Standards Interaction
- Process - Consultation Interaction
- Process - Critical Services Interaction
- Process - Data Component Interaction
- Process - Event Interaction
- Process - Governance Interaction
- Process - Lessons Learned Interaction
- Process - Location Interaction
- Process - Organization Structure Interaction
- Process - Performance Interaction
- Process - Principles Interaction
- Process - Process Dependency Interaction
- Process - Role Interaction
- Process - Stakeholder Interaction
- Process - Strategic Context Interaction
- Process - Technology Interaction
- Process - Value Stream Interaction

Example Interaction: Process - Performance Interaction.

There are several elements to the Process Catalog and the Performance

Catalog. Therefore, there are many possible ways to map this interaction. In this example, the interaction maps the relationship between processes and performance measurements.

The process for creating this interaction table involved selecting the element 'process name' from the Process Catalog and the element 'performance measure' from the Performance Catalog.

This selection process is illustrated in the following diagram.

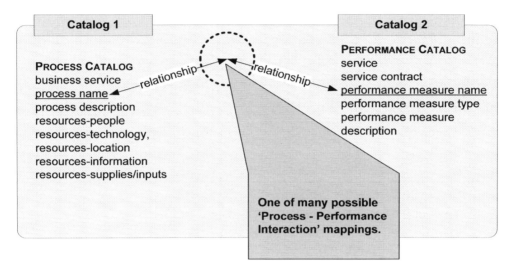

The resulting interaction table looks like this:

Interaction	Performance			
Processes	Measure 1	Measure 2	Measure 3	Measure N
Process 1	X	X	X	X
Process 2			X	
Process 3	X	X	X	X
Process N				X

Chapter 111

Role Interaction

Role interactions describe the relationship between one or more of the elements from the role catalog—organizational unit, business function, business service, role, actor, actor type—and other catalogs and the elements that they contain.

The key Role Interactions are:

- Role - Application/System Interaction
- Role - Business Profile Interaction
- Role - Business Services Interaction
- Role - Consultation Interaction
- Role - Critical Services Interaction
- Role - Event Interaction
- Role - Lessons Learned Interaction
- Role - Location Interaction
- Role - Organization Structure Interaction
- Role - Process Interaction
- Role - Value Stream Interaction

Example Interaction: Role - Application/System Interaction.

There are several elements in the Role Catalog and the Application/System Catalog and, therefore, many possible ways to map their interactions.

In this example, the interaction maps the relationship between enterprise roles and the enterprise's applications. Harmonizing roles and access to enterprise applications is a particularly challenging task in very large organizations.

This example is a ground-level approach to understanding the role-application perspective (horizontal-row relationships), but also the multiple roles/application perspective (vertical-columnar relationships).

The process for creating this interaction table involved selecting the element 'role' from the Role Catalog and the element 'application name' from the Application/System Catalog.

This selection process is illustrated in the following diagram.

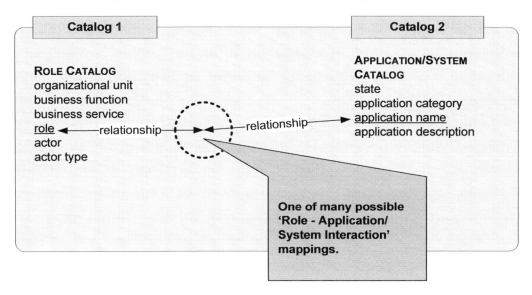

The resulting interaction table looks like this:

Interaction	Application/System Interaction			
Roles	App 1	App 2	App 3	App N
Role 1	X	X	X	X
Role 2			X	
Role 3	X	X	X	X
Role N				X

Chapter 112

Prioritization Interaction

Prioritization interactions describe the relationship between one or more of the elements from the prioritization catalog—activity name, activity description, priority level, priority ranking—and other catalogs and the elements that they contain.

The key Prioritization Interactions are:

- Prioritization - Business Alignment Interaction
- Prioritization - Business Profile Interaction
- Prioritization - Consultation Interaction
- Prioritization - Critical Services Interaction
- Prioritization - Governance Interaction
- Prioritization - Lessons Learned Interaction
- Prioritization - Organization Structure Interaction
- Prioritization - Performance Interaction
- Prioritization - Stakeholder Interaction
- Prioritization - Strategic Context Interaction
- Prioritization - Value Stream Interaction

Example Interaction: Prioritization - Critical Services Interaction.

There are several elements in the Prioritization Catalog and the Critical Services Catalog and, therefore, many possible ways to map their interactions.

In this example, the interaction maps the relationship between enterprise priorities and critical services.

The process for creating this interaction table involved selecting the element 'activity name' from the Prioritization Catalog and the element 'service' from the Critical Services Catalog.

This selection process is illustrated in the following diagram.

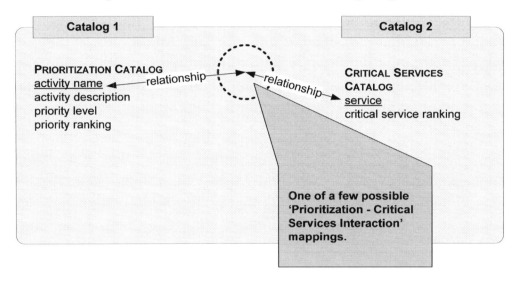

The resulting interaction table looks like this:

Interaction	Critical Services			
Prioritized Activities	Critical Services 1	Critical Services 2	Critical Services 3	Critical Services N
Activity 1	X	X	X	X
Activity 2			X	
Activity 3	X	X	X	X
Activity N				X

Chapter 113

Lessons Learned Interaction

Lessons learned interactions describe the relationship between one or more of the elements from the lessons learned catalog—lesson date, submitting organization, lesson title, lesson summary, description of driving event, lessons learned (list), recommendations (list), related documents—and other catalogs and the elements that they contain.

The key Lessons Learned Interactions are:

- Lessons Learned - Application/System Interaction
- Lessons Learned - Architecture Decisions Interaction
- Lessons Learned - Business Alignment Interaction
- Lessons Learned - Business Issues Interaction
- Lessons Learned - Business Profile Interaction
- Lessons Learned - Business Services Interaction
- Lessons Learned - Business Standards Interaction
- Lessons Learned - Consultation Interaction
- Lessons Learned - Critical Services Interaction
- Lessons Learned - Data Component Interaction
- Lessons Learned - Event Interaction
- Lessons Learned - Governance Interaction
- Lessons Learned - IT Terms Interaction
- Lessons Learned - Location Interaction
- Lessons Learned - Organization Structure Interaction
- Lessons Learned - Performance Interaction
- Lessons Learned - Policy Interaction
- Lessons Learned - Principles Interaction

- Lessons Learned - Prioritization Interaction
- Lessons Learned - Process Interaction
- Lessons Learned - Role Interaction
- Lessons Learned - Stakeholder Interaction
- Lessons Learned - Strategic Context Interaction
- Lessons Learned - Technology Interaction
- Lessons Learned - Threat Interaction
- Lessons Learned - Value Stream Interaction

Example Interaction: Lessons Learned - Policy Interaction.

There are several elements in the Lessons Learned Catalog and the Policy Catalog and, therefore, many possible ways to map their interactions. In this example, the interaction maps the relationship between recommendations and the policies those recommendations impact .

The process for creating this interaction table involved selecting the element 'recommendations (list)' from the Lessons Learned Catalog and the element 'policy' from the Policy Catalog.

This selection process is illustrated in the following diagram.

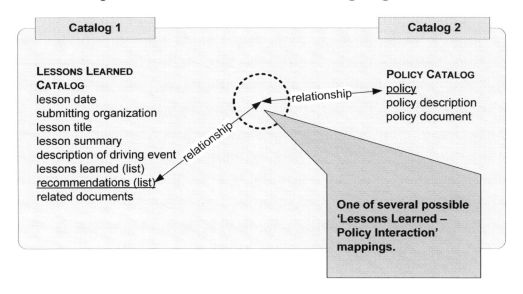

The resulting interaction table looks like this:

Interaction	Policy			
Lessons Learned	Policy 1	Policy 2	Policy 3	Policy N
Recommendation 1	X	X	X	X
Recommendation 2			X	
Recommendation 3	X	X	X	X
Recommendation N				X

Chapter 114

IT Terms Interaction

IT terms interactions describe the relationship between one or more of the elements from the IT terms catalog—IT term, definition, acronym, reference, synonym—and other catalogs and the elements that they contain.

The IT Terms Interaction is:

- IT Terms - Consultation Interaction

Interaction: Lessons Learned - Policy Interaction

This interaction maps the relationship between IT Term updates and consultations.

The process for creating this interaction table involved selecting a pseudo-element 'IT Terms Version' based on the IT Terms Catalog and the element 'audience organization' from the Consultation Catalog.

This selection process is illustrated in the following diagram.

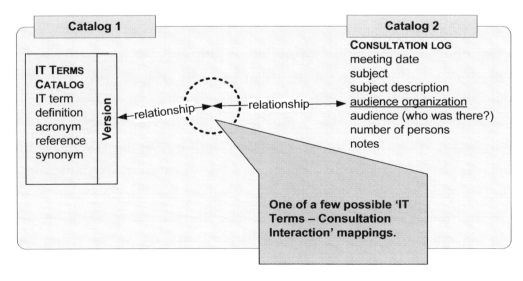

The resulting interaction table looks like this:

Interaction	Consultation			
IT Terms	Org 1	Org 2	Org 3	Org N
IT Terms Version 1	X	X	X	X
IT Terms Version 2			X	
IT Terms Version 3	X	X	X	X
IT Terms Version N				X

Chapter 115

Application/System Interaction

Application/system interactions describe the relationship between one or more of the elements from the application/system catalog—state, application category, application name, description—and other catalogs and the elements that they contain.

The key Application/System Interactions are:

- Application/System - Application/System Interaction
- Application/System - Business Alignment Interaction
- Application/System - Business Profile Interaction
- Application/System - Business Services Interaction
- Application/System - Business Standards Interaction
- Application/System - Consultation Interaction
- Application/System - Critical Services Interaction
- Application/System - Data Component Interaction
- Application/System - Event Interaction
- Application/System - Governance Interaction
- Application/System - Lessons Learned Interaction
- Application/System - Location Interaction
- Application/System - Organization Structure Interaction
- Application/System - Performance Interaction
- Application/System - Principles Interaction
- Application/System - Process Interaction
- Application/System - Role Interaction
- Application/System - Stakeholder Interaction
- Application/System - Strategic Context Interaction
- Application/System - Technology Interaction
- Application/System - Value Stream Interaction

Example Interaction: Application/System - Business Services Interaction.

There are several elements in the Application/System Catalog and the Business Services Catalog and, therefore, many possible ways to map their interactions. In this example, the interaction maps. The dependencies between applications and business services.

The process for creating this interaction table involved selecting the element 'application name' from the Application/System Catalog and the element 'Business Service' from the Business Services Catalog.

This selection process is illustrated in the following diagram.

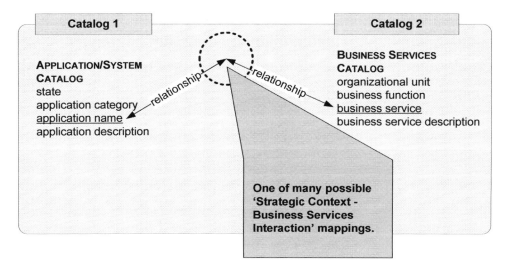

The resulting interaction table looks like this:

Information Interactions	Business Services			
Application/System	Service 1	Service 2	Service 3	Service N
Application 1	X	X	X	X
Application 2			X	
Application 3	X	X	X	X
Application N				X

Chapter 116

Data Component Interaction

Data component interactions describe the relationship between one or more of the elements from the data component catalog—state, data category, data component name, description—and other catalogs and the elements that they contain.

The key Data Component Interactions are:

- Data Component - Application/System Interaction
- Data Component - Business Alignment Interaction
- Data Component - Business Profile Interaction
- Data Component - Business Services Interaction
- Data Component - Business Standards Interaction
- Data Component - Consultation Interaction
- Data Component - Critical Services Interaction
- Data Component - Data Component Dependency Interaction
- Data Component - Governance Interaction
- Data Component - Lessons Learned Interaction
- Data Component - Location Interaction
- Data Component - Organization Structure Interaction
- Data Component - Performance Interaction
- Data Component - Principles Interaction
- Data Component - Process Interaction
- Data Component - Stakeholder Interaction
- Data Component - Strategic Context Interaction
- Data Component - Technology Interaction
- Data Component - Value Stream Interaction

Example Interaction: Data Component – Business Alignment Interaction

There are several elements in the Data Component Catalog and the Business Alignment Catalog and, therefore, many possible ways to map their interaction.

In this example, the interaction maps the relationship between 'conceptual date components' and 'business functions. The interaction is based on a scenario where the conceptual date components impact the business function, revealing the scope of change implied by a roadmap for transforming the conceptual date components into logical and, finally, physical date components that support business function.

The process for creating this interaction table involved selecting the element 'conceptual date components' based on the 'state' (conceptual) and 'data component name' elements from the Data Component Catalog and 'aligned business functions' from the Business Alignment Catalog.

This selection process is illustrated in the following diagram.

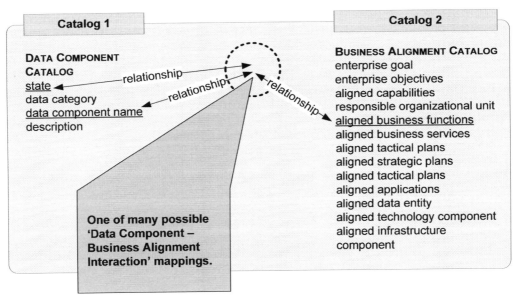

The resulting interaction table looks like this:

Interaction	Aligned Business Function1			
Conceptual Data Components	Business Function 1	Business Function 2	Business Function 3	Business Function N
Data Component 1	X	X	X	X
Data Component 2			X	
Data Component 3	X	X	X	X
Data Component N				X

Chapter 117

Technology Interaction

Technology interactions describe the relationship between one or more of the elements from the technology catalog—state, technology category, technology component name, description—and other catalogs and the elements that they contain.

The key Technology Interactions are:

- Technology - Application/System Interaction
- Technology - Business Alignment Interaction
- Technology - Business Profile Interaction
- Technology - Business Services Interaction
- Technology - Business Standards Interaction
- Technology - Consultation Interaction
- Technology - Critical Services Interaction
- Technology - Data Component Interaction
- Technology - Event Interaction
- Technology - Governance Interaction
- Technology - Lessons Learned Interaction
- Technology - Location Interaction
- Technology - Organization Structure Interaction
- Technology - Performance Interaction
- Technology - Principles Interaction
- Technology - Process Interaction
- Technology - Stakeholder Interaction
- Technology - Strategic Context Interaction
- Technology - Technology Dependency Interaction
- Technology - Value Stream Interaction

Example Interaction: Technology - Application/System Interaction.

There are several elements in the Technology Catalog and the Application/System Catalog and, therefore, many possible ways to map their interactions. In this example, the interaction maps the relationship between physical (current state) supporting technology and the physical (current state) applications that depend on them.

The process for creating this interaction table involved selecting the element 'state' (physical) and the element 'technology component name' from the Technology Catalog and the element 'state' (physical) and the element 'application name' from the Application/Systems Catalog.

This selection process is illustrated in the following diagram.

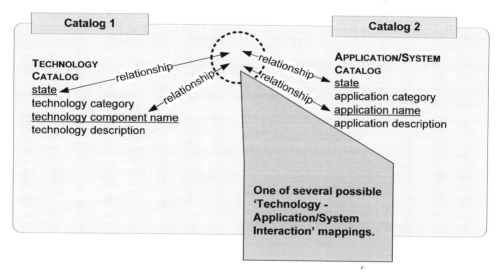

The resulting interaction table looks like this:

Interaction	Applications			
Technology Components	Application 1	Application 2	Application 3	Application N
Technology Component 1	X	X	X	X
Technology Component 2			X	
Technology Component 3	X	X	X	X
Technology Component N				X

Chapter 118

Business Profile Interaction

Business profile interactions describe the relationship between one or more of the elements from the business profile catalog—organizational unit, profile document name, document title, document date—and other catalogs and the elements that they contain.

The key Business Profile Interactions are:

- Business Profile - Application/System Interaction
- Business Profile - Business Alignment Interaction
- Business Profile - Critical Services Interaction
- Business Profile - Data Component Interaction
- Business Profile - Event Interaction
- Business Profile - Governance Interaction
- Business Profile - Lessons Learned Interaction
- Business Profile - Location Interaction
- Business Profile - Organization Structure Interaction
- Business Profile - Performance Interaction
- Business Profile - Principles Interaction
- Business Profile - Prioritization Interaction
- Business Profile - Process Interaction
- Business Profile - Role Interaction
- Business Profile - Stakeholder Interaction
- Business Profile - Strategic Context Interaction
- Business Profile - Technology Interaction
- Business Profile - Value Stream Interaction

Example Interaction: Business Profile – Organizational Structure Interaction.

There are several elements in the Business Profile Catalog and the Strategic Context Catalog and, therefore, many possible ways to map their interaction. In this example, the interaction maps the existence of a current business profile against the current organizational structure—gaps along the left to right diagonal axis of the table indicate where alignment may be required.

The process for creating this interaction table involved selecting the element 'organizational unit' and the element 'document date' (where less than two years old) from the Business Profile Catalog and the element 'organizational unit' from the Organizational Structure Catalog.

This selection process is illustrated in the following diagram.

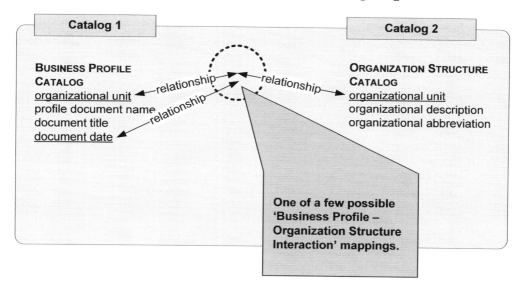

The resulting interaction table looks like this:

Interaction	Organizational Structure			
Business Profile	Organizational Unit 1	Organizational Unit 2	Organizational Unit 3	Organizational Unit N
Org Unit 1	X			
Org Unit 2				
Org Unit 3			X	
Org Unit N				X

Chapter 119

Business Standards Interaction

Business standards interactions describe the relationship between one or more of the elements from the business standards catalog—standard category, standard name, standard, description, status, effective date—and other catalogs and the elements that they contain.

The key Business Standards Interactions are:

- Business Standards - Application/System Interaction
- Business Standards - Business Alignment Interaction
- Business Standards - Business Standards Interaction
- Business Standards - Critical Services Interaction
- Business Standards - Data Component Interaction
- Business Standards - Governance Interaction
- Business Standards - Lessons Learned Interaction
- Business Standards - Performance Interaction
- Business Standards - Policy Interaction
- Business Standards - Process Interaction
- Business Standards - Stakeholder Interaction
- Business Standards - Strategic Context Interaction
- Business Standards - Technology Interaction

Example Interaction: Business Standards - Application/System Interaction.

There are several elements in the Business Standards Catalog and the Application Catalog and, therefore, many possible ways to map their interactions. In this example, the interaction maps the relationship between new business standards and applications—this interaction is a first step in exploring the implication of a new standard on existing applications

The process for creating this interaction table involved selecting the new standard — a composite of element 'standard name', element 'status' (sunrise) and element 'effective date' — from the Business Standards Catalog and the element 'state' (physical) and the element 'application name' from the Application/System Catalog.

This selection process is illustrated in the following diagram.

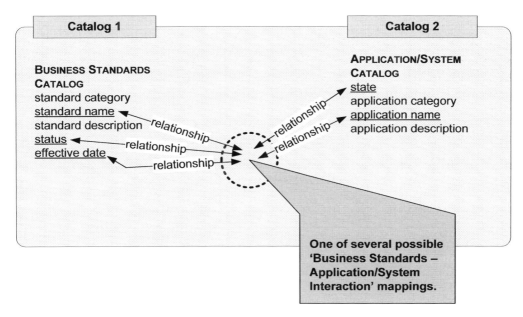

The resulting interaction table looks like this:

Interaction	Applications/Systems			
Standards	App 1	App 2	App 3	App N
Standard 1	X	X	X	X
Standard 2			X	
Standard 3	X	X	X	X
Standard N				X

Chapter 120

Architecture Decisions Interaction

Architecture decisions interactions describe the relationship between one or more of the elements from the architecture decisions catalog—issue, issue description, related organizational unit, project name, date, architecture decision—and other catalogs and the elements that they contain.

The key Architecture Decisions Interactions are:

- Architecture Decisions - Business Alignment Interaction
- Architecture Decisions - Business Issues Interaction
- Architecture Decisions - Critical Services Interaction
- Architecture Decisions - Governance Interaction
- Architecture Decisions - Lessons Learned Interaction
- Architecture Decisions - Performance Interaction
- Architecture Decisions - Policy Interaction
- Architecture Decisions - Stakeholder Interaction
- Architecture Decisions - Strategic Context Interaction

Example Interaction: Architecture Decisions - Business Issues Interaction.

There are several elements in the Architecture Decisions Catalog and the Policy Catalog and, therefore, many possible ways to map their interactions.

In this example, the interaction documents the relationship between architecture decisions and policy.

Architecture decisions are often promoted to policy when they apply, beyond a specific project or program, to the entire enterprise.

The process for creating this interaction table involved selecting the element 'architecture decision' from the Architecture Decisions Catalog and the element 'policy' from the Policy Catalog.

This selection process is illustrated in the following diagram.

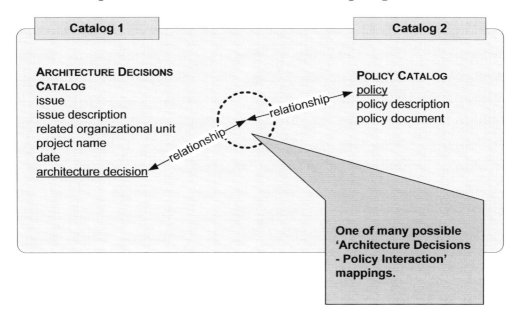

The resulting interaction table looks like this:

Interaction	Policy			
Architecture Decision	Policy 1	Policy 2	Policy 3	Policy N
Architecture Decision 1	X			X
Architecture Decision 2		X		
Architecture Decision 3		X	X	
Architecture Decision N				X

Chapter 121

Policy Interaction

Policy interactions describe the relationship between one or more of the elements from the policy catalog—policy, policy description, policy document—and other catalogs and the elements that they contain.

The key Policy Interactions are:

- Policy - Architecture Decisions Interaction
- Policy - Business Alignment Interaction
- Policy - Business Standards Interaction
- Policy - Critical Services Interaction
- Policy - Governance Interaction
- Policy - Lessons Learned Interaction
- Policy - Performance Interaction
- Policy - Stakeholder Interaction
- Policy - Strategic Context Interaction

Example Interaction: Policy – Critical Services Interaction.

In this example, the interaction maps relationship between policies and the critical services the policies apply to. In other words, the interaction identifies which policies govern which critical services.

This is an important relationship to keep current. Why? Identifying critical services is often the most important aspect of a crisis management and business continuity plan. When a crisis event occurs, up-to-date policies need to be accessible to the crisis management team—these policies (and how they apply to any given critical service) will inform critical decision-making.

The process for creating this interaction table involved selecting the element 'policy' from the Policy Catalog and the element 'service' from the Critical Services Catalog.

This selection process is illustrated in the following diagram.

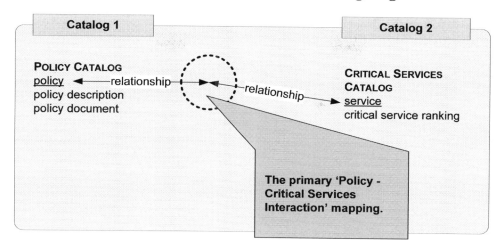

The resulting interaction table looks like this:

Interaction	Critical Services			
Policy	Service 1	Service 2	Service 3	Service N
Policy 1	X	X	X	X
Policy 2			X	
Policy 3	X	X	X	X
Policy N				X

Chapter 122

Threat Interaction

Threat interactions describe the relationship between one or more of the elements from the threat catalog — threat category, threat name, likelihood/probability, impact-health & safety, impact-assets, impact-critical service delivery, threat ranking—and other catalogs and the elements that they contain.

The key Threat Interactions are:

- Threat - Critical Services Interaction
- Threat - Lessons Learned Interaction

Example Interaction: Threat - Lessons Learned Interaction.

There are several elements in the Threat Catalog and the Lessons Learned Catalog and, therefore, many possible ways to map their interactions.

In this example, the interaction map identifies which lessons learned apply to which threats, informing the task of updating the threat mitigation strategies used in business continuity plans.

The process for creating this interaction table involved selecting the element 'threat name' from the Threat Catalog and the element 'lesson name' from the Lessons Learned Catalog.

This selection process is illustrated in the following diagram.

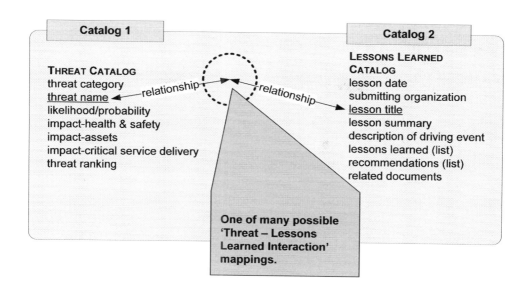

The resulting interaction table looks like this:

Interaction	Lessons Learned			
Threats	Lessons Learned 1	Lessons Learned 2	Lessons Learned 3	Lessons Learned N
Threat 1	X	X	X	X
Threat 2			X	
Threat 3	X	X	X	X
Threat N				X

Chapter 123

Consultation Interaction

Consultation interactions describe the relationship between one or more of the elements from the consultation log—meeting date, subject, subject description, audience organization, audience (who was there?), number of persons, notes—and other catalogs and the elements that they contain.

The key Consultation Interactions are:

- Consultation - Application/System Interaction
- Consultation - Business Alignment Interaction
- Consultation - Business Issues Interaction
- Consultation - Business Services Interaction
- Consultation - Critical Services Interaction
- Consultation - Data Component Interaction
- Consultation - Event Interaction
- Consultation - Governance Interaction
- Consultation - IT Terms Interaction
- Consultation - Lessons Learned Interaction
- Consultation - Location Interaction
- Consultation - Organization Structure Interaction
- Consultation - Performance Interaction
- Consultation - Principles Interaction
- Consultation - Prioritization Interaction
- Consultation - Process Interaction
- Consultation - Role Interaction
- Consultation - Stakeholder Interaction
- Consultation - Strategic Context Interaction
- Consultation - Technology Interaction
- Consultation - Value Stream Interaction

- Consultation – Enterprise Business Architecture Asset Catalog

Example Interaction: Consultation - Stakeholder Interaction.

There are several elements in the Consultation Catalog and the Stakeholder Catalog and, therefore, many possible ways to map their interaction. In this example, the interaction maps the relationship between stakeholder groups and the various consultation subjects. Other interactions in this list are subject specific.

The process for creating this interaction table involved selecting the element 'subject' from the Consultation Catalog and the element 'stakeholder type' (group) from the Stakeholder Catalog.

This selection process is illustrated in the following diagram.

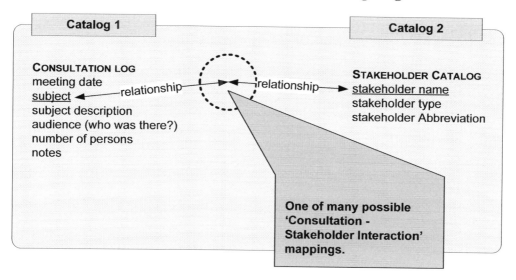

The resulting interaction table looks like this:

Interaction	Stakeholders			
Consultation	Group 1	Group 2	Group 3	Group N
Consult Subject 1	X	X	X	X
Consult Subject 2			X	
Consult Subject 3	X	X	X	X
Consult Subject N				X

INDEX

11774119R0029

Made in the USA
Lexington, KY
31 October 2011